PEASANTS IN THE PACIFIC

PEASANTS IN THE PACIFIC

A Study of Fiji Indian Rural Society

by

ADRIAN C. MAYER

Second edition

UNIVERSITY OF CALIFORNIA PRESS

Berkeley and Los Angeles

First published 1961
Second edition 1973
University of California Press
Berkeley and Los Angeles
California

© *Adrian C. Mayer 1961, 1973*

Library of Congress Catalog Card No.: 72-91618
ISBN 0 520 02333 1

Printed in Great Britain

TO
KAIA

CONTENTS

Contents

PLATES

ix

INTRODUCTION TO THE SECOND EDITION

Twenty years after the stay in Fiji on which the first edition of this book was based, I attended the XXVII International Congress of Orientalists in Canberra and stopped in Fiji on my way back to England, to renew old acquaintances and to see in what ways the settlements I had described had changed.

I spent from mid-January to mid-March 1971 in Fiji, and I was able to visit both Vunioki and Delanikoro for a fortnight, and Namboulima for a couple of days. There had indeed been changes. The main trends that first struck me were towards an increased economic importance of sugar cane in one case, and towards part-time farming coupled with urban employment in the other. Each change had its social concomitants, and my short stays enabled me at least to discuss these with residents, if not to document or explore them fully. My return to Fiji was not in any sense a research project, nor could it be compared to the study carried out in 1951; but sufficient interest was shown in my impressions, however hasty, by colleagues and others in Fiji and elsewhere, to embolden me to add them to the 1951 account as a concluding chapter.

In doing so, I am happy to acknowledge with thanks the aid of a great many people who gave me their views on changes in the decades since my first visit. To Messrs K. P. Mishra and Moti Lal my thanks are again due, as well as to Messrs Siv Prasad, Rajaram and Parmanand Singh, and to the officials of the South Pacific Sugar Mills, of all grades of seniority, who were helpful with information and generous with their time. Individuals are too numerous to mention; but I especially want to thank the residents of Vunioki, Delanikoro and Namboulima. Our meetings, after almost a generation, were a continuous pleasure for me, clouded only by the inevitable gaps left by those no longer living. I hope, and think, that people were also pleased to renew our links and to think back to earlier days of youth and childhood. Lastly, I acknowledge with thanks the comments of R. G. Crocombe and Peter Stone on a draft of this chapter.

London, 1972

INTRODUCTION

INDIAN settlement overseas has a history of many centuries. One of its most notable features is the recruiting in the nineteenth century of Indian labourers under indenture. These people were sent to such British colonies as Trinidad, Natal, Mauritius, Guiana and Fiji. There they started permanent communities, most of whose members were farmers, in contrast to the mainly mercantile character of traditional settlement which was later followed in such places as East Africa.

The first aim of this book is to provide an account of the rural section of the Fiji Indian community, for people either living in Fiji or interested in the Colony. Such an object should need no justification in a country where populations with such varied interests and customs live side by side. The ignorance of people of one community about the ways of life of another can be a hindrance, if not a danger, in the days of rapid social change into which Fiji is now entering. This account should help to broaden the knowledge held of Fiji Indian society, by describing the rural part of it.

The book will also, it is hoped, aid comparative study when more data on other overseas Indian communities are available. One of the objects of such study would be to examine the social structure of these immigrant communities, seeing the degree to which economic, religious, political and other social behaviour is institutionalized. Hence, an analysis of Fiji Indian rural social structure forms the theme on which the descriptive material of this book is based. Such a theme was, in fact, suggested by a first view of the Fiji countryside, and by initial enquiries into the Indian backgrounds of immigrants. For Indians coming to Fiji were usually unrelated and from many castes, and had come from widely separated districts. They were allowed to settle wherever they could lease land, and formed settlements of scattered homesteads instead of villages. What interests bound such a potentially heterogeneous community? What groups were formed, and how did they operate under physical conditions which favoured an individualistic way of life?

Research on such questions was undertaken for a year during 1950–1, shortly after a stay in India. The difference between the highly stratified and controlled Indian, and the freer Fiji Indian society was striking. In contrast to Indian villages, settlements in

Fiji were both officially and socially ill-defined; there was no settlement headman, and only for sugar production and for education was it necessary to submit to a local association in which fellow residents had the power to enforce rules. The reader should therefore bear in mind the author's acquaintance with India as one of the implicit factors in the fieldwork, since it may have led him to stress the 'looseness' of the Fiji Indian settlement.

Fiji Indians live in three main regions and it seemed best to stay in a settlement of each, to see if there were variations between them. The first five months were spent in Vunioki, where specific questions on the theme of research were formulated, and where the basic ethnography was collected. Three and two months were then spent in Delanikoro and Namboulima respectively. The three settlements contained all major cultural and religious variations and represent what was judged to be the average economic pattern. Together, they contained something over 1 per cent of the total Fiji Indian rural population at the time. It cannot be said that any was a 'typical' settlement, if such a place exists; but it is thought that a good cross section of the population was observed. Stays were made in a homestead separated by one hundred yards from its nearest neighbour in Vunioki, in a homestead only twenty yards from a neighbour in Delanikoro, and in a hut which formed part of a homestead centred on a single compound in Namboulima. The opportunity was thereby gained of assessing both the isolation of homesteads and the intimacy of people in dwellings within a single homestead. Research was carried out in Hindi, the *lingua franca* of Fiji Indians, without an interpreter. Proper and place names used are fictitious.

The first chapter of the book sets out the historical background of the community. The next chapter is mainly concerned with the degree to which the rural settlement can be said to be a separate geographical and social unit, comparable to the village in other societies. Chapters III to VI deal with economic, religious and political affairs of the settlements in turn, seeing how people co-operated and what groups were formed to do so. Chapter VII isolates three main bases for these groupings—caste, kinship and 'culture'—and examines their roles more closely. Finally, a concluding chapter sets these rural settlements within the wider society of Fiji, and outlines their contacts with India.

The book has been made possible through the help of many people. Most important are the inhabitants of the three settlements, who accepted two strangers with immediate hospitality and friendliness. It would be unfair to mention any single person, and it is hoped that all who took an interest in the research will find in this book a true interpretation of their views and actions.

Introduction

Many other people in Fiji have contributed to this book, too, in particular Messrs. Moti Lal, J. Madhavan, Krishna Prasad Mishra, Sursenap R. Sharma, Venkat Swami and the late Pandit Ami Chandra. Officials of the Government of Fiji and the Colonial Sugar Refining Company gave great help and showed much kindness.

The research was suggested by Professor Raymond Firth, and any virtues the book may have are largely due to his guidance. It has also profited from the comments of Professors C. von Fürer-Haimendorf, D. G. Mandelbaum and the late S. F. Nadel. The manuscript was read by Sir Ronald Garvey, K.C.M.G., K.C.V.O., Mr. G. K. Roth, C.M.G., O.B.E., Dr. Burton Benedict, Dr. K. C. Rosser and the Hon. Vijay R. Singh, M.L.C., all of whom provided a great deal of stimulating and helpful criticism.

Lastly, a debt is gratefully acknowledged to the Australian National University, Canberra, under whose auspices the research was carried out.

London, December 1959

I

THE BACKGROUND

INDIANS have been in Fiji since May 14, 1879, when the first 498 indentured labourers arrived in the *Leonidas* from Calcutta. They came to a newly-established British Crown Colony, which had been ceded by the Fijian chiefs to Queen Victoria in 1874. Hitherto, plantations of cotton and coconuts had been run with labour from nearby island groups, such as the New Hebrides. But new regulations, designed to check the abuses in the 'blackbirding' of these natives, had made it hard to obtain recruits. The Fijians themselves provided the obvious answer to this labour shortage. But Fiji's first Governor, Sir Arthur Gordon, refused to run the risk of a plantation system's effects on the Fijian way of life. He felt that the recruitment of young men to labour camps, with the consequent disorganization of family life and of the structure of the Fijian village economy and authority system, was not a course open to a Government which had pledged itself in a Deed of Cession to look after Fijian interests. Nor did the Fijians themselves wish to neglect their lands for routine work which they disliked.

Various proposals for outside labour were made during the years after Cession of which the recruitment of Indian labour proved the most fruitful and easy to negotiate. Under agreement with the Government of India, labourers were to be brought by the Fiji Government to Fiji for five years of compulsory work as the Government directed, under penal sanctions. After this they were free to go back to India at their own expense, though at the end of a further five years their return passages, and those of their children, were to be paid by the Government. Most important, there was no necessity for them to return to India at all, for the Fiji Government saw, in a permanent Indian settlement, the prospect of a growing labour supply without the costs of repeated transport from India.

A year after the first Indians arrived in Fiji the Government persuaded the Colonial Sugar Refining Company (CSR Company) of Sydney to extend its operations to Fiji, and this started the important

1

commercial exploitation of sugar. It quickly proved to be a crop well suited to Fiji, and the expansion of the sugar industry, especially in the first years of the twentieth century, made certain the continued immigration of Indians. A total of 60,537 Indians arrived in Fiji under indenture.[1] 24,655 were repatriated during the indenture period under the indenture contract,[2] the remainder staying on in the Colony, together with a small but influential number of 'free' immigrants,[3] many of whom came as traders and teachers in the years after indenture was abolished. By 1951, the majority of Indians in Fiji were Fiji-born, and less than 10 per cent of the population could claim to have known the indenture ships and a land of birth beyond the seas. Nevertheless, significant features of the present-day rural society of the Fiji Indians derive from immigration, and to understand them something must be known of the conditions of people brought to Fiji, and the kind of lives they led during, and immediately after, their period of indenture.

Enlistments were made in India by recruiters licensed by the magistrate of the district in which they worked. A potential recruit would be brought to the sub-agent appointed by the Fiji Government's agent in Calcutta and, later, Madras. The sub-agent then took the recruit before the magistrate of the district, where the terms of the contract were explained, and he formally accepted a term of indenture. He was then sent to the main depot, where he was medically examined and kept until a ship sailed for Fiji.

Indians had a dislike and fear of going abroad which was largely due to the loss of caste which an emigrant suffered. This made the recruiting of labourers difficult, if not physically hazardous. Conditions of life in India helped to counteract this fear, but even the spur of depressed economic conditions could not entirely overcome customary prejudices. It was left to other incentives, and to the deceptions of the recruiters, to supply many of the people required. Incentives included disputes with kin, and desire for adventure and, in a few cases, trouble with the police.[4] Recruiters played on the ignorance of the peasants, saying, for instance, that Fiji was a place near Calcutta; or exaggerating the value of the wages to be earned, whilst saying nothing of the penal nature of the indenture contract.

The people who enlisted were mainly Hindus belonging to castes—endogamous bodies ranked in a hierarchy of status, membership of which could only be acquired by birth. Of the people leaving from the Calcutta depot 16·1 per cent were classed as of high castes, 31·3

---

[1] Gillion 1956: 139.   [2] Derrick 1951: 138.
[3] No figures are available for their total number.
[4] Andrews estimated that some 10 per cent were thus involved (Gillion 1956: 150).

per cent as of middle agricultural castes, 6·7 per cent as of artisan castes and 31·2 per cent as of low and untouchable castes; there were also 14·6 per cent Muslims and 0·1 per cent Christians.[1] Only a few people were refused by the immigration authorities, notably Brahman priests not used to agriculture, some of whom are said to have enlisted by falsifying their occupation and caste. Except for these, all strata were included and many of the castes from the districts of major recruitment were represented. However, a caste system was not 're-formed' in Fiji, for other factors intervened and made a full caste complement irrelevant to relations between Fiji Indians in their new home.

Not all parts of India were covered by the recruiters. The first areas were in the lower Gangetic plain (Bengal and Bihar), activity slowly shifting to the northwest,[2] and centring in Uttar Pradesh. (No great numbers were recruited in Central and Western India.) By the end of the century, recruitment in North India became difficult and labourers were brought from South India, both from Tamil-speaking districts near Madras city, and also from the northern Telugu-speaking areas and from Malabar on the West coast. In all, 45,833 Indians came from Calcutta as compared with 15,132 coming through the southern depot at Madras. The fact that fewer South Indians were indentured, and that they formed the bulk of the later immigrants, is important when the present social concomitants of place of origin in India are considered.[3]

Fiji Indians came from only a fraction of the hundreds of districts in British India.[4] But the size of even these districts made it unlikely that people would have known each other in India, unless they had actually emigrated together. A minimum of 40 per cent female emigration was enjoined, and this proportion was maintained, though never greatly exceeded.[5] Some 30 per cent of adult women were recorded as accompanied by their husbands;[6] and there are records of male kinsmen coming together. But one should not conclude that a large number of people emigrated in families. For a great many men were no more than 'depot husbands', men classed as husbands through the persuasion of the sub-agent because no married woman could be recruited without her husband's permission. The majority of emigrants were, in fact, single men and 68·7 per cent were between twenty and thirty years old.[7]

[1] Gillion 1956: 152.   [2] Gillion 1956: 143 and 145.   [3] See p. 144 seq.

[4] Later 'free' immigration was mostly from the Punjab and Gujarat.

[5] Figure for the total Calcutta emigration was 43·72 per cent (Gillion 1956: 150).

[6] Collation of figures given in Calcutta Emigration Reports 1879–1916, as given in Gillion 1958.

[7] Gillion 1956: 154.

These facts are stressed by Gillion as a major reason why the emigrants were able to ignore the rules of the society in which they had been reared. For they were, on the one hand, young and able to adapt to the very different conditions which they found on the immigrant ships and on their arrival in Fiji; and, on the other hand, they were unattached people, able to adopt different patterns of behaviour without suffering the sanctions imposed by the public censure of their orthodox relatives and caste mates.

On arrival in Fiji, the immigrants were assigned to plantations which needed labour. At first, many worked for small copra planters as well as on the estates of the sugar companies. But the copra planters had gone deeply into debt for their share of the costs of transporting the immigrants, and were driven out of business when prices fell in 1884. Henceforth, immigrants went mainly to the sugar companies' estates, some of which were operated directly by the companies and others through planters to whom the companies leased them. There were three main areas of sugar production, and Indian settlement centred there, both during and after indenture.[1]

Work on the sugar plantations followed a seasonal cycle. The cane was planted, the land weeded and if necessary drained, and finally the crop cut and loaded on wagons to be sent to the crushing mill. *All* Indians did this work,[2] regardless of previous occupation and economic status in India. Not only did this have the important effect of overlaying patterns of hereditary occupation, which had existed in India, but it also rendered the Fiji Indian community superficially undifferentiated. All Indians were thought of by the European planters as 'coolies' and it was this outlook that, in part, led to their severe treatment. If the community had had differences of wealth and occupation it would have been more familiar to the planters who might have been less disposed to see Indians as mere sugar-producing machines.

Besides having, in many cases, to learn a completely different occupation, immigrants were subjected to several other social pressures. They were housed in 'lines', the name for the barracks of wood and corrugated iron which were situated at the centre of each estate. Inside was a double line of rooms, usually eight on each side. By law, each room was a minimum of 10 feet by 7 feet (changed to 10 feet by 12 feet in the last eight years of the system), and housed three single men, or one man, his wife and not more than two children. The occupants had to cook in their rooms during most of the indenture period, and there was little privacy since the partitions between rooms did not go right up to the ceiling. This kind of hous-

[1] See map (p. 14).
[2] A few were later made interpreters and personal servants of the plantation overseers.

4

ing represented a sharp break from conditions in the village, where, though there were often streets of closely packed houses, each person felt that he had his own dwelling, rather than a single room within a larger dormitory. Moreover, the crowded lines, in addition to the low proportion of women, produced conditions conducive to immorality and crimes of violence.

The pattern of authority differed radically from that with which the immigrants had been familiar. The main leader, appointed by the European overseer of the sugar estate, was the *sardar*. Briefly, his duties were to see that immigrants performed the tasks set them, and to keep order. He did not have any explicit duties of a social nature (e.g. to be a spokesman for the people on the plantation in their contacts with the overseer and the Government, or to be an arbiter of their disputes). The *sardar's* qualifications for his job were partly those which would have made him a leader in his village in India—membership of a high caste, and an education of at least a rudimentary sort. Partly, however, *sardars* were chosen for their ability to get the immigrants to complete their tasks in the fields by methods which were anything but diplomatic. Here, 'toughness' was needed and a capacity to lead, rather than education or caste status. *Sardars* needed considerable courage and self-confidence, for some immigrants would avenge themselves on the *sardar* or the overseer in return for the assaults made on them in the cane fields. There were therefore *sardars* from a wide range of castes, including some of the very lowest, from which there would never have sprung village leaders in India.

Little more can be said about patterns of leadership in the lines—to show, for example, how far other leaders existed and how far *sardars* were also the most influential men outside their jobs. But it is clear that the conditions of the lines represented an extreme change for a group of young men and women, used to a pattern of firm hereditary authority in the family, the caste group and the village. Nobody could be a leader either through his birth or his knowledge of customary procedure; for immigrants came from districts between which there were variations of custom. The groups most likely to evolve were factions—groups recruited over one or more disputes; but even in 1951 faction leaders had only a weak kind of authority, with fluctuating support.[1]

In some ways the social conditions of the indenture period can be seen as a 'breakdown' of those of the parent society. But after indenture the immigrants did not rebuild their old society. Instead, they were forced to build an entirely new one—the Fiji Indian—which was a response to conditions in Fiji, even though many of its ways were still Indian.

[1] See Chapter VI.

In 1916 the indenture system was abolished, and in 1920 all outstanding contracts were cancelled. The abuses with which it had become associated (overwork, immorality, cruelty, an abnormal number of suicides and murders) were too serious to be overcome by the Government's and the CSR Company's efforts at reform during the last years of the system, and attempts by Europeans in Fiji to renew large-scale Indian immigration after the First World War failed.

At the level of humanitarian principles, the indenture system was clearly indefensible; for labour enforced by penal sanctions cannot be condoned. But it is possible to qualify one's condemnation of the system in view of the general *laissez faire* attitude held towards labour at that time, and in view of the attitudes of many of the labourers themselves. On balance, misery may well have prevailed over happiness; but many Fiji Indians, looking back on those times, have something good to say about them. As one old man said, 'The time of indenture was better than now. You did your task, and you knew that this was all. You knew you would get food every day. I had my shipmates with me, and we weren't badly off when there was a good *sardar* and overseer. Of course, if these were bad, then you had to be careful. But now, what do I do? I have cane land, bullocks and a house. Yet, every night I am awake, listening to see if someone is not trying to burn my cane, or steal my animals. In indenture lines we slept well, we did not worry.' For some people the indenture period may now seem like a golden age which they certainly would not have recognized at the time. Yet perhaps there is some truth in the old man's remarks. The disorganization of many people's lives had occurred in India before they ever left for Fiji; and, for all its hardships, life in the lines may have been preferable to a life with quarrelling brothers, or with a savage mother-in-law or, maybe, under the shadow of the police. Again, the indenture system presented each migrant with definite tasks, in contrast to the decisions he had to take when he became a 'free man'; and the tie between ship brothers (*jahazi bhai*) which has often been close enough to endure to this day, suggests a certain solidarity among some, if not all, of the migrants on an estate.[1]

POST-INDENTURE SOCIAL PATTERNS

The Fiji Indian community changed greatly, even before the end of the indenture system, for many immigrants did not make use of their

---

[1] A difficulty in considering past conditions is the possibility that only those who did, in fact, adjust themselves to the new conditions stayed in Fiji, and an unduly favourable picture may be derived from questioning them alone.

free passage back to India, but instead settled in Fiji as free men.
Over the years the proportion of free men to indentured Indians
grew. By 1904, for example, about 10,000 of the 22,700 Indians in
the Colony were in this category.[1] At the time the indenture system
was abolished, the indentured people formed only a minority of the
whole Fiji Indian community.

The history of the 'free' Fiji Indian community can be summed up
in two words—expansion and diversification. First there has been a
purely physical expansion of population, as the table shows.

TABLE 1

Category	*Census Numbers:*					
	1956	*1946*	*1936*	*1921*	*1911*	*1901*
Chinese	4,155	2,105	1,751	910	305	—
European	6,402	4,594	4,028	3,878	3,707	2,459
Fijian	148,134	117,488	97,651	84,475	87,096	94,397
Fiji Indian	169,403	120,063	85,002	60,634	40,286	17,105
Part-European	7,810	6,142	4,574	2,781	2,401	1,516
Rotuman	4,422	3,313	2,816	2,235	2,176	2,230
Pacific Islanders	5,320	2,508	2,353	2,060	2,758	1,950
Others	91	3,425	204	293	812	467
Total	345,737	259,638	198,379	157,266	139,541	120,124

Sources: Appropriate Fiji Censuses.

The Fiji Indian population nearly trebled itself in the thirty-five
years after indenture, and has almost become an absolute majority
in the Colony. This high rate of increase has been little helped by
immigration since 1916, and is almost entirely due to natural growth.
The population being predominantly youthful—85,668 were under
fourteen years in 1956—and the percentage of women to men being
fairly equal at 478 to 622 per thousand (having recovered from the
disproportion of the indenture period) the Fiji Indian population will
increase even faster in the future, and it is forecast that by 1967 it will
exceed 250,000.[2] As to diversification, no fewer than fifty-four
categories of Fiji Indian occupation are listed in the 1956 Census,
from farming to hotel-keeping and motor body-building to dentistry.
Fiji Indians have, in fact, gone into almost every occupation in Fiji.
Amongst farmers there are different categories, too. It was estimated
in 1953 that of the 14,000 Indians, farming on their own account,
some 9,000 were mainly cane farmers, the rest, who had farming as
their main work, growing rice, mixed crops, or dairying.[3] Only one

[1] O'Loughlin 1956: 5. [2] H.M.S.O. 1958: 9. [3] O'Loughlin 1956: 58.

economic pursuit has been denied to Indians. There are almost no landlords living on their rents in Fiji, for no land was alienable to non-Fijians after the Cession.[1] Although Indians own a proportion of the freehold land made available before that time, the great majority have to rent land from the Fijian owners, from the Crown, or from other freeholders or tenants, such as the CSR Company. Land ownership has thus been a minor source of revenue for them, and mainly concerns the few who sub-let part of their leaseholds.

With differences in occupation have come differences in wealth. The 1953 income per head of the Indian population was estimated to be £F64 4s. 0d.[2] But various occupations provided different average remuneration. From O'Loughlin's figures of the total sum earned in different occupations, and the total number of Indians engaged in each, it can be seen that the estimated income per earner from transport and communications was £120 per year, from wholesale and retail trade £222, from agriculture £111 and from sugar mill labour £130. As might be expected, there are differences of wealth within each of these categories. There are, for example, large storekeepers in major towns, and there are the small village storekeepers who maintain with difficulty a reasonable selection of stock and whose turnover is correspondingly small.

The community as a whole is too new to have any very rich people. But there are men with large businesses which will no doubt be passed on to their descendants. A wealthy class is developing as well as a professional group made up of those who return from universities overseas, mainly in Australia and New Zealand, as lawyers, doctors, dentists or teachers.

Country people are to some extent looked down upon as bumpkins by people from the Colony's capital, Suva, which, in 1956, had 37,371 inhabitants. But other towns are much smaller, those with under 3,000 people being hardly more than large villages save that they supply goods and services for a wider hinterland than would a normal village. Townspeople tend to have friends and relatives in the surrounding country districts, whom they meet for a drink at the local bar on Saturdays. People of Suva are criticized for not giving time or hospitality to their country cousins much more often than are the residents of smaller towns where there is not the social gap which exists, say, in India, where town life differs greatly from country life and where almost any white-collar worker sees himself as infinitely superior to the villager, and seldom treats him as an equal.

---

[1] A small amount of land not occupied by Fijians at the time was alienated between 1905 and 1909, as the sole exception.

[2] O'Loughlin 1956: 72. There are £F111 to £100 sterling. Amounts in this book are given in £F.

From the first, most of the immigrants were Hindus, and the Muslim and Christian proportions of the community have not greatly changed since the indenture period, being 15·0 per cent and 2·6 per cent in 1956. There has, however, been some proliferation of sects and socio-religious associations within each of the major religious communities. Within the orthodox Hindu (Sanatan Dharm) population, groups of the Kabirpanthi and Ramanandi sects were formed.[1] The latter suffered eclipse when its founder died, but the former still exists. Larger and more influential is the Arya Samaj reformist sect.[2] An Arya Samaj association was started in 1902, and has played an important part in the religious and social affairs of the Colony. Finally, a branch of the Ramkrishna Mission was established in recent years, and this has played an especially important role among Fiji Indians who came from South India.

On the Muslim side both Sunni (orthodox) and Ahmadiya[3] Muslims have founded mosques, and have imported teachers (*maulvi*) when necessary. The Christian community is divided into Methodists, Roman Catholics, Anglicans and Seventh Day Adventists, according to the missions working in the particular locality.

Important social activities have developed from these religious allegiances, of which education provides a good example. The first two successful schools for Fiji Indians were started in 1898 by the Methodist Mission and the Marist Brothers. Later the Anglicans entered the field and by 1916, the year that the Government set up a Department of Education, there were also schools operated by the Arya Samaj and by the Muslims (some being attached to the mosques themselves, and some run by the Islam Teaching Society). In 1926 South Indians formed the Then India Sanmarga Ikya Sangam, which was an association devoted to social and educational work among Fiji Indians as well as to the preservation of the South Indian languages. The Sangam also started a chain of schools in the Colony, and received help from Ramkrishna Mission teachers. In 1956 there were 154 Indian schools in Fiji, all but 13 of which were Government-aided;[4] of these, 129 were run by non-denominational settlement committees and by Indian socio-religious associations of the type described, and 11 directly by the Government.[5] There were also a few schools under Christian missions.

There were also several associations for more general social welfare

[1] Followers of the Saints Kabir and Ramananda.

[2] Founded by Dayanand Saraswati (1824–1883) who went to the ancient Vedic texts to reform Hindu practice and counteract Christian influences in India.

[3] The name of a sect founded by Mirza Ghulam Ahmad in 1879, and regarded as heretical by other Muslims for its various unorthodox tenets.

[4] Indians were also enrolled in some of the 30 multi-racial schools.

[5] H.M.S.O. 1958: 40–1.

9

and advancement. One already mentioned was the Southerners' Sangam. Another was the Indian Reform League, founded in 1924, which had been operated by the more westernized Hindus of the community. In 1934 the Indian Association was formed, and in 1946 a dispute over the political allegiance of its senior members resulted in a split and the founding of the Central Organization. There was also a branch of the Muslim League (open to Sunni Muslims), as well as the Muslim Association of Fiji, which was controlled by the Ahmadiyas. All these bodies had political aims as well as social programmes. They wanted to organize schools and educational gatherings and help in national emergencies; but they also wanted to institute, at their meetings, reforms which would require Government action, and to support candidates at the elections to the Legislative Council.

POST-INDENTURE POLITICAL PATTERNS

Fiji is a Crown Colony, with a Governor and Civil Service appointed by the Secretary of State for the Colonies. In addition, there is a Legislative Council, with power to enact and advise on legislation (subject to veto by the Secretary of State in London). In 1951, there were thirty-one members of the Council, sixteen being officials and fifteen representing each of the three major communities: Fijian, Fiji Indian and European. The five Fijians were nominated by the Governor from a panel of ten names submitted to him by the Great Council of Chiefs, and of the five Europeans and Fiji Indians two were nominated by the Governor and three elected from constituencies dividing the Colony into south, northeast and north zones. Elections were held every three years, and suffrage on the Fiji Indian electoral roll was reserved for those over twenty-one years who had certain financial, property or education qualifications.[1]

This degree of Fiji Indian participation in government came into being after a steady expansion of responsibility. In 1916 the first Fiji Indian was nominated to the Legislative Council; in 1929 Fiji Indian elected members were admitted and in 1937 the number of Fiji Indian members was made equal to that of the Fijian and European representatives. Ten years later the first Fiji Indian took his place on the Governor's Executive Council, a consultative body whose advice the Governor could not ignore without giving his full reasons to the Secretary of State in London.

No Fiji Indian political parties existed with specific names and

---

[1] They had to be literate in English or one of the major Indian languages used in Fiji, and had to have an annual income of £75 or own property of at least £5 annual value.

10

organization, but each leader had a group of close supporters. Some of these belonged to the associations listed in the previous section. Others were members of trade unions who declared their support for particular leaders. There were thirty such unions in 1956, having from 25 to 5,000 members. They covered all major occupational categories; farmer, teacher, stevedore, etc. Most of them contained Fiji Indians, and some, like the cane growers' unions, had few people from other communities. Yet other supporters belonged to no association, but gave their support on lines of religion, common background in India, etc. Thus, a politician might have the backing of the Sangam association, of Southern Indians who did not belong to the Sangam but who supported him because he was linked to a cane growers' union dominated by Southerners, of Gujarati-speakers because he was himself one, and perhaps of a Muslim group with whom he had formed an electoral alliance.

The political situation, as such, is not going to form part of this account, but various kinds of political allegiance reached into the rural settlements and were able to influence relations between their inhabitants. Especially significant were the cane farmers' unions, whose activities affected large numbers of people in the settlements. The history of these unions provides yet another example of the growing complexity of the society. In 1943 the first two unions were registered (though they had been operating for several years before this). By 1950 there were seven, and by 1956 no fewer than eleven unions on the books of the Department of Labour.[1] Many of these unions were formed with political ends in view, and thus the farmers who joined were themselves affected by the pattern of allegiances and oppositions between the leading public figures of the Fiji Indian community.

POST-INDENTURE INTER-RACIAL RELATIONS

Fiji Indians have had little social contact with other communities in the Colony. Their position *vis-à-vis* their European masters in the indenture period needs no elaboration, and relations with the Fijians were also distant. In the early days, when some Fijian and South Sea Island labour was still employed on the estates, people of the three communities were quartered in the same lines. Several serious disputes broke out between them, born of differences in behaviour, which were exaggerated by the close proximity in which the people were living. As a result of this, and for fear of unsettling influences on the Fijian way of life, efforts were made by Government to keep Indians and Fijians apart, and Indians were forbidden to live in

[1] Leg. Co. Paper No. 20 of 1957: 13.

Fijian villages.[1] The pattern of those days still existed in 1951 in many rural areas, where the economic activities of Fijians and Fiji Indians continued to be different. The latter cultivated sugar cane in the valleys around the coasts of the large islands; the former occupied the high lands of the interior as well as parts of the coast (and the smaller islands) and were the main producers of copra and bananas. In 1951, areas of Fijian-owned land were being demarcated as reserves for the present and future use of that community, and only outside these were Fiji Indians to be able to lease land. This may further crystallize the separation of the two communities.

Only in the towns and in parts of the coastal strip had there been much mixing of Fiji Indians with Fijians. In the former men of both communities filled the middle and lower posts in multi-racial Government and commercial offices. Here, also, Fiji Indians met Europeans in close contact as fellow Government servants or as members of a single firm. They also competed in certain professions, such as law and medicine. In rural settlements, however, there was little close contact.

CONCLUSION

This chapter has described the outlines of a community which has taken the opportunities offered in its new homeland. From humble and sometimes tragic beginnings, in which they played the simple role of a labour force, Indians in Fiji have become a community with an important place in all aspects of the Colony's life. Business and professional men, experienced political leaders, craftsmen, mechanics and farmers all exist in the Fiji Indian community. Because of the restriction on ownership of land, capital has tended to be invested in towns on urban enterprises. But the farmer nevertheless remains the most important person in the Fiji Indian community, and a major factor in the Colony. The cane which is his main crop provides revenue for the Government (through export tax, wharfage and income or company tax) as well as livelihoods for such non-agriculturalists as traders and sugar mill workers.[2] Numerically, too, the farmers are by far the largest category of Indians in Fiji, and a study of Fiji Indian rural society is an essential part of the knowledge of the whole community.

[1] Europeans were also forbidden to live with Fijians (Fiji C.S.O. 739/93, 3608/99, 4016/93, quoted in Gillion 1958).

[2] Of a total export value of £11·3 million in 1956, cane comprised £5·0 million as contrasted with £2·2 million for coconut oil, the next most important product (H.M.S.O. 1958: 20 and 23). New primary and secondary industries (e.g. manganese mining and banana growing) have somewhat lessened the importance of sugar production, but the latter is still Fiji's major activity.

II

HISTORY AND PATTERNS OF SETTLEMENT

ANY account of Fiji Indian rural settlements cannot ignore ecological features, for the pattern of housing and the location of homesteads influence the ways in which the inhabitants act together. A knowledge of the history of these settlements is important, since the degree of permanence of settlement and the lengths of stay, will help to explain people's relationships.

There are more than 300 islands in the Fiji Group. Many of these are tiny and uninhabited, and only about 100 are permanently settled. They are scattered over an area of some 300 miles square of the Pacific Ocean 2,000 miles northeast of Sydney, Australia, and 1,300 miles north of Auckland, New Zealand. Many islands are only a few square miles in size, and have no more than a handful of Fijian villages; and almost all the land is contained in the two islands of Viti Levu (4,011 sq. miles) and Vanua Levu (2,137 sq. miles). Both have mountains of between 3,000 and 4,000 feet, with systems of steep valleys and swiftly flowing rivers, whose valleys open out into flat plains when they near the Pacific Ocean. It is here that the indenture estates were founded and where the majority of Fiji Indians have settled, as the map on p. 14 shows.

Both islands contain two quite different climatic zones. The prevailing winds come from the south and east, and the windward sides of the islands have an almost constant amount of rain throughout the year. The western and northern portions, however, receive rain only during the hot season (December–March) when frequent northerly winds cause rain of a monsoonal kind. Even the casual traveller in Fiji will find this difference most marked. A journey on the main road round Viti Levu will start from Suva in the southeast with more than fifty miles of travel in either direction through a countryside of thick, tropical vegetation. But then, within the space of a few miles, the leeward zone is reached and the road continues through grasslands which are green only during the short rainy season. The temperatures for both zones are similar, averaging about 77 degrees throughout the year, though there is more difference between winter and summer in the 'dry zone'. But the rainfall in Suva is nearly double (123

13

inches) that in the western town of Lautoka (70 inches). Sugar cane will not grow well in wet conditions, requiring intensive weeding and a good drainage system. Though the initial plantations were in the wet zone, most cane is now grown on the west side of both islands,

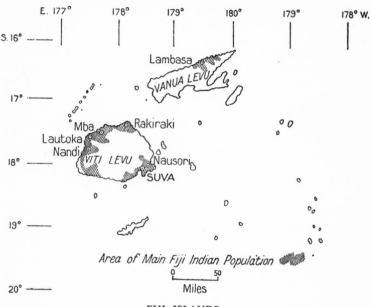

FIJI ISLANDS.

and Fiji Indians living around Suva and Navua have been turning to rice and other suitable alternative crops.[1] Two of the settlements studied lay in the dry zones of Viti Levu and Vanua Levu, and the third was in the Suva region.

GEOGRAPHY OF THE SETTLEMENTS

The settlement of Vunioki had, in 1951, a population of 514. It was near the northern coast of Viti Levu, at the head of a valley which reached south from the sea and ended in the first of the inland ranges. The river flowed through Vunioki after emerging from a small gorge to the south, and had built up small areas of flat land on either bank. From these the land sloped gently upwards, though there were steep little hills overlooking the river in some places. Three creeks

---

[1] The CSR Company closed their Nausori mill in 1959, and cane may be abandoned in this area also.

14

twisted through the area before joining the main river. They were easily fordable in dry weather, but rose with great rapidity in the wet season and were usually impassable for several hours after the almost daily storms. A motor road crossed the northern part of Vunioki; other paths were not fit for traffic and were seas of mud in the wet weather. It was often easier to reach the road and so get to the market town five miles away than it was to visit other parts of Vunioki.

The settlement covered about $1\frac{1}{2}$ by $1\frac{1}{4}$ miles as the crow flies, though considerably more by path. Cane was grown chiefly on the river flats and on the higher ground not too far from the railway line laid and operated by the CSR Company for transport of cane to its mill in the town. The rest of the land was given to mixed farming and to grazing. Beyond Vunioki to the south the country was too inaccessible for cane growing. 410 acres were under cane in Vunioki; mixed farming took up another 300 acres or so of the remaining 510 acres, the rest being used for grazing. Thus, the geographical position of a man's land determined both the crops he could grow and the ease with which he could visit other parts of the settlement.

Habitation in Vunioki was not clustered, and is called a 'settlement' rather than a 'village'. Houses were scattered all over the area, with very little concentration except near the point at which the road crossed the river, where there was a small rice mill and two shops (see map). There was no gap in settlement beyond Vunioki to the north and south; in the north the cane fields continued in unbroken succession, and in the south the homesteads of Fiji Indian farmers continued until they gave way to Fijian villages. In the other directions, however, Vunioki was sharply defined. To the east, a ridge of hills separated it from another cane-growing valley, and to the west were a gorge and some steep uninhabited hills.

Houses in Vunioki were usually extremely simply built, being of grass thatch lashed to a wood and bamboo framework. Omitting separate kitchen huts, there were 115 such houses (known by the Fijian word *bure*) as against 44 houses made of corrugated iron sheets nailed to a wooden frame. Each house usually had only one room and a family would live in, say, two houses, a storehouse and a kitchen hut, often made from opened-out kerosene tins or some such non-inflammable material. All these dwellings formed a homestead set around a compound of grass or smoothed earth. There were in Vunioki 63 such homesteads; some were half a mile from each other, others were so close that, had it not been for their separate grouping round their own compounds, they would have appeared to be one homestead (see map). If the family grew, it was easy to add to the number of houses in such homesteads, as long as there was land

15

around the central compound;[1] and the largest homesteads had half a dozen or so houses with perhaps two or three kitchens. However close the houses might be, no streets were formed. The pattern was of groups of houses looking on to their own central space. Only in towns were houses found in rows with uniform entrances on to a street.

The second settlement, Namboulima, resembled Vunioki. It lay in the dry zone of Vanua Levu, covering a wide river valley enclosed by steep and rocky hills. To the south there were paths leading to the less settled parts of the island; to the north the river flowed into the Pacific some six miles away. There were 820 acres of cane land, mostly in the valley flats, as in Vunioki; the hillsides were used for mixed farming and grazing. From Namboulima the CSR Company's railway ran the twelve miles to its mill in the market town, and there was also a newly built road. The latter only penetrated a short distance into the settlement, and most movement was along footpaths. There were fewer creeks here than in Vunioki and communication was easier.

Namboulima covered an area of about 2 miles square and had in 1951 a population of 678. Houses were almost always built of thatch, and were grouped around the compound as in Vunioki. A local variant of the *bure* was the *belo*, a house with thatch roof whose walls, of plastered and whitewashed woven bamboo, were only three or four feet high, leaving a gap between wall and roof. Inside there was a sleeping platform reached by a ladder, and the usual beaten earth floor. There was little concentration of homesteads in Namboulima, save in one spot where the road ended and where the indenture lines had stood (see map). The settlement was bounded to the west and east by uninhabited hills; to the north and south, settlement continued along the river without a break.

Delanikoro, the other settlement studied, lay in the wet zone at the edge of a wide river valley. It composed an area of about one mile square of the flat land, and the edge of some bluffs which enclosed the plain on its eastern side. Behind the bluffs lay Fijian villages, and under them a road ran for four miles to the town and its sugar mill. A large proportion of houses in Delanikoro were within one hundred yards of this road, which gave easy communications within the settlement—though the last few yards to any house might run through mud or marsh. Because they were flat and situated in the wet zone, the fields of Delanikoro were not good for cane-growing, unless they were well-drained with canals. In 1951 about half the land (145 acres) was under cane, and the rest (171 acres) was used for rice cultivation and grazing.

[1] By law every plan for a new house had to pass certain official standards of hygiene; but in practice many were constructed without these permits.

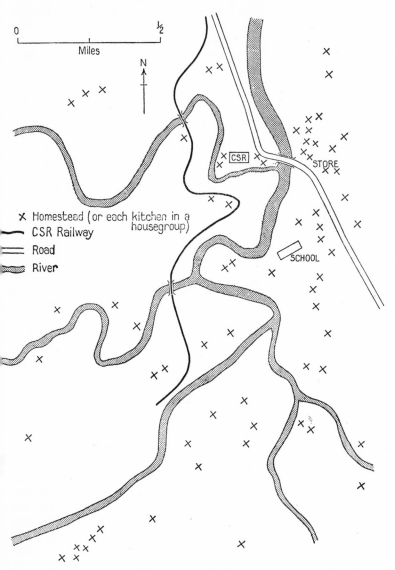

0   ½

Miles

N

CSR

STORE

✕ Homestead (or each kitchen in a housegroup)
➤ CSR Railway
═ Road
▨ River

SCHOOL

VUNIOKI SETTLEMENT.

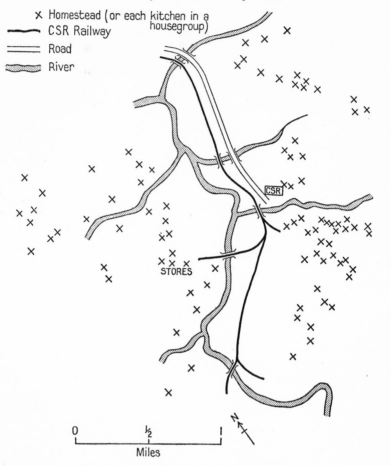

NAMBOULIMA SETTLEMENT.

The pattern of settlement differed slightly from that in Vunioki and Namboulima. Houses were often built on the higher land (see map) both as a precaution against floods and also to save the better land for agriculture. People also tended to live nearer to each other. This was partly because of the restricted area used for houses, and partly because there was greater population density, since the leases were usually smaller than in Vunioki and Namboulima.

Housing also tended to be different, for many of the settlement's 457 people lived in multi-roomed dwellings set on wooden piles a foot or so high and made of corrugated iron, which withstood the heavier rainfall better than thatch. The kitchen was also of iron and was connected to the house by a covered veranda. As with the *bure,* there was a compound in front of the house. There were, in Delanikoro, 46 iron houses compared with 45 thatched houses, and 29 of the 54 homesteads consisted of a single iron house. A growing family would try to fit into the house by partitioning off more rooms, for a new house was expensive to build; and this contrasted with the custom in the dry zone of building a new *bure* if the family got too cramped.

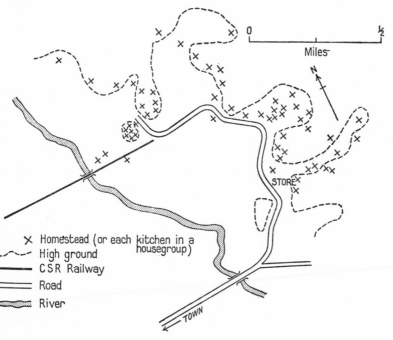

DELANIKORO SETTLEMENT.

Delanikoro also differed from the other settlements in that it was territorially cut off on all sides. To the south the road wound for nearly a quarter-mile through hillocks before reaching the nearest settlement, and to the north there was a mile of open ground. To the west the cane and paddy fields stretched right to the town; and behind ran paths to the Fijian villages. Of the three settlements, Delanikoro was most nearly a village. Yet even here the houses stretched for about a mile, and there was no street, no square or temple which provided a central meeting place. What is the reason for this pattern of settlement? Was it deliberately planned, or was it the result of chance? Short histories of the settlements will give the answers.

Indian settlement in Vunioki started at the turn of the century. The nearest estates of indentured labourers were several miles to the east, and it was from there and from the coastal estates that 'free' men came, each man leasing land from its Fijian owners, until houses were dotted throughout the area, except on some freehold land near the river.

In 1910, Europeans converted these river flats into a cane plantation, selling the crop to the CSR Company. Some of the labourers employed by them were taken straight from the indenture lines, but others were men who had already settled in Vunioki. Many built houses on land provided around the plantation's cane land, while leaseholders continued to occupy the higher ground. This pattern remained for the next thirty years, though there was a continual replacement of people—some would move out to other leases or would return to India and others would take their place. During this time shopkeepers set up businesses near the principal ford of the river.

In 1939 the CSR Company took over the cane plantation and, in accordance with its policy of operating through small tenant-farmers, split up its holding into blocks of an average of ten acres. Some of these farms were leased to men who had previously been labourers on the plantation; and the rest were given to newcomers who lived up to fifty miles from Vunioki, but who were known to the CSR Company as good farmers. The pattern of settlement now changed, for farmers built houses in the centre of their own fields which had previously been reserved for cane land by the plantation owners.

Thus settlement in Vunioki was haphazard in the sense that there was no initial centre of population acting as a nucleus for the settlement. There had been a constant flow of arrivals and departures, marked by main movements in 1910 and 1939. The table provides a measure of this mobility:

TABLE 1

	Number	Per cent
Men* born in Vunioki	27	28
Men who came before 1920	10	11
Men who came in 1920–38	27	28
Men who came after 1938	31	33
Total	95	100

* By 'men' are meant males over seventeen years (i.e. full-time worker, usually married).

It is impossible to calculate the number of people who left Vunioki during these periods, but it is said to have been considerable. There were in 1951, nineteen men and nine women who had come to Fiji under indenture, or 5·5 per cent of the total population.

Unlike Vunioki, the first settlement in Namboulima was made by the CSR Company through a cane estate. Lines were built to house indentured workers, and these were at first the only Fiji Indians to live there. Slowly the number of free men grew who took leases in the hills above the limit of the cane. After the abolition of indenture the CSR Company leased the estate to European planters. But after four or five years the shortage of labour drove these men out of business, and the CSR Company then made ten acre blocks and distributed them to farmers, some of whom were Namboulima men who had come down from their more remote leases which had frequently grown unproductive after over-cropping. The map shows a fairly uniform scatter of homesteads over the settlement; for the site of the indenture lines had not developed into a settlement centre, nor had the area around the two shops.

There had been relatively little movement of population in and out of Namboulima. Until recently, the settlement was without a road, and to go to the town meant several hours' walk. The picture of a fairly remote and stable settlement is supported in Table 2:

TABLE 2

	Number	Per cent
Men born in Namboulima	51	37
Men who came before 1920	21	15
Men who came in 1920–38	40	29
Men who came after 1938	26	19
Total	138	100

There were forty male and sixteen female survivors of the indenture era, or 8·6 per cent of the population.

As in Namboulima, settlement of Fiji Indians in Delanikoro began in the late nineteenth century when cane cultivation was started by Europeans for the CSR Company, and the foundations of the indenture lines could still be seen in 1951. After the abolition of indenture, the CSR Company divided the land into five acre blocks, whose tenants were supposed to spend half their time on their land and the remainder on the nearby estate of the CSR Company. The experiment failed after a two-year attempt (1918–20) and ten acre blocks were then made in most other settlements. But the smaller blocks survived in Delanikoro, and more than half of these were still held by the same people and their families. Though nobody had lived in Delanikoro for more than forty-five years, there was a fair percentage of men who had served their indenture there and had stayed ever since. More recent arrivals included a storekeeper and men who had bought portions of a block of freehold land which had formerly been held by a European. Table 3 sets out the development.

TABLE 3

	Number	Per cent
Men born in Delanikoro	27	30
Men who came before 1920	15	17
Men who came in 1920–38	26	30
Men who came after 1938	20	23
Total	88	100

Twenty-seven men and nineteen women (10 per cent of the population) had been indentured.

The settlements might vary in the details of their histories but they were similar in two main respects. One was that permanent settlement started with free men taking leases, whether or not indenture lines existed. The other was that there had been considerable movement in and out of the settlements, reflected in the number of men who had come in recent years. Both features were connected to the system of land tenure.

There are several categories of land in Fiji. By far the largest is that held by the Fijians themselves. Under Fijian custom land is owned by social groups (*matanggali*) of which each member is a coparcener. Much land was sold to Europeans in the days before the Cession of Fiji, sometimes for the traditional whisky and fire-arms. One of the first acts of the new Government, after Cession, was to prohibit the alienation of land by the Fijians, and a Lands Commission was appointed to examine the claims of freeholders to their titles. It validated some 400,000 acres, found that another 88,000 acres were unclaimed by either Fijians or Europeans, and classed the remainder (about 4,012,000 acres) as Fijian *matanggali* land. This latter area was later diminished, firstly, by further sales of land during 1905-9; secondly, by sale of 75,000 acres to the Government which has become Crown land; and thirdly, by the reversion of 120,000 acres to the Government when *matanggalis* became defunct. The total amount alienated in these ways has brought the Fijian *matanggali* land holdings to 3,756,000 acres, with 459,000 acres of freehold land held by individuals of all communities in the Colony, including Fijians.[1]

These figures show how large a proportion of land is under Fijian control. When free men left the indenture lines and decided to farm, they usually had to go to the head of the *matanggali* to negotiate a lease. This was a complicated procedure. For they first had to obtain the verbal consent of the *matanggali* and then make an application to the Government, which was passed on to the Fijian Administration[2] whose local officials finally gave their permission after contacting the head of the *matanggali*. Not only did this take a long time, but the approval of the *matanggali's* head had to be maintained with presents throughout the period; and, as the Fijians became more sophisticated and competition for the better land became more lively, the value of the presents increased. The system was later simplified, and the Fiji Indian had merely to apply to the European District Commissioner, who then negotiated with the Fijians. But even then, pressure could be brought to bear on the applicant by the *matanggali* head, to the latter's advantage. It was not until 1940 that a Native Land Trust Board was inaugurated, which henceforth issued leases for thirty, instead of the previous ten years, and which had full power to lease any Fijian-held land and collect the rent on behalf of its owners, and to distribute it to them.

The result of the early system of leases was that Fiji Indians sometimes had to lease land wherever they could find Fijians willing to give them plots without too much expense. They might settle near or far from their shipmates; they might have to search for land at some distance from where they had served their indenture; and they might only find land which was far from any neighbours. All this made for 'haphazard' conditions of settlement, in which Fiji Indians could not have controlled the form of their settlements, even had they wanted to. There was, in any case, no pressure towards forming closely packed settlements of the type which most immigrants had left behind them in India. There was no danger of attack, necessitating a fortified village; nor was the country heavily wooded, resulting in settlement in a nuclear clearing; there were no inland roads at the time of settlement which might have stimulated a ribbon settlement along them, and the small track used by the CSR Company for hauling cane was hardly the public artery near which settlement might have been beneficial.

Later occupation of land did nothing at first to crystallize the initial pattern of settlement by a continued use of the same

[1] H.M.S.O. 1958: 25; Shephard 1945: 16.
[2] Within the Colonial Government there is a separate system of local government for all Fijians.

homesteads. For the CSR Company's land policy after indenture meant that some of the land was abandoned and new homesteads were built on the newly-formed CSR Company blocks. Also, there was a continuing turnover of Fijian leases, as free men went back to India after their ten years in Fiji, with newcomers not necessarily settling in the same places as their predecessors.

This pattern changed after about 1925. In the first place, fewer people gave up leases and returned to India after indenture was abolished. In the second, land tenure was made more secure, mainly by the CSR Company's decision to break up its holdings into family-sized blocks, which resulted in the creation of a class of peasant cane farmers, and much later by the creation of the Native Land Trust Board. In 1943, the CSR Company had 21,000 acres of freehold land and 29,000 acres of Fijian and other leasehold land which it considered suitable for growing cane. Of this area, no less than 19,000 acres and 27,000 acres respectively were leased in small blocks, almost entirely to Fiji Indian growers.[1] These leases were renewable after every ten years, but there was almost complete security of tenure if the tenant kept to the conditions of the lease. These included several clauses designed to maintain the land in good condition—for example, that there should be rotation of crops, that the land should be kept weeded, and that artificial manures should be applied as the CSR Company directed. When a tenant died, the lease was normally transferred to an heir.

Another factor which made for continuity of settlement was that most Fiji Indians were now members of kin-groups. When a person temporarily left a settlement, a relative sometimes informally took over cultivation until the owner himself returned. Formerly, if a man left the settlement his lease lapsed too, for he had nobody to act on his behalf. On the whole, it appears that mobility, though considerable when compared to non-immigrant societies, had lessened in the years before 1951, especially when inhabitants had an interest in land. The competition for work in the towns, and the pressure on the available land elsewhere, was too great to allow it.

DEFINITION OF SETTLEMENT BOUNDARIES

This account has dealt with each settlement as if it were a definite unit of area and population. But this was not always the case; for the boundaries of a settlement were to some extent only where the inhabitants of contiguous settlements said they were, rather than where they had been placed by official demarcation.

Several factors influenced the pattern of settlement boundaries;

[1] Shephard 1945: 16.

the position of Fijian *matanggali* land, the limits of the CSR Company's cane sector, and physical features which made a boundary easily visible. The point can be elaborated with reference to Vunioki settlement.

The non-Fijian population of the Colony lived in one of three Districts at the time of fieldwork, each of which was under a District Commissioner who had a number of District Officers to help him.[1] Though there was no official division smaller than the District,[2] the District 'out-stations' in which the District Officers resided were, in effect, Sub-Districts. Each one had a small court-house, and machinery for collecting taxes and carrying on other official business.[3] Below the Sub-District, however, there were no administrative boundaries at all. There were no people with official status in the settlements, and any Fiji Indians, Chinese, Europeans or other Pacific Islanders living in settlements had to go to the Sub-District town for any business with the Government.

Vunioki, then, had no official existence.[4] The name of the settlement was taken from the name of a small area of Fijian land within the settlement. This land lay in the north of the present settlement, and tradition had it that a Fijian village had once stood there. But the area of the settlement was much larger than the extent of 'Vunioki'. An area which nearly approximated it was named Vunioki by the Europeans who used to operate the plantation. They might well have chosen any of the other Fijian names for plots lying within their plantation, but they may have chosen Vunioki because of the previous Fijian village. Later the CSR Company also called the cane land there 'Vunioki' and gave it separate existence in their records as one of two sub-sectors in the sector controlled by their European Field Officer. This Vunioki sub-sector of the CSR Company varied in size, for some of the cane land was on Fijian leases, and could be put under other crops by its tenants.

The area covered by the CSR Company's sub-sector did not comprise the whole of Vunioki settlement, however. Settlement and sub-sector boundaries coincided at the northern end of the valley, where

---

[1] Fijians had their own structure of fourteen provinces and their sub-divisions, based on areas owned-in-common by Fijian social units; within these were the nuclear villages.　　　　　　　[2] H.M.S.O. 1958: 88.

[3] The reason that these Sub-Districts were well-defined may be because in former times they formed the Units of administration. It was only in 1938 that the number of administrative Districts was reduced from eighteen to five, and later to four and then three.

[4] In the decennial census, some settlements are listed separately (e.g. Delani-koro is mentioned, perhaps because it forms a discrete settlement), and have a quasi-official status thereby. On other occasions, however, the CSR Company's sector is made the unit of enumeration. Vunioki settlement is not listed separately, for example.

the cane fields continued unbroken into the other sub-sector super-vised by the Vunioki CSR Field Officer. But in other directions there were homesteads of farmers growing rice, tobacco and other crops, who had nothing to do with the CSR Company and the production of cane, and yet were known as Vunioki residents. Those on the eastern and western slopes of the valley had obviously to form part of any settlement which was based on the cane-growing farms in the valley, for behind them for some distance stretched uninhabited hills. But those to the south merged with the homesteads of the next settlement which also had no cane and so had the possibility of belonging to either settlement; and, indeed, there was some am-biguity about the affiliation of some of these marginal homesteads with the inhabitants of Vunioki.

Discussion of these cases often revealed that the main criterion for belonging to the settlement involved some sort of inter-action with the people of that settlement. A man living on the margin of settle-ment lands, who rarely shopped at the settlement's store, went to town by bus from a bus stop near or outside the settlement boundary, had no cane land and no school-going children, and in fact seldom participated in the major economic and social activities of the settle-ment, might well be called an inhabitant of the next settlement. Similarly, people of the latter settlement might be dubious of his affiliations there. A homestead could never be completely isolated, but some met most of the criteria just listed, and the lack of official boundaries might make the status of such a homestead debatable.

On the criterion of inter-action, the CSR Company's sub-sector was the most important of the boundaries just discussed. For the cane farmers of a sub-sector provided a settlement with what was often its only sustained and co-ordinated associational activity, in the Gang organized for cane cutting. But the boundaries of settlements remained to a large extent undefined and officially unrecognized.

INTERNAL STRUCTURE OF THE SETTLEMENT: WARD AND CULTURAL GROUP

Looked at from the outside, the settlement was an entity, though its boundaries might be indefinite. Within the settlement, however, there was the notion of a division into what can be called wards. It was a 'notion' because the boundaries of these wards were no more definite than those of the settlement itself. All the ward names recorded in Vunioki and Namboulima were at the same time names of Fijian tracts of land within the settlement. Their boundaries should therefore have been definite enough. But people gave widely differing accounts of the areas of various wards as the map shows.

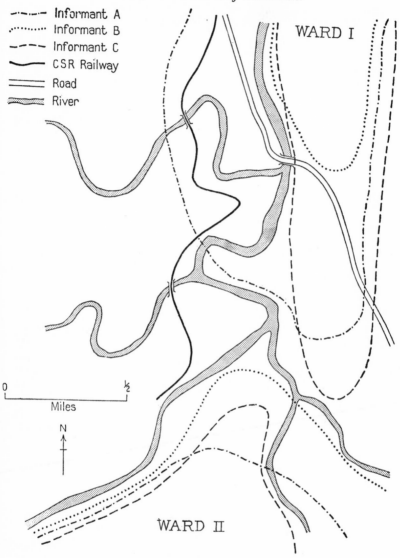

VUNIOKI WARDS.

These wards did not appear to be important in the life of the settle-ment. People used the ward name in casual conversation to tell a questioner where someone had gone, for example; but there was no organization of associations or kin groups on the basis of wards. The

Hindi word *toli*, which was often used to refer to the ward, was said to be traditionally connected with the division of a village into sections of different caste—a division which was irrelevant in Fiji, it was said, because these caste distinctions did not exist. The neutral word *jagah* (place) was therefore also used. There were four wards in Vunioki and three in Namboulima; in Delanikoro people did no more than occasionally refer to 'the Madrassi corner' or to 'Baburam's corner'. This may well be because Delanikoro covered so much smaller an area that there was no need for sub-division.

More important than these wards in the sub-division of the settlement was the tendency for people with the same socio-religious background to form separate clusters of homesteads. There were three main divisions into what may be called 'cultural groups', that is, groups whose members were distinguished either by religion or the retention of some customs of the area from which they came in India. In India itself, of course, the people of each province, and sometimes of much smaller regions, may vary in their behaviour. But it would be impossible to apply such a restricted yardstick to Fiji Indians, since many differences in dialect, dress, diet and so forth had disappeared in the new country. Nevertheless, definite cultural variants remained between Hindus from North and South India, and between them and the Muslim community; and members were conscious enough of their differences for them to be called 'groups' rather than 'categories'. A few discernible sub-divisions existed within each of these cultural groups, too. South Indians could be divided into those with Tamil and those with Telugu as their 'mother tongue'; the Northerners had both orthodox members and Arya Samaj reformists; and the Muslims, who were almost all North Indian, were divided into the Sunni and Ahmadiya sects. But these divisions were mainly important to those within the cultural group. People outside tended to see all Muslims, for example, as undifferentiated.

The proportions of each cultural group in the three settlements were as follows:

TABLE 4

Cultural Group	Vunioki §	Delanikoro †	Namboulima
Northern Hindus	53·7	54·0	60·2
Southern Hindus	21·2	37·0	21·3 *
Muslims ‡	25·1	9·0	18·5
	100·0	100·0	100·0

* Six of these were nominal Roman Catholics (roughly 1 per cent).
† There were also twelve Sikhs in Delanikoro.
‡ There were no Ahmadiyas in any settlement studied.
§ Vunioki contained one Gujarati.

28

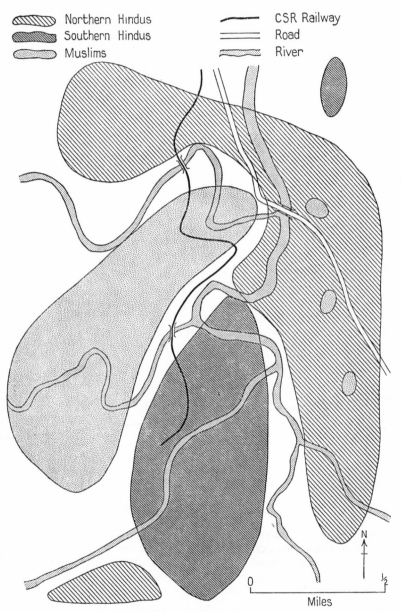

Northern Hindus
Southern Hindus
Muslims

CSR Railway
Road
River

VUNIOKI CULTURAL GROUPS.

N

0   Miles   ½

In all cases Northerners comprised the largest cultural group, and they and the other cultural groups were present in roughly the same proportions as for the entire community. Members of different cultural groups to some extent lived separately from each other.

The three maps show Vunioki with the clearest distinction between what one might call 'cultural neighbourhoods'.[1] The other two settle-

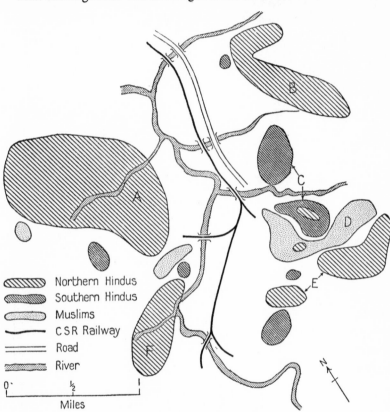

Northern Hindus
Southern Hindus
Muslims
C S R Railway
Road
River

0   ½   1
Miles

NAMBOULIMA CULTURAL GROUPS.

ments showed a mixture of cultural groups with certain degree of differentiation; for example in Namboulima one would see A, B, E and F as Northern neighbourhoods, C as Southern and D as Muslim, and disregard the smaller clusters. Again, Delanikoro contained a Southern (A) and two Northern neighbourhoods (B and C). These cultural neighbourhoods did not correspond to the wards. Their physical boundaries were not the same, and their survival was

[1] These have been called 'wards' in an earlier publication (Mayer 1953).

governed by different factors. For the ward was based on named plots of Fijian land, whereas the cultural neighbourhood was no more than a concomitant of settlement at a particular time.

INTERNAL STRUCTURE OF THE SETTLEMENT: THE HOMESTEAD

The lack of emphasis on wards and neighbourhoods gives the individual homestead an added importance in the settlement pattern.

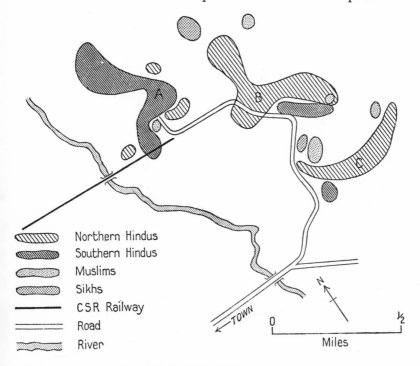

Northern Hindus
Southern Hindus
Muslims
Sikhs
CSR Railway
Road
River

DELANIKORO CULTURAL GROUPS.

The word 'homestead' denotes any separate group of houses—i.e. set in their own compound—regardless of who is living in them. It is a sociologically neutral word, and several categories of homestead should be distinguished. Thus, 'simple household' will mean a group of people—of unspecified kin ties, if any—living in the same homestead with a common kitchen and budget, with only one adult wage-earner, any other male being an unmarried youth.[1] 'Joint household'

[1] The average age of marriage for youths was about 17–18 years, and there were few unmarried men over that age. Girls usually married from fourteen to sixteen years.

31

will mean a group having a common kitchen and a single budget with more than one adult wage-earner. Finally, 'house group' will mean a group living in a single homestead but with several separate kitchens and budgets. None of these terms implies the existence of kin ties within these homesteads; this is deliberate, because there were several homesteads in which unrelated people were fellow-members. Generally speaking, however, each type of homestead corresponded to a particular kinship unit, when applied to the settlements. The elementary family went with the household, the 'joint family' with the joint household and the extended family with the house group. Below are listed the main types of homestead in the three settlements.

TABLE 5

Type	Vunioki	Delanikoro	Namboulima	Total
Simple household	40	37	47	124
Joint household	15	14	21	50
House group	8	3	11	22
Total	63	54	79	196

These figures show that the proportions of types were fairly uniform in the three settlements. The only major difference was the relative lack of house groups in Delanikoro. However, it must be remembered that, owing to the heavier rainfall, people in Delanikoro tended to live in large corrugated iron houses containing both sleeping accommodation and kitchen under one roof. It was obviously less easy to make a separate kitchen in such a house,[1] than it was to build a new thatched kitchen in a compound already composed of several thatched houses. If there was a family division in Delanikoro, people tended to build an entirely new house for themselves and, at the same time, to build it apart from the one they were leaving, so that two simple households were formed, rather than a single house group.

The majority of homesteads comprised simple households. Table 6 shows that those who lived in these simple households were, in fact, in a numerical minority, though they comprised the largest category.

TABLE 6

Type	Vunioki	Delanikoro	Namboulima	Total
Simple household *	234	221	312	767
Joint household	169	184	209	562
House group	111	52	157	320
Total	514	457	678	1,649

* Including households of single people.

[1] There are no examples of sections of an extended family with separate budgets using the same kitchen in rotation.

History and Patterns of Settlement

The more complex types of homestead were mainly composed of agnates and their dependants, a fact which was consistent with a society recognizing patrilineal inheritance. Below is a table showing the types of relationships existing in joint households and house groups.

TABLE 7

Type	Vunioki No.	Pop.	Delanikoro No.	Pop.	Namboulima No.	Pop.
Joint household of agnates	13	150	12	170	17	177
Joint household of affines	1	14	2	14	3	25
Joint household—no kin ties	1	5	—	—	1	8
House group of agnates	3	52	1	29	8	125
House group of affines	4	53	2	23	2	21
House group—no kin ties	1	6	—	—	1	10
Total	23	280	17	236	32	366

There were various possible combinations of kin in each type of household. Thus 'agnates in joint households' might include brothers living together, or a father living with his sons; affinal groups might contain two brothers-in-law or a man with his daughter's husband. There were one or two homesteads whose populations fell between the various types; thus there was a house group of a man with his married son as well as his daughter's husband. These cases have been classified by taking into account the relative importance of the inhabitants. In the above instance the son was young and only recently married, whereas the son-in-law was older with a large family of his own, and the homestead has thus been classified as a group of affinally related kin.

Table 7 indicates that joint households were primarily composed of agnates; so close an arrangement, involving a common housekeeping fund, was apparently unsuitable for affines. The latter were more suited to the loose organization of the house group, and only in Namboulima did affines live in joint households more often than in house groups.

Both types of homestead sometimes contained people unrelated to the other residents. This was usually the result of indenture. Older men who had been shipmates and companions in the labour lines still lived together; or sometimes a family would have an India-born man to help them, who had remained single not by choice but because of the scarcity of women during and immediately after indenture. None of these homesteads were formed of Fiji-born people alone, and they will probably cease to exist when the India-born die out.

33

INTERNAL STRUCTURE OF THE SETTLEMENT:
THE EXTENDED KIN GROUP

The preceding section has shown the varied composition of home-steads at a particular moment—in the middle of 1951. Many of these differences can be better understood if it is clear that they portray only a stage in the development of the homesteads. As many anthro-pologists have shown, such differences can help one to reconstruct the cycle of a family's, or a homestead's, life. Thus, the simple house-hold of a couple and their children grows into a joint household when the couple's sons grow up and marry; later, these young men may either split to form several simple households in different home-steads, or may manage their own affairs in the same homestead, which then becomes a house group.

The evolution of extended kin groups is of interest here because it provides one way in which settlement patterns can be seen in terms of kinship. When a joint household or a house group divided, and some of its members went to live in a different homestead, the ties of kinship remained, unless the split had been accompanied by such bad feeling that the two households were not on speaking terms—a rare event, at least after the first few years. The members of the extended kin group thus formed might co-operate in economic, religious or associational affairs, as will be shown in the following chapters.

The growth and splitting of homesteads was only one way in which an extended kin group was formed. Another was by the immi-gration of relatives. A man who got into difficulties in a settlement might, for example, come to live in the settlement of his mother's brother, his wife's father or his agnatic collaterals (father's brother and his sons, etc.). He would, of course, only come if he were on good terms with these kinsmen, and they would perhaps give him work, or arrange for him to obtain a lease of Fijian or CSR Company land. But he would usually form his own homestead separate from that of his relatives.

A third way of creating an extended kin group was by marriage between members of the settlement itself. It was not considered wrong for two people of the same settlement to marry[1] and this often hap-

[1] This runs counter to the traditional values of the majority of Northern Hindus. For villages in North India are generally exogamous. From this change we can infer that Northerners did not regard the settlement as an equivalent of the villages they had left, and this reinforces a view of the Fiji situation as a new situation, rather than an attempted reconstruction of the old. South Indians were traditionally allowed to marry within the village; but it cannot be said that the change in Northern customs was due to Southern influence, since Southerners only started coming to the settlements towards the end of the indenture period, when the pattern appears to have been established.

I (a). Scattered homesteads in Vunioki settlement.

(b). A thatch homestead in Namboulima.

II (a). An iron homestead in Delanikoro.

(b). The 'centre' of Vunioki (store on the left).

III (a). Canefield; dry zone of Viti Levu.

(b). Storm clouds; wet zone of Viti Levu.

IV (*a*). Transplanting paddy.

(*b*). Harvesting paddy.

pened when eligible spouses existed. Table 8 shows the number of such matches in each of the three settlements.

TABLE 8

Settlement	No. of Matches
Vunioki	3
Delanikoro	10
Namboulima	11

The figures refer to matches between households whose members still lived in the settlement at the time of fieldwork. One would expect a higher number for Delanikoro and Namboulima since there had been less mobility there than in Vunioki and so less chance for the kin of one of the partners to have moved away. In terms of total population, the number of intra-settlement matches was highest in Delanikoro. This adds a social aspect to the physical and demographic contrast between the settlements of Delanikoro and Vunioki —the former geographically separate, with easy communications and a higher population density, the latter intersected by its creeks, with long distances between homesteads, and in places no definite boundary with neighbouring settlements. Delanikoro, in short, seems to emerge as a more compact settlement with closer social ties than Vunioki. Nevertheless, even the few matches within Vunioki when combined with the other factors, had produced extended kin groups, which included a large proportion of the entire settlement's population. An example is provided by the extended Southern kin group in Vunioki. The main linkages were as follows, omitting children and those who had emigrated from the settlement.

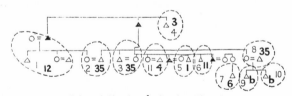

I = household number. **b** = born in settlement
I = years of settlement. ▲ = deceased

**VUNIOKI SOUTHERN
EXTENDED KIN GROUP.**

There were eleven homesteads and a population of ninety-three; the number of years the head of each homestead had spent in Vunioki is marked in bold type and shows the development of this extended kin group. At first two brothers (in homesteads 2 and 3) came to

Vunioki as free men, with their sister's husband (8), whose household grew to be a joint one and then split into separate homesteads (9 and 10). Two affines of these men came when the CSR Company formed its cane blocks in 1939—one of them (6) was given a Company block, the other (1) obtained a Fijian lease of cane land. More recently other relatives had come to live in the settlement (4, 5, 7 and 11).

The degree to which the extended kin groups dominated the settlement populations is shown in the following table.

TABLE 9

Group	Vunioki Homestead	Pop.	Delanikoro Homestead	Pop.
Southern Hindu—kin group A	11	93	12	139
—others	2	16	5	25
Northern Orthodox—kin group A	13	111	7	81
—kin group B	5	25	6	59
—kin group C	—	—	4	30
—kin group D	—	—	3	29
—others	13	106	8	41
Arya Samaj	2	34	—	—
Muslims—kin group A	12	104	3	24
—kin group B	3	18	—	—
—others	2	7	3	17
Sikhs	—	—	3	12
Total	63	514	54	457

The table shows that Vunioki contained three large groups of kin —one in each of the main cultural groups of the settlement—which together amounted to more than half the settlement's homesteads, and 308 of the 514 people. Similarly, in Delanikoro there were three large kin groups, including two kin groups of Northerners[1] which contained about half the number of homesteads and 61 per cent of the population.

These extended kin groups sometimes, but not always, formed separate parts of the settlement's territory. The extended kin group, given in diagrammatic form above, did, for example, fit the Southern cultural neighbourhood in Vunioki[2]—the two remaining Southern homesteads being isolated at the northern end of the settlement. The large Northern extended kin group, on the other hand, took up part of the cultural neighbourhood in the north of Vunioki but also comprised the small group of Northern households isolated at the

[1] These groups were kept separate by differences of caste which prevented the inter-marriage of their members.
[2] See map on p. 29.

extreme south of the settlement. Sociologically, the extended kin groups might be distinct; but this did not necessarily coincide with a spatial distinction.

A knowledge of the history and geography of the settlements and the spatial distribution of major social units forms an important background to the later chapters. The haphazard pattern of settlement and the frequent difficulties of communication; the lack of official recognition of settlement boundaries and their unimportance to residents themselves; the minor role of territorial sub-divisions within the settlement, in contrast to the significance of kinship and common cultural background as social links, must be remembered in the discussion of economic, political and religious activities which now follows.[1]

[1] Readers familiar with Indian society may wish to read about the place of caste in Fiji Indian settlements (see pp. 156-64) before starting accounts of these activities, for caste is so important in Indian social organization that they may well wonder why it is not more often mentioned below.

III

ECONOMIC ACTIVITIES

AGRICULTURE

IT has already been said that the main productive activity in Fiji Indian settlements was agriculture, and that the major crop in most places was sugar cane. About one million tons of cane were produced each year, giving between 110,000 and 130,000 tons of raw sugar, which were manufactured at the five mills operated by the CSR Company.[1] Towns had grown up around each mill, and most Fiji Indian settlements were in one of the mills' hinterlands and looked to it as the last link in the chain of sugar production started in their fields. Sugar cane production was almost entirely an Indian monopoly. In 1943, Indians occupied 94 per cent of the land under cane, Fijians 3 per cent, and 3 per cent was reserved by the CSR Company for experimental and nursery purposes;[2] the proportions had changed little by 1951.

Cane was cultivated on the one hand by tenants of the CSR Company, and on the other by farmers with their own freehold land or land leased from Fijians or the Crown. The latter were under no obligation to sell their cane to the CSR Company, but since all the mills were in the Company's hands, they did indeed sell it under a ten-year contract with the Company,[3] and were known as 'contractors'. The land held by tenants and contractors was roughly equal (51 and 46 per cent respectively of the land under cultivation in 1944). But almost all tenants had blocks of from 8 to 16 acres (seven-eighths in 1944) whereas contractors tended to have smaller blocks (35 per cent had between 2 and 6 acres) and also a few much larger holdings (350 contractors, as contrasted with 14 tenants, had holdings of over 24 acres of cane land).[4] It was general to find the CSR Company's tenants on the lower and more fertile valley land,

---

[1] This was the size of harvests in the few years preceding 1951. Production has considerably increased since that time.

[2] Shephard 1945: 42.

[3] Called a Memorandum of Purchase of Cane.

[4] All figures from Shephard 1945: 38–9.

with the contractors occupying the higher land, where the soil was less productive and the costs of cultivation higher. This difference in location, coupled with the greater control exercised by the CSR Company on the husbandry of its tenants, through the clauses of the Tenancy Agreement,[1] made the average tenant's cultivation more efficient and his cane yield higher than that of the contractor. But in this general account both tenants and contractors are considered together.

Sugar cane was planted each year from March until the end of May, and was harvested about fifteen to eighteen months later. Most planting took place during the hot, wet months of March and April, when conditions were suitable for a quick 'strike' of new shoots from the nodes of the seed cane. Before sowing, the land had to be thoroughly ploughed and harrowed, and furrows made a yard or so apart. The seed cane was then cut and brought to the field, laid in the furrows, chopped into six-inch lengths, pressed into the ground, and covered lightly with soil (see Plate V*a*). The cane which did not germinate could be replaced in May, after which the weather became too cold for growth.

An element of risk and uncertainty attended the planting of cane. Good weather was most important; too much rain would waterlog the seed cane and rot it, whereas a week or ten days without rain, immediately after planting, would dry out the land to such an extent that there would be little germination. The weather in Fiji was variable at this time of year; rain normally fell but not always in exactly the right quantities and with the right timing to suit the farmer. Hence, when the decision to plant was made in good conditions, there was a rush by all the cane farmers to get their crop sown quickly. The entire family went to the field to help, the men wielding their choppers on the seed cane, and quite small children covering it with earth.

Cane two or three months old was artificially fertilized with ammonium sulphate and was weeded every couple of months from the time the shoots were a foot or so high until the next rains at the end of that year. By November or so it was as high as a man, and there was danger that the first heavy rains of the hot weather would beat down the cane; as many crops were damaged for this reason as from bad weather at the time of sowing.

[1] The Memorandum of Purchase of Cane gave the CSR Company the right to determine the variety of cane grown by the contractor, and said that the crop must have been cultivated and harvested 'to the complete satisfaction of the Company' but did not specify the need for application of artificial fertilizer, the fencing of livestock and the adequate weeding that was contained in the Tenancy Agreement (Shephard 1945: 57 and 51).

There was little to do in the cane fields from this time until the harvest started in the cooler weather of June. This process was highly organized by the CSR Company; for the individual grower did not harvest the cane himself, but joined with all the farmers of a sub-sector in a harvesting Gang, operated along lines laid down by the CSR Company itself.[1]

The Gang completed the harvest in about four months, and cane farmers were given considerable economic benefit by this co-operative effort. Shephard compares the ten- to twelve-acre Fiji Indian family block with the maximum of about five acres which a Trinidad Indian family could cultivate by itself. He attributes much of this difference to the 'chaotic' carting of cane in Trinidad, where each farmer brought his cane by cart to the mill, and might wait most of the day to have it weighed on the purchasing scale.[2]

In harvesting, the stem of cane was cut at ground level where it first sprouted from the seed cane. The top fronds were cut off and lay drying in the fields. After they and the grass in the fields had been burnt—and the cane districts on an August night were full of the dull red glow of these fires—new shoots sprouted from the old seed cane. These provided a second crop, known as 'rattoon', which was cut, together with the first crop, during the next season's harvest. It was even possible to grow a second rattoon crop during the third year; but the cane was by this time fairly weak, and such crops were rare and mainly produced by contractors.

The two cane crops took nearly two and a half years to grow. This period formed part of one of two systems of rotation. In the four-year cycle, when a man's block was divided into quarters, a further nine months was taken up with fallow or the cultivation of a green manure such as a pulse crop, and the fourth year with the cultivation of plant cane for seed. This was the cycle recommended by the CSR Company, and in fact specified as one of the conditions on which tenancies were granted. The other was a shorter cycle; soon after the harvest a quick-maturing paddy[3] crop was sown and harvested in February, when the land was ploughed and new cane was sown. This was known as the three-year or 33 per cent rotation. It gave the land little rest, and could only be successful in the more fertile areas. It had the advantage, from the farmer's point of view, of not only producing cane more quickly, but also of giving him a crop of paddy for his domestic consumption.

Paddy was the Fiji Indian's second most important crop, his two staple foods being rice and coarse wheat flour (sharps) imported from Australia. Before the Second World War, Fiji imported most of her rice, and the CSR Company did not allow its cultivation by its

---

[1] See p. 98 seq.   [2] Shephard 1945: 14.   [3] Paddy is unmilled rice.

40

tenants. But as soon as the Japanese stopped the export of rice from southeast Asia, Fiji suffered a severe shortage, and the CSR Company allowed paddy to be grown by tenant farmers as an emergency measure. Since the war the growing population and the continued world shortage of rice had combined to maintain the growing of paddy on cane lands, and the three-year rotation system had become common. Almost all farmers grew paddy for their household needs, selling the surplus.

There were two methods of paddy cultivation. The first was to sow seed broadcast on lands never flooded during the rainy season. The second, used on lower fields which flooded,[1] was to grow seedlings in nursery plots and transplant them, after a month or so, in bunches of half a dozen plants into fields which had been well puddled with a plough and leveller. Quick-growing paddy was planted on cane lands, maturing within three or four months from the time it was sown in October–November. On land used exclusively for paddy, however, a six- or seven-month seed was used, since the slower maturation gave a better ear, and so more grain, to the plant.

Dry paddy needed little labour. One man could sow it, there was no weeding to be done, and help was only needed at harvest, done with hand sickles. Paddy grown in wet lands needed much more co-operative effort. The field had to have the right amount of water when the seedlings were transplanted, and farmers liked to get all transplanting done while conditions were favourable. Men, women and children might turn out for this back-breaking work, standing up to their knees in the slushy mud (see Plate IV*a*). Weeding was also necessary between the clumps of paddy, and people liked help for this long, dull chore, saying that three people working and talking together would accomplish far more than one person working three times as long by himself. The crop had to be cut when it was ripe, and not left too long to burn in the sun; for this, too, helpers were welcomed.

There were many other minor crops. Maize was grown from March to July, or could be cultivated between cane growing, from October to February. Tobacco was planted in March or April, and in May or June, after the rains, the seedlings were transplanted. Harvest was at the end of the year, and the leaf was cured locally and used in hand-made 'country' cigarettes. Besides this, vegetables, spices and other minor crops were grown.[2] Every cane farmer had a small vegetable

---

[1] Artificial irrigation, if practised at all in Fiji, was confined to purely paddy-growing areas.

[2] Fiji's other two main crops—bananas and coconuts—were produced mainly by Fijians; pineapples were produced commercially in plantations but did not form part of the settlements' agricultural pattern.

41

plot on which he cultivated some or all of these crops; but their main production was in the hands of either contractors having only part of their land under cane, or people who had no cane at all and who can be called 'mixed farmers'.

The proportion of each type of farm in the three settlements was as follows:

TABLE 1

	No. of Farms			
Type of Farm	*Vunioki*	*Delanikoro*	*Namboulima*	*Total*
Cane farm *	24	7	59	90
Cane and mixed farm †	11	18	16	45
Mixed farm	22	29	14	65
Total	57	54	89	200

* These farms were almost entirely devoted to cane, though paddy might be grown in the short fallow season.

† These farms produced more mixed crops than were needed by their owners though cane might still be the major crop.

The table shows distinct variations in the agricultural patterns of the settlements. Vunioki had an equal proportion of cane farms and mixed farms—most of which were on Fijian leases, but a few of which were on land sub-leased from other Indians at much higher rents.[1] The price of cane at the time of research was sufficiently attractive to cause all who could grow it to do so—hence the small number of farms having mixed as well as cane crops. In Delanikoro, by contrast, there were few purely cane farms, and the emphasis was on paddy production. The price of paddy was also good, and had strengthened the feeling against growing cane in the wet zone, where draining systems of canals and ditches were difficult and costly to maintain.[2] All but eight of the 'cane' or 'cane and mixed' farms were in part or whole on CSR Company land, and the tenants could not have changed from cane even if they had wished to. The rest of the land in Delanikoro was under Fijian lease, however, where there had been a trend towards paddy. Namboulima was almost entirely devoted to cane production. The CSR Company controlled nearly all of the

[1] The scale of rents levied by the CSR Company and the Fijian Native Land Trust Board ran from 5s. to £1 per acre per year. Tenants-at-will, on the other hand, might pay £2 or £3 per acre.

[2] This trend towards paddy production does not necessarily apply to all settlements in the wet zone. When the CSR Company announced in 1958 their intention to close their Nausori mill, which served these settlements, there were protests from many areas, and a plan was suggested in which cane growers in the Viti Levu wet zone would operate a co-operative mill.

valley land, and their tenants grew cane. There were a few mixed farms in the more inaccessible parts of the settlement.

The different patterns of agriculture in the settlements had social implications. The greater the percentage of cane farmers, for example, the greater the number of people in the cane harvesting Gang. Similarly, more cane farmers meant higher credit ratings at the store and a different pattern of debt.

The farms were not of the same size, nor were all of exactly the right size for the labour force of the tenant's household. The CSR Company's ten-acre cane blocks in Namboulima and Vunioki were intended to fit the needs of a single man and his family but the family was frequently larger—and blocks in Delanikoro averaged only about five acres. Again, the optimum size of a family paddy plot appeared to be about two and a half acres; but some holdings were less than this, or were larger without a correspondingly large family of farmers.

Farmers would offer their services as labourers if their holdings were too small to keep them permanently occupied, and some of the younger household members were almost permanently employed by others. But almost everyone had some sort of interest in land, though it might not be enough to fill all his needs. Women might work too, transplanting or weeding rice, and sometimes hoeing and planting cane—doing almost any work which did not entail driving draught animals.

Wages varied in different parts of the Colony; in 1951 a male labourer earned between 3*s*. and 5*s*. per day, plus two meals and morning tea, when working for a Fiji Indian, and 6*s*. to 7*s*. without food when paid by the CSR Company. A day's hoeing of cane in Namboulima entailed work from 7.30 until 9.30 and again from 10.15 to 12.30 in the morning, and from 1.30 to 5.00 in the afternoon —a total of nearly eight hours. Sometimes work was done on a task basis. For instance a farmer of Delanikoro paid labourers 5*s*. for each thirty-chain row of cane that they planted. There were also seasonal engagements when a cane farmer sent a man to act as his alternate in the work of the Gang. This man was hired for the entire cutting season, but was paid for the work he did each day, as well as being given a signing-on bonus, and certain perquisites—a pair of trousers and a shirt, a cane knife. In some cases, the same alternate would represent a man for several seasons. Apart from this, anything longer than daily employment was rare. In one case, a farmer of Namboulima hired a youth for £12 and his keep for six months' work; in other cases single old men were kept in the homestead of a farmer in return for their labour. But the general pattern was one of repeated daily engagements; even if the same labourer worked for a master for several months, there was no compulsion for him to continue to do so.

A great deal of labour was available on a reciprocal basis rather than for payment of wages. A man would do a day's work in another farmer's field, and would then have an equivalent amount done on his own land. Such return had to be made within the space of a few days, it was said, or cash would be demanded from the defaulting partner. Sometimes the arrangement was more complicated than this. In Delanikoro, for example, five farmers in 1951 formed a collective paddy transplanting Gang; they went to the fields of each in turn, and at the end reckoned up the total amount of work each farmer had put in and settled any differences in cash. Such arrangements were more likely to occur with paddy cultivation than with cane growing; the latter required a lot of labour during the sowing season alone, whereas 'wet' land paddy needed continual manual work. Perhaps two-thirds of these exchanges of labour were within the cultural group, often between members of an extended family.

During times of major agricultural activity there were also a great many deals involving draught animals. Not everyone owned a pair of bullocks and few a pair of horses, and others would borrow animals, repaying with their own labour. A typical arrangement was one whereby a man worked for three and a half days in return for a pair of bullocks with which he ploughed half an acre of paddy land.[1]

Variables in the pattern of co-operation were the relative isolation of homesteads, which might make the recruitment of help difficult, or even completely prevent it: and the distribution of kin in the settlement, which, if scattered, could well result in the co-operating group being from different kin or cultural groups.

There seemed to be few positive correlations between the type of crop grown and the organization of the homestead. For example, there was no prevalence of joint households amongst, say, paddy farmers which might imply that paddy farming required a *permanent* group of co-operating kin. The figures for Vunioki illustrate this point:

TABLE 2

Type of Homestead	Cane	Type of Farm Cane and Mixed	Mixed	Total
Simple household	13	6	15	34
Joint household	8	2	5	15
House group	3	3	2	8
Total	24	11	22	57

---

[1] An increasing number of settlements contain tractors since 1951. The owner uses the machine for his own work and rents it for the day to others for ploughing and cultivating.

The only correlation to be noted is that mixed farms were primarily operated by farmers in simple households. This is probably because such farms were often less paying and unable to support a larger population.

NON-AGRICULTURAL OCCUPATIONS

In each of the settlements there were some people whose main work was not agricultural. Most, however, were at the same time part-time farmers, with a small plot of land, be it only a vegetable garden and a half-acre of paddy farmed by labourers or their relatives, on which they might help during the sowing and harvest seasons.

The numbers engaged in non-agricultural work varied in the three settlements. In Vunioki fifteen men fell into this category in 1951; of these, two were storekeepers, three were regular and two casual transport drivers, one was a barber, one an 'inviter' [1] and two attended to the CSR Company Field Officer's household and stable. One man worked regularly in the CSR Company's mill, returning to Vunioki each day, and three others worked there during the cane crushing season. In short, only four of these men had regular work outside the settlement. Two or three men left Vunioki each year for work in the town and these sometimes returned to see relatives or to take part in festivities.

There was a different pattern at Delanikoro. Here, out of a slightly smaller population, twenty men were working full-time in Suva and the nearby market town, as drivers, tailors, shop assistants, shoemakers, carpenters, etc. These men bicycled or went by bus to work each day, returning in the evening. In addition, twelve men worked at the mill during the crushing season. Finally, a storekeeper and a priest lived in the settlement. Delanikoro differed so markedly from Vunioki, not because it was very much nearer to town, but because of the better bus service and the flat countryside which made bicycling easier. Vunioki men who got outside jobs generally left the settlement; but Delanikoro men could easily go to work each day, and retain a little land in the settlement to grow paddy. The existence of outside workers partly explains the greater population density in Delanikoro, for not all the people there had to live off the limited available land.

Namboulima was far more remote than either of the other settlements, being twelve miles from the town and until recently without a road. There were no daily travellers to the town from the settlement,

---

[1] Traditionally a man of the Barber caste was matchmaker, major-domo and general factotum at rites, and issued auspicious invitations. The man in Vunioki who had taken over this work was not of the Barber caste, however.

and the only people who did not have farming as their major activity were four storekeepers, three tailors, two priests, a bus driver, a barber, and the CSR Company's cook and groom. Very few men had gone to town from Namboulima, and the influence of town life had been much less than in the other settlements. However, the arrival of a bus service, a year or two before 1951, meant that Namboulima's contacts with the town were becoming more similar to those of the other settlements.

THE STORE

The most important non-agricultural work in the settlements was storekeeping. The first trade with the Fiji Indian community had been done by free men who became itinerant hawkers or small shop-keepers near the indenture lines, and by the European trading houses which had started to cater for Fiji Indian customers. The latter had continued to do considerable business, and branches of such firms as Morris Hedstrom and Burns Philp existed in all market towns. But they, as well as the first Fiji Indian storekeepers, had met increasing competition from Indian immigrants who had arrived more recently. These men had mainly come to Fiji after the First World War, from Gujarat and Punjab, the former being Hindus and the latter Sikhs. Some of the Sikhs had settled on the land, where they had often formed Punjabi-speaking settlements grouped around their temple-cum-meeting-place. Others had become traders and mechanics in the towns, and had produced some very prosperous merchants. The Gujaratis had also formed a separate cultural group —speaking the regional language, not marrying the local Fiji Indians, and maintaining the customs of their birthplace. They had not taken to farming at all, but kept on with the occupations they had in India —mainly as storekeepers, tailors, and gold and silver smiths.[1] In a decade or two they had taken over much of the retail trade in the rural settlements,[2] as well as a great deal of the urban retail business and some of the wholesale importing from overseas, notably of Indian foodstuffs, cloth, etc.

There were a number of reasons given for their success. They felt that they were a separate community and therefore helped each other and combined to fight any non-Gujarati competitor. Then, too, they were shrewder businessmen than other Fiji Indians, for whom trade was a new rather than a hereditary occupation. They were also more

---

[1] The first Gujarati to come to Fiji in 1906 was a goldsmith from Surat (the main district of recruitment) who had heard of Fiji whilst in South Africa (Gillion 1958).

[2] Chinese traders provided some of their main rivals.

46

frugal than Fiji-born Indians and so saved money and took a lower margin of profit if it was necessary.

Some Gujaratis had gone into real estate and other profitable businesses in the towns, but it was as merchants that they most closely affected the economic patterns of the rural settlements. For the kind of credit structure which existed in the rural settlement forced the country storekeepers into considerable dependence on their urban suppliers—and these were often either Gujaratis or Sikhs.

In 1951 there was only one general store in Vunioki, run by a Gujarati who had come from Broach, near Surat, some twenty years before. Two other establishments operated by young men of the settlement could hardly be called stores. One was really a tailoring shop, whose proprietor usually had a few bolts of cloth to sell to his clients, and perhaps some fly-blown tins of pilchards and pineapple juice. The other was run by the settlement's barber who would make petty sales to his clients of *yanggona*,[1] tobacco, cigarettes and chewing gum. The Gujarati's store, on the other hand, was stocked with staple foodstuffs, such as flour and sharps, oil, sugar, salt, pulses, etc.; necessities such as soap, kerosene and matches; luxuries such as tinned fruits, fish, meats, children's toys; and a small selection of cloth. He also had a kerosene refrigerator, which produced water ices for younger customers. Each Friday, he brought in a stock of bread to sell to the Fijians who passed by on their way to the Saturday market in the town.

The Gujarati had been the proprietor of this store for some seventeen years; but his shop was sixth in a row of such commercial enterprises which had started in about 1925. Of all these stores, his and the tailor's 'shop' were still working; one had been closed by the death of its owner; three had been put out of business, and the corrugated iron houses in which they had operated sold to farmers in whose homesteads they could still be seen. This mortality rate is partly explained by the inexperience and incompetence of the non-Gujarati owners. One of these still lived in Vunioki, and consoled himself with petty trading in tobacco and vegetables in nearby market towns. He would talk proudly of his disdain for accounts, his generous credit terms to favoured customers, and the reputation he had once had as a financier. He was no penny-pincher, like the Gujaratis, he would assert, and he almost took pride in having sailed so handsomely into bankruptcy. His sons, on the other hand, reproached him, in private, for having gambled and given away his lucrative position as the

---

[1] The root of the *yanggona* plant (*piper methysticum*) is pulped with water, making a drink beloved of all communities in Fiji. Neither the plant nor the beverage have for Fiji Indians the ritual and social properties they possess in Fijian society. (See Roth 1953: 106 seq.)

47

settlement's first storekeeper. There is no doubt that many store-keepers were not qualified. But even Gujaratis could get into difficulties under a system where large amounts of credit had to be extended to many customers.

This system had evolved because the CSR Company paid the cane farmers most of their money only twice a year—once shortly after the harvest, and again some six months later—with a third less substantial payment. Shephard notes that in August 1944 cane farmers were expecting a payment of 3s. 6d. (out of the total price of about 23s. per ton) on cane harvested in 1943, the preparation for some of which might have started early in 1941.[1] Few farmers could finance themselves for such a long time without borrowing, and so they ran up credit accounts at a store. In theory, of course, they could have used their last cane payment to purchase with cash—but in practice they always used the payment to settle accounts retroactively. Because purchase of the entire cane crop by the CSR Company was guaranteed by contract, the income of the cane growers was assured. The precise amount could not be calculated, but a rough estimate could be made from the state of the cane and the probable size of the harvest. This the storekeepers did—whilst trusting that a hurricane would not wipe out the entire crop—and on this basis they were prepared to give credit of up to £150 or so for the larger producers.[2]

There were dangers in such a system, quite apart from a soft heart or a bad head for accounts. The client might be indebted to others, who would collect their money before the storekeeper could do so; or he might spend his cane payments, defy the storekeeper, and start an account at another store. Even if affairs ran smoothly, the month or two before one of the cane payments would see a greatly depleted stock on the shelves of the store, and a reduced turnover as farmers slacked off on all but essential purchases. The present storekeeper in Vunioki was bankrupt on one such occasion, and was only saved by loans from another Gujarati in the town who felt obliged to help him.

Lack of capital restricted the service which the local store could give to the settlement; and part of the reason for this lack was that the country stores were, on the whole, doing less trade than in former times. The process was, in fact, a circular one—people went less to the country stores because there was less range and choice of goods, and so the stores had an ever diminishing number of goods to offer. The proprietor of the Vunioki store said that his turnover in 1950 was around £1,200. It allowed him an income of less than £200,

---

[1] Shephard 1945: 19.

[2] Stores in the towns, having more capital, were prepared to advance up to £300–£400 in appropriate cases.

which was no great sum. Indeed, the Vunioki proprietor often talked of closing up his store and devoting himself entirely to his bus service—a much more lucrative occupation, and one which provided the major part of his income, since he reckoned to clear £50 per month on it.[1]

Not only did people find it advantageous to shop in town, but the weekly journey was an enjoyable opportunity to meet friends from other settlements, to transact such business as the buying of a horse or the selling of a bullock and, often, to go to the hotel and drink cold beer.[2] Comparatively few men went to town to sell their wares in the market each Saturday (see Plate XIV*b*); the greater number thronged in to buy from the stores and to spend a pleasant day.

The store had only a limited importance as a social centre. People in the ward around it came of an evening and sat on the store veranda, and men from further afield would stop for a while as they passed by on their way to town. But the latter tended to send their young boys on horseback for goods which ran short during the week, and came rarely themselves. Thus the store was the centre for only casual, rather than regular, social gatherings on any scale.

Besides trade in stores, there was also a good deal of small-scale, informal trading done by people of the settlement. Mention has been made of an ex-storekeeper who was in 1951 just such a petty trader. He dealt mainly in tobacco and vegetables in season. His son was a bus driver, who gave him news of the latest prices in the nearby towns. Farmers who went to town to trade in the market were not so fortunate. They had no advance information, and were forced to sell, often at a bad price, when they went or their vegetables would have rotted in the ensuing week. Because of this, some preferred to sell to this small entrepreneur. Similarly, a man employed as a lorry driver

---

[1] Several men of the settlement had tried to run bus services in the old days. But the repayment of loans raised to buy the vehicle, and the costs of maintenance, proved too much for them. The worst failure was that of a man who ended with £500 unpaid on his bus and a garage debt of £100. The transport business was in 1951 a paying one. The storekeeper in Vunioki had a franchise granted by the Road Transport Board for a bus service from Vunioki to town. This rising profitability and frequency of bus services indicated a growing economic dependence on the town, as the goods piled on the roofs of buses testified.

[2] In 1951 Fiji Indians could only drink at hotels, or purchase liquor to take home, by having permits. These were granted fairly freely, and most people who wanted them appeared to have them. But there was a considerable trade in bootleg liquor for those whose consumption over-ran the permitted limits. These varied with the status of the applicant. A common permit was for unlimited beer at a hotel, and a bottle of spirits and a dozen bottles of beer to take home per month.

bought mangoes picked by the school children, put them on his lorry, and sold them in Suva or other centres in the wet zone, where their price was much higher. People also bartered or bought *yanggona* from Fijians.

There had never been more than a single store in Delanikoro, it seems. The first had been run during and after the period of indenture by a Northerner who had gone back to India when his wife died. After this, there had been a time without a store, and Delanikoro people had had to buy from two establishments in a settlement a mile to the southwest. In 1943 a Sikh had started to trade, and when he died in 1949 a fellow Sikh had taken over the business and was still in charge in 1951. This man had come to Fiji from Simla district in 1938, and had previously worked in other Sikh stores. Delanikoro does not have Vunioki's more picturesque trading history of bankruptcies.

As might be expected, with buses running to the town only four miles away, and with the many daily town-goers, the store's turnover was hardly as large as that of the Vunioki establishment, though the range of goods stocked was approximately the same. However, the owner had smaller credit problems than his counterpart in Vunioki; for there were far fewer cane growers in Delanikoro, and even these had smaller blocks and so less security on which to run up an account. Hence, the storekeeper was able to use his capital to make loans,[1] and the larger part of his income was said by clients to come from money-lending.

The store in Delanikoro was in 1951 hardly a centre for the settlement. Only two or three neighbours could be met with each evening, as well as a few Fijians from villages in the hilly land behind the settlement, who used the store as a place to rest and catch the bus into town. Despite the fact that homesteads in Delanikoro were less scattered, no central place had evolved for casual meetings. People either sat with their immediate neighbours, or kept to themselves in the evenings.

As in Vunioki, there were several small traders. One old man made a round of Fijian villages, selling tobacco, and the settlement was visited each week by a Chinese, who bought chickens and eggs. There were also occasions when an intelligent man could make a little money with a quick deal. The Easter Saturday market in town provided a good example. A Delanikoro resident calculated that the

[1] The accounts at the store were formally without interest. Many customers asserted, however, that the storekeeper added enough items on to the bill to ensure himself some return for the credit he had given. Only a few farmers kept written accounts of their purchases, and the rest could hardly be expected to recall the amounts they had bought six months previously.

V (a).   Sowing sugar cane.

(b).   A Gang member harvesting sugar cane.

VI (*a*).   The Gang linemen.

(*b*).   Hauling trucks to the permanent way.

Fijians would be anxious to sell their wares, so that they could make Easter purchases. He therefore went to the market early, and bought coconuts from them at 1*s*. 6*d*. a dozen. Later that day he was re-selling these for 2*s*. a dozen—some to neighbours in Delanikoro.[1] Again, bootleggers existed in all settlements, not least in Delanikoro. They sold liquor brewed on the premises, or arranged to supply beer and Western spirits.

Trade in Namboulima had started at the time of indenture, with a store operated by a European. He had sold the business at the end of indenture to a South Indian who had recently finished his contract in the Namboulima lines. This man had gone bankrupt—owing more than he could pay to a wholesaler in the town—and the store passed to a fellow Southerner. He, in turn, had been unable to carry on—bankrupted, it was said, by the extravagance of his son—and in about 1925 had sold the building to a Northerner called Narain. The history of rapid bankruptcies was not to be continued, for Narain had built up his store into a flourishing business which went to his widow at his death in about 1945. The business was in 1951 mainly run by Narain's sometime assistant, a man called Ramnath; he was assisted, and sometimes hindered, by advice from Narain's widow as well as her brother, sister and other relatives who had come to live with her since Narain's death.

Narain's had been the only store in Namboulima for many years. Then, in 1937, a man called Dayal had leased a plot of land and set up a store. He had previously been a partner in a store run by his brother, and had good commercial connections, including a tie by marriage with the only Fiji-born wholesaler in the town. So he had been helped in the first difficult years, and had started to build up a good business in opposition to Narain and Ramnath. Recent factions in Namboulima stemmed largely from the rivalry between Dayal and Ramnath,[2] which was both commercial and political.

The Namboulima stores differed from those already described in that both storekeepers were Fiji-born.[3] It was noticeable that these men took far more part in the settlement's affairs than did the Gujarati and Sikh traders in Vunioki and Delanikoro. The latter could remain 'culturally neutral', whereas Fiji-born traders were involuntarily members of cultural groups, whose influence (and hence their trade) depended on their role as cultural group leaders as well as that of good businessmen.

---

[1] Women in Delanikoro made their own coconut oil, by scraping the flesh from the inside of the coconut and then boiling it. One bottle of oil was made from about a dozen coconuts. Some settlements possessed bullock-drawn oil presses.

[2] See p. 129 seq.   [3] It is likely that this was exceptional.

The other difference which marked the stores in Namboulima was the amount of trade they carried on. The annual turnover of Ramnath's store was said to be £8,000, and that of Dayal's about £6,000. In Ramnath's store there were, in addition to the range of essentials and luxuries stocked in the Vunioki store, a full range of aluminium kitchen equipment, farm supplies, such as rope and ploughs, all kinds of fancy goods and patent medicines, and a large stock of cloth attended by two resident tailors who sat on the veranda of the store and took orders from the customers as they bought the cloth. Dayal's store had only one tailor, no farm equipment, and a smaller range of goods, but there was still more stock than in Vunioki. Namboulima was, in fact, far enough from the town, and the road had been opened for a sufficiently short time, for the stores not to have lost their former economic importance.

Trade had fallen off a little, however. A small weekly market, which provided a centre for exchange with farmers living further in the interior of the island, had been stopped a few years before 1951. The reason could be seen in the people waiting at the end of the road for buses to take them to town. The shops, unfortunately for their owners, were at some distance from the road's end. Although they still provided a meeting place for the people in their ward, it was said that far more men had been accustomed to come there in past years.

CREDIT AND DEBT

Storekeepers were obliged to give considerable amounts of credit and cane growers, having the best security, also had the highest credit rating.[1] Cultivators of mixed crops were much less sure of their income, for there were no fixed prices for their crops; they were consequently seldom allowed credit of over about £20 or £30. And young men who had not yet negotiated an economic lease of land, and who worked mainly as agricultural labourers, seldom had store debts of over £4–£5. As others have pointed out, the relation between the dispenser and the receiver of this kind of credit is by no means one-sided.[2] The creditor must not hound his man for repayment, or the latter may abscond to another store. Yet he must also take care not to over-extend the customer's credit. In the three settlements there were two or three men indebted to the store for amounts which they could not hope to pay off in the foreseeable future. The storekeeper

---

[1] To set this discussion within the wider framework of rural income, material has been furnished by O'Loughlin who estimates the 1953 gross income from a 'typical' farm with a father and his adult son as £794, net income being £576, with a net profit of some £223. This was 'an outstandingly good year' however (O'Loughlin 1956: 59).

[2] E.g. T'ien 1953: 44.

had presumably misjudged appropriate credit ratings, and had given them too much latitude. He knew now that he would probably never be repaid the £50–£150 which was outstanding. But he also knew that by keeping them as customers he could recover his debt in the normal run of trading profits. This could not happen if he let them go to another storekeeper. The clients knew this, and made it an excuse to try to get further small advances; and they had a continual battle with the storekeeper, who was forced to meet their wishes to some extent, but who tried, as much as possible, to make them pay in cash.[1]

A second type of loan was made in cash, on security of the cane crop. The CSR Company made loans to its tenants and contractors, at a rate of 4 per cent, which were geared to the amount of income received from the crop. It gave this money for purchase of livestock, farm equipment, building materials and so forth; but it did not countenance loans made for ritual expenses, of which weddings were the largest, or for the payment of the high premia involved in the transfer of leases of Fijian land. Since the Company did not allow its tenants to use their crops as security with any other moneylender, the tenants had to make other kinds of loans to meet the expenses which the Company tried to discourage.[2]

Contractors were not bound by the Company's rules. Besides borrowing from the Company under the conditions just described, they could make other liens on their crops to moneylenders, who then collected the cash with some 10–12 per cent interest directly from the Company when cane payments were made. The relatively small demand of cane growers for loans to meet expenses sanctioned by the Company compared with that for other expenses, was shown by the fact that contractors took £301,509 in 'free' liens and only £26,299 in CSR loans in 1943.[3] This worked out at an average of £280 for each lien made by a contractor. Many liens about which data were collected were given by new contractors to pay for the lease they had just negotiated. Every transfer of Fijian leaseholds had to be approved by the Native Land Trust Board; but it seemed that few difficulties were raised by that body, and that there was an almost 'free market' in Fijian leases among the Indians. Leasehold cane land was in short supply in 1951,[4] and high premia were asked

---

[1] This can be compared with the position of Indian cane farmers in Mauritius, where clients had a continuing store credit appropriate to their general economic position (Benedict 1958: 215–16).

[2] Since this fieldwork was done, the CSR Company has agreed to let its tenants assign crops to cover existing debts or advances.

[3] Shephard 1945: 42.

[4] There was, in fact, a general shortage of Fijian land; one reason was said to be because large regions were not being given in lease until the extent of the Fijian reserves there had been ascertained.

for its transfer—a common way of raising the needed money being to place the crops under a lien for several years.

Other types of loans to be had were those which involved bills of sale made on the security of house, livestock or implements; those made under mortgages which could be taken on all land save that held on tenancy from the CSR Company; and those contracted under simple promissory notes, which were usually valid for one year only, when a new note was executed for the amount of principal and outstanding interest. Interest was limited to 12 per cent by the Moneylenders Ordinance of 1938. But there were unofficial ways of exacting a higher rate if the need of the borrower were great enough.

It is worth making a rough estimate of the extent of debt. This is based both on the statements of informants about the general position in their settlement and upon samples taken in each settlement, covering between one-quarter and one-half of the households. These were not random samples, because some of the men interviewed were reluctant to give details of their financial position. But the material can serve as a rough indication, and perhaps as an aid to further economic studies.

A quantitative statement of debt in 1951 would have shown a good majority of household heads in the settlements with debts ranging from £10 to £150. But this would obscure the fact that many of these debts were store debts or liens based on the security of a crop already planted and cultivated. True, a hurricane or severe drought might turn such debts into more permanent liabilities. But they should normally be distinguished from a mortgage or promissory note, for at the end of each agricultural year the farmer was generally free of debt to the storekeeper and lienor. He was not, however, necessarily free of his commitments under a mortgage.

We should therefore distinguish between heavy debts and debts which could be called operating debts. The former are debts roughly equal to at least a year's income and exclusive of store credit and annual liens. The amounts involved were clearly different for each individual. A debt of £150, for instance, was heavy for a man who had a small plot of land on which he grew only a little paddy and some vegetables, depending for his main income on wage labour in the fields. For an average cane farmer, on the other hand, the equivalent sum would have been around £300. It was obviously hard to clear a debt of this nature in a short time. The credit at the store alone might amount to one-third or one-half the man's annual income, and only a fraction of this more permanent debt could be paid off in an average year. Some men could not do even this much. For example, a farmer in Delanikoro had borrowed £100 on a promissory note from the storekeeper, and for the last two years had simply paid the annual interest. As he said, if he let the principal start to grow, the debt would never end; and he was at present content merely to limit the debt to its original' size.

In 1951 about 25 per cent of households in the three settlements had serious debts of a more permanent kind. Some debts were of considerable antiquity. Perhaps the record was held by a debt of £150 contracted to buy a lease in about 1920 by a Delanikoro man with a Sikh of the town. Over the years the sum grew to around £500, with interest and additional small loans of £5 or £10. The debtor had been repaying since about 1940, however, and by 1951 no longer had a serious debt, for he hoped to give the last instalment in the following year or two.

That many people had repaid debts during the past five years was clearly due to the fall in the value of money which had caused debts to 'shrink' to easily payable proportions. Between one-fifth and one-third of the households surveyed were free of all but operating debt, many of them quite recently. But it is not certain that the number of serious debtors had greatly decreased. Though some men said that this was the case, others maintained that there were just as many large debtors—and that the lower value of the currency merely meant that their debts were numerically larger. An economic survey might well find out whether freedom from debt has mainly applied to smaller debtors, and whether the point made by Darling for India also holds true in Fiji—that the extent of debt varies with the extent of credit, there being greatest debt in times and areas of greatest prosperity.[1]

Even if it were established that serious debt had decreased in the years before 1951, there appeared to be a point below which the number of these debts would not drop. For there were two types of debtor who continued to exist, however favourable the possibilities of repayment.

The first type consisted of people with extravagant and lazy habits. Such people did not usually manage their farms well. They found excuses to sit and talk in their houses, or to go and while away the time in the market town. Higher prices and more liberal credit merely resulted in larger debts; eventually their credit diminished, but they extended it as far as they could, their farms under lien and their houses encumbered with bills of sale. Drink—either of *yanggona*, home-made beer, or Western liquor—was an important item of extravagance. It was easy for men to spend the Saturday at the hotel, drinking with friends; it was easy, too, for them to drink at home, and to pay high prices for extra liquor when the permitted quota had been consumed. India-born people often used to say that the new

[1] Darling 1947: 210.

generations were too easy-going and spend-thrift, giving the money spent on liquor as a favourite, and in some cases not unjustified, illustration of this tendency.

The other type of debtor was the man of sober and hard-working habits, who was nevertheless forced into debt by certain common situations. For example, a farmer of Vunioki had sixteen children, only two of whom were working; the raising of such a large family had forced him into debt. The size of this family was exceptional, but the rapidly expanding Fiji Indian population created many similar cases. Also the transfer of leases could be accompanied by large premia which resulted in crop liens or mortgages. Shephard says the 'evidence submitted to me in every mill area suggests that many contractors have incurred crippling obligations in the form of premia for the transfer of native leases'.[1] Evidence gathered in 1951 suggests that premia had risen with the general fall in the value of the currency and the increased pressure of the Indian population on the available land. Many smaller transfers were made without debt—but there were enough large transactions centring on good cane lands to make premia (and purchase prices of rare freehold land) a cause of serious debt.

There were certain unavoidable social expenses, too, of which the most important were the costs of marriage. Parents of brides in the three settlements were said to pay £100 on average. Detailed expense accounts were kept for two marriages. The first cost £72, with about £14 on the preliminary engagement party; but at least another £30 must be set aside as invisible costs—the loss of wages and labour during the week of preparations, the obligations entered into in terms of physical help by friends, which would later have to be repaid. The second example was an occasion where two daughters were married at the same time—the total cost was £86 10s., with another £20 or so for the engagement parties, which shows why parents liked to have a double wedding if they could manage it.

It is noteworthy, however, that very few men had become seriously indebted through over-spending on marriages or other rites. Such occasions were far more likely to result in a crop of small debts; for some money was usually saved for the marriage, and most of the rest could be borrowed informally, and in small amounts, from relatives. Again, though marriages were always celebrated with as much pomp and hospitality as the household could muster, it was not essential that the expenses be wildly incommensurate with the economic status of the household. A poor resident of Vunioki, for example, was said to have spent no more than £40 on a marriage, with £2 for the engagement ceremony. Doubtless extravagance increased with the

[1] Shephard 1945: 17–18.

56

wealth of the host—and hence his power to borrow extra amounts—but this survey does not make these kinds of social expense the most important single contributors to serious debt. Their main significance was as unavoidable commitments which might push someone with concurrent problems into serious debt. Thus a man trying to pay off a large premium for land might find that at a crucial stage, when he had to give a substantial instalment to keep the lease, a wedding was to occur in his household. This might divert the sum required for the lease, and might force him into a high-interest debt.

Where were loans made, and who were the chief moneylenders? Of the seven men who were most frequently mentioned in the three settlements as large moneylenders, and who were most often patronized by the people, only one lived in the settlement itself—the Sikh storekeeper in Delanikoro. Of the others, two were in market towns near to Vunioki and Delanikoro respectively, and four were in adjacent settlements. It is only when the class of smaller lenders is reached that local men were more prominent.

This pattern was not just the result of chance, but was the deliberate decision of the rich men in each settlement. In Delanikoro, for example, one of these had entirely stopped making loans, having grown tired of the endless disputes they occasioned. He had lent £20 to one man, for example, and when he did not repay it had obtained a court order for payments of £1 5s. each month. The borrower did not pay any of these instalments for seven months, and it took the further expense of putting the case on the court calendar again before the loan was repaid. The other Delanikoro moneylender also refused to do any business inside the settlement for this reason, and instead loaned considerable amounts to people in a settlement some ten miles away. The pattern was repeated in the two other settlements. The moneylenders were not always of the same cultural groups as their clients; in fact, most of the lenders in the three settlements were Northern Hindus—Muslims not being allowed by Islamic law to lend on interest, though some did so.

One feature which emerged from data on people's financial histories was that the older people talked of having borrowed from men in the town, whereas more recent loans were from nearby moneylenders. This might be because urban moneylenders had come to prefer other forms of investment, such as transport, buildings and import agencies. It is a point which specific economic surveys would clarify.

The network of smaller financial transactions existed mainly within the settlement. Almost everyone with money saved would make loans to neighbours who were less wealthy, or who were temporarily short of money. The main outsiders who made such loans were those who lent to kin at times of ritual expense, as has been suggested. Some people had £200 or more given out in small loans, preferring to spread their risks in this way, rather than make a single larger loan with most of their capital. One man even found it profitable to borrow £100 at 10 per cent from a large moneylender, and lend the sum out on short-term loans of a few months, often at 20 per cent. Formerly, when most people were illiterate, such loans had often been made by word of mouth, in front of witnesses. In 1951, people were more sophisticated—and less honest, said the ancients—and would usually insist on a properly executed promissory note. Even small loans of £2 or £3 might have an IOU written out by a third party.

CONCLUSION

The economy of these three settlements had two major features. In the first place, the most important place in the agricultural system was taken by an exported cash crop rather than locally consumed products. This was, of course, due to the historic fact of the introduction of sugar cane, which had provided the *raison d'être* of the Fiji Indian community. There was some cultivation of other crops, the surplus of which was sold for cash to cane farmers and townsmen. But few, if any, farmers subsisted on their own crops, since major staples of diet were either entirely or mainly imported, like wheat flour, onions and potatoes. Thus, the rural economy of Fiji Indians was sensitive to external economic conditions—the world price of sugar, the cost of wheat in Australia.

Secondly, important socio-economic relations existed in, but did not define, the settlement. The harvest Gang ensured the efficient flow of cane to the mill, and also made for economic co-operation between farmers as well as the only long-term contractual relationship between landed tenants and labourers in a situation marked by a fluid pattern of daily labour. The CSR Company's pattern of cane payments had also resulted in important credit relations with the store. Nevertheless, the settlement was not itself an economic unit. There were, for example, no craftsmen whose exclusive right it was to serve the settlement population, and who would have resisted outsiders practising there. There were few craftsmen in any case, for skilled carpenters, blacksmiths, cobblers, etc., were in the towns. The nearest approach to an economic activity defined by the settlement's boundaries was the cane harvesting Gang, but in none of the settlements did this comprise all farmers.

The settlement was not self-contained with respect to trade or to investment and credit. The rural storekeeper was undoubtedly important as a source of credit. But the services of the towns had grown in this respect, and both economically and socially the store had lost importance. Moneylenders existed in every settlement, but major ties went outside, though not in this case so much to the town as to nearby settlements.

The account suggests a distinction between cane farmers and others. This would be to some extent correlated with wealth, for cane was the most profitable crop. It was also related to social features, notably the participation of cane farmers in the co-operative and political aspects of the Gang, which gave them added prestige, as later chapters will show. Thus, interest groups existed, formed through economic differentiation, but also expressed in leadership and social status. But it would be wrong to look for too clear a class structure on this basis, though economic interests sometimes cut across kin and cultural affiliations.

IV

RITUAL ACTIVITIES

O NE aspect of religion in a society is the ways in which social relationships and groupings are made manifest in the rites performed. Who are the people attending a ceremony? What part do they play in it? What ties link them in other social spheres? These questions underlie the following general description of Hindu and Muslim ritual in the settlements. The first rites to be considered are those of the individual's life cycle; then follow the periodic rites initiated by individuals or groups of kin; last come the rites which were centres of festivals to which the entire settlement or cultural group subscribed, though all its members might not actually participate.

MINOR RITES OF THE LIFE CYCLE

Traditionally, ritual notice is taken of successive stages in a Hindu's or Muslim's social progress. In Fiji, all save the most important of these rites were optional.

Shortly after birth, a priest was called to calculate, from the Hindu child's horoscope, his name—or rather, the first syllable from which a name could be chosen.[1] The first rite for both Southerners and Northerners was directed towards the malignant goddess (Hindi —Chatthi) who was allegedly responsible for post-natal mortality. Chatthi's power was said to be greatest during the sixth night after birth, and female neighbours, both relatives and others, were invited to stay with the mother and child and to sing songs to keep Chatthi away. Only after this night was the father allowed to see the child, and the latter to leave the room in which it had been born. The participants brought small gifts of clothes, cash or such accessories as talcum powder. It was not an occasion to invite kin from a distance. Southerners were also said to have a small rite of propitiation at the spot where the baby first touched the ground.

After a minimum of two or three months, and up to a year, the

---

[1] E.g. the priest would say that the auspicious syllable was 'Ra' and the child could be called Ram Das or Rattanlal, etc.

Hindu infant's baby hair was shaved in a rite of purification (see Plate IX*a*). On the same occasion, or at a later date, the child's ears, and nostril if a girl, were ceremonially pierced. A supplementary rite confined to Southerners was one in which a calf was named after a child. It was decked with flowers, sprinkled with purificatory water, and donated to a temple, whose custodian took charge of it. The animal and the child were in a close relation, and the former might not be harmed. In one case, for example, a boy's father sold the special calf and misfortunes befell the family for several years. During 1951 he decided to buy another calf and donate it to a small Southern temple in a nearby settlement.

All these rites were usually minor ones. Few nearby outsiders were invited; there were few special roles for particular kin; and the cost was small. For example, at the head shaving of a North Indian boy the 'inviter' was paid 4*s*.,[1] the girl who took the hair away and put it in a stream got 2*s*. 6*d*. and that evening the priest gave a sacred reading (*katha*) at which were present the household members, the 'inviter' and three people from the next homestead, of the same cultural group although not kin.

It was difficult to estimate in how many cases these minor Hindu rites—and the equivalent Muslim ceremonies of purification on the fortieth day after birth and, later, of circumcision[2]—were performed. It is possible that they were more faithfully marked for the first-born, and for sons rather than daughters; but no satisfactory statistics of frequency exist. It is doubtful, however, that, except for circumcision, they were fulfilled in more than a quarter of cases. Nevertheless, as long as they were recognized at all, they helped to create a feeling of cultural homogeneity, however slight.

Traditionally, Hindus of the upper castes underwent a rite of ritual birth at, or shortly before, puberty; this made them 'twice-born' and separated them from the lower castes. The symbol of this ritual birth was the sacred thread (*janeo*) whose investiture was the climax of the rite. People in the settlements usually combined the rite with the general marriage ceremonies, if they observed it at all. An informant estimated that only about 10 per cent of both orthodox and Arya Samaji Northerners held this rite.

One such occasion concerned a Delanikoro Northern Brahman youth of about sixteen. It took place on the day before he went to the bride's house for his wedding. The boy dressed up in a turmeric-dyed loincloth (*dhoti*), and put on wooden clogs. He slung two cloth

---

[1] This compares with the 3*s*. to 7*s*. given for a day's farm labour.

[2] The actual operation was now usually done by a doctor, it was said, and a few days afterwards there was a small rite attended by the *maulvi* and followed by a dinner.

bundles of rice over one shoulder, and placed a bamboo yoke over the other, on which were suspended on turmeric-dyed thread two small earthen pots. Under his arm he carried a bundle of purifying *kus* grass, and he held a small brass pot. Thus arrayed, he walked about in the compound of the homestead and collected alms from his father's sister and father's brother's wife. He was teased by the male guests there, who were from other Northern castes, and the Southern cultural group. They would call him over as if to give him alms, then look in their pockets and say they had no money; or they would laugh at his donning of an ascetic's costume and wonder what had made him suddenly so holy. The boy was most self-conscious. He complained that he could not walk on the wooden clogs, which had no strap over the feet, but simply a small peg to be held between the large and second toes; and he was plainly ill at ease in his loincloth, a dress which is never worn by the Fiji-born and which is considered comically old-fashioned by most of them. The priest was angry at all this chaff. He said that it was an important step for the boy, and he gave him a short talk on his responsibilities as a member of the twice-born population, ranging from the need to render service to humanity to the prohibition on speaking whilst defecating. After this, all men present, including non-Brahmans and non-Northerners, took hold of the sacred thread and raised and lowered it three times to the chanting of the priest before putting it over the boy's shoulder in traditional fashion. At once the boy divested himself of his clothes—with some relief—and the wedding went on in the usual way. The rite was of little importance for most people in the settlements, and was probably a landmark only in the lives of those who became priests, of those who valued it as a symbol of spiritual development, or of those few who used it as a means of asserting a caste status to which they might not be traditionally entitled.

MARRIAGE RITES

Only two stages in a person's life were always ritually observed—his marriage and his funeral. Of the two, the former was structurally more important, since by it social ties were created as well as reaffirmed, and it followed a procedure of match-making involving parents and other kin.

THE SELECTION OF A SPOUSE

The selection of a spouse was limited by rules which rendered a large number of people ineligible. First, the cultural group was almost entirely endogamous. It is easy to see why Hindus did not marry

Muslims; but within the Hindu fold the people coming from North India rarely married those from South India.[1] Similarly, most people preferred not to marry outside their caste. When people were asked what they looked for in an eligible spouse for their child, they gave as the first criterion that 'he should be of the same caste'. It cannot be asserted that this was an overriding consideration, for men might not invariably reject an eligible suitor of another caste of roughly the same status for a less favoured person of their own caste. Though caste endogamy was at the least an ideal and at the most a preferred pattern, it was not a rule whose infraction brought serious consequences. Nevertheless there were very few marriages reported between castes having adequate representation in Fiji, in each of which there must have been an eligible suitor. It was different, of course, for people having few fellow caste members in Fiji; for they had often to contract marriages outside the caste whether they wished it or not.[2]

Limitations of choice within the caste centred around the unilineal descent group, and the circle of close kin. A person was not supposed to marry anyone of the same patrilineal clan. Clan membership was shown by a common name, but in Fiji there appeared to be numbers of people who did not know their clan name and who were, therefore, not sure that they were not violating the rule of clan exogamy when they married. But, as one man of Vunioki said, after a long discussion with his brothers had failed to produce any result, 'No, I do not know my clan name. But this does not matter in Fiji, for I know *all the people who are related to me here*. If a woman is not a relative, I can marry her.' Relationships through links in Fiji were thus more important than traditional Indian unilineal affiliations.

Fiji Indians followed traditional practice in saying that some categories of close kin could not inter-marry, each cultural group differing in details. Thus, Muslims allowed the marriage of parallel and cross cousins; South Indians married cross cousins only;[3] and Northerners prohibited both types of match, and disapproved so strongly of what they called incestuous unions that the other two cultural groups were slowly dropping the custom. The prohibitions on marriage with more distant kin were less clear-cut. In general, marriage was forbidden with *anyone* with whom cognatic or affinal kinship could be traced; for instance, a Vunioki Northerner said that it would be wrong to marry one's brother's wife's brother's wife's sister. It was possible to have such a wide exogamous spread in the early days, for indentured migrants were hardly ever related, and so neither were their children. It was only in the third generation, for instance, that

---

[1] See p. 144 seq.   [2] See p. 160.
[3] A common and preferred match for some people in South India is that of a man with his elder sister's daughter; no such cases were recorded in Fiji.

the possibility of cross-cousin marriage had arisen—and in the homes of post-1900 immigrants the third generation had only reached marriageable age in the years immediately before 1951. The ties of marriage contracted by the previous generation were, however, starting to hinder the marriages of those who took literally the injunction that no related people should marry, and for whom the endogamous caste population and the exogamous group within it were now starting to coincide. It seems likely that prohibition on marriage will be limited to nearer kin (and perhaps that clan exogamy will grow in importance). In fact, this was already taking place, for cases were recorded in which distant kin had married, under the disapproval of some of the conservatives, perhaps, but married nevertheless.

Within these limitations of endogamy and exogamy, the parents of the prospective spouses started to search, the mother's voice in the search and final approval being at least as important as that of the father. Among Northerners and Muslims, it was the girl's father who made the first enquiries, among Southerners the boy's parent. Initially no direct contact was made. Parent A mentioned to a close friend or relative that he would not be displeased if he found a spouse for his daughter; the friend then surveyed his acquaintances until he found a suitable boy, to whose parent (B) he indirectly suggested that A was on the marriage market. B's interest was relayed to A, who in turn considered whether B and his son were suitable. If he indicated that he was satisfied the next step was for B, his women folk and close kin, to go and view the bride.

Formerly, the prospective groom did not go with his parents; but by 1951 quite a large proportion of boys had seen their brides before marriage, though only a very few had actually exchanged words with them.[1] It was considered modern to see one's bride; but some educated men in the settlements had preferred not to do so. They felt that it cast a reflection on the ability and solicitude of their parents in their interests and it embarrassed them if they did not agree with them; moreover, it made any subsequent breaking of these delicate negotiations more of a disgrace for the girl, and more likely to produce bad blood between the families. In the towns there were instances of boys choosing their own spouses in the Western manner, but in the settlements the boy's freedom had gone no further than to see the person chosen for him. If the visit of the people from B's side passed off well, and if a comparison of the couple's horoscopes showed that the match would be auspicious, the marriage was approved and the initial stage was over. If, on the other hand, either

[1] The couple was so hedged around with chaperones, however, that platitudes alone could be exchanged, as several men ruefully admitted.

side was not satisfied, there was no direct refusal. Instead, there were delays to consult other kin, to consider the matter further, etc., until the other party understood that the match would not be made.

What was looked for in a desirable mate? As indicated, the first attribute was that he should be of the same caste, though this was sometimes qualified in practice. Next was physical fitness; particular attention was here paid to the girl since she had been more secluded in the years before marriage[1] and might have some defect unknown to the match-maker. She might cook a meal for the visiting party, which was critically tasted to see if she would be a good housewife. The complexions of both spouses were considered; for a light complexion was preferred by country people, and it was best for the couple to be of roughly the same shade. Education was not mentioned by informants as a criterion, but this was increasingly required amongst townspeople. The girl's parents were interested in the character of the boy,[2] and wealth was important, though not the only consideration. There was, for instance, a very wealthy man in a settlement near Vunioki who was having great difficulty in getting his daughters married. For he drank and led what was held to be a dissolute life. As one man said, 'X paid £10 for some dancers from Suva, but gave only £5 to the school fund. He cannot get men as rich as himself to be his daughter's father-in-law when people know this.'

Generally, it was considered better to have affines in a settlement at some little distance. Relations between the respective families were then formal, and any quarrels between the couple would be less likely to involve the two kin groups. Nevertheless, enough marriages existed within the settlement to link the different homesteads of the same caste into large extended families. It was the members of these families who took part in the selection of the spouse; for the 'viewing party' usually contained three or four of these close kin, rather than kin from outside the settlement. Only the matchmaker was often a person from outside the settlement—he might even be of a different caste or cultural group, for his main asset was that he had contacts elsewhere, and his main recommendation was that he was a reliable friend of both parties, not necessarily a kinsman.

The ages of the couple were relevant. The legal minimum age for a girl's marriage was fourteen and for a boy's eighteen years.[3] In general this was observed, though some of the girls married in 1951

---

[1] There was no *purdah* in Fiji; but girls after the age of about ten tended to take on household duties and to stay indoors and this, coupled with the isolation of many homesteads, made it necessary to check their physique.

[2] There is a significant difference from matchmaking witnessed in India, where matches were usually made when the couple had not yet reached puberty, and it was held to be useless to ask about the character of a mere child.

[3] The minimum girl's age is to be raised to sixteen years in 1961.

must have been very close to this age and perhaps below it. The main reason for early marriages was that parents did not wish the responsibility of having their girls unmarried for long after puberty. People distrusted the youths of the settlement, and were afraid that secret assignations would be made, with what to them were inevitable results.[1] To some extent they were justified; for the complete lack of any social contact between adolescents of the two sexes made it impossible for them to meet for innocent amusement, such as going to the cinema in town together. Contacts tended therefore to be made for the ends feared by the parents. Nevertheless, by no means all girls were married at puberty, and a common age was around sixteen years. People were not averse to later marriages, saying that matches of young people resulted in weak children, but their suspicion of adolescents weakened this attitude.

If a girl was not married by the time she was about twenty, matchmaking became difficult.[2] People would wonder why she had remained single for so long, and would start to fear some reason which would render her ineligible for their sons. Boys were married between seventeen and twenty, on the whole; similarly, they started to find it hard to get wives if they remained bachelors after, say, twenty-five years. It was thought best for the husband to be five years or so older than his wife; and marriages of people with disparate ages were mocked, and disparaged. The storekeeper in Delanikoro, for example, was the butt of some ridicule, for he had married a girl of fifteen. His own age could not have been less than forty-five, but it was said that he had tried to turn himself into a young groom by writing it as twenty-five in the marriage banns.

THE ENGAGEMENT

When the spouses had been chosen, a formal engagement followed. This was often held a week or two before the wedding, but could occur on the day of the ceremony itself at less expense to the parties. There follows a description of the engagement rites of an orthodox Northern girl of Delanikoro, whose wedding was of average size and expense. They started at the girl's house; the Delanikoro priest

[1] There were, indeed, cases of unmarried girls becoming pregnant; and these had then to be married off hurriedly, often making a worse match than would otherwise have been possible, and not necessarily having an astrologically auspicious partner.

[2] It must be recalled that the account refers to the conditions found in rural settlements. People in the towns were much more liberal about these matters, though even here there was restriction in the mixing of the sexes and distrust of co-educational institutions (e.g. the Nasinu Teachers' Training College was regarded with great suspicion by many townspeople as well as rural folk).

blessed the gifts to be given to the boy, as the bride handed them over to her 'inviter' or factotum, and then made a *tilak*[1] on her forehead. This, it was said, showed that the bride was in earnest and that the gifts symbolized the firm decision of the bride's side to go ahead with the wedding.

The engagement party then left the settlement in a special bus. There were eighteen people, all men. Of these, six were the bride's close relatives, seven were other Northerners, two were the priest and his kinsman and three were Southerners. Except for the lack of Muslims, the group formed a fair cross-section of the extended families in Delanikoro. The number was calculated by the bride's father as being respectable, but not too large for the boy's parents to entertain.

On arrival at the groom's house, the party was shown into a separate house, and left there, with cigarettes, tea and *yanggona*, for about an hour. During that time nobody came to speak, save to ask if members had all they required. Men and children peered in at them, and there was the definite feeling of being in strange territory. Finally, the party moved outside to a space cleared for the rite. On one side sat the groom, with his priest and his factotum; and on the other side the bride's brother with *his* priest and factotum. Both priests conducted purificatory rites for their subjects, after which the bride's brother washed the groom's feet and, taking a betel leaf on which was a white paste of curd and rice flour, put it on the groom's forehead as a *tilak*. He then presented him with a tray bearing £5 0s. 6d. in cash, a basin of rice, a coconut, cloth for a shirt and loin-cloth, and a handkerchief. The groom's priest took the tray, examined what was in it, and then announced the items to all assembled. Speaking in Hindi, the rites having been in Sanskrit, he said that the groom had now made the contract by accepting these presents, and asked the bride's priest whether the period from 7 p.m. till midnight on February 21 would be auspicious for the wedding.[2] The bride's priest looked up this time in his almanack and agreed to it. The engagement was then complete, and the bride's party returned home, after having accepted dinner with a show of formal reluctance.

The main items of interest on this occasion are—the obeisance of the bride's representative to the groom's (a subordination which is present throughout the wedding), the public announcement of the

[1] An auspicious mark made, in this case, with red powder.
[2] As one priest said, any calculation of auspicious times was complicated by the fact that most almanacks used were printed in India. The times they gave had therefore to be corrected by 6 hours 35 minutes. But, as he said, most people regarded as auspicious the same periods as existed in India (e.g. they had their weddings at night, as in India).

contract, and the representative nature of the party coming from Delanikoro.

Southerners had a similar preliminary to the wedding, except that it was the groom's party which went to the girl's house. They made gifts of cash, clothes and a set of ornaments to be worn at the wedding and exchanged betel leaf as a symbol of their agreement over the match. On one such occasion a party of Namboulima people consisted of three men and two women from the groom's immediate family, one other Southerner and a Muslim. All lived in the same ward as the groom; it is interesting to note that women went in the party, and this supports the picture of the bride's side, and women generally, being in less of a 'weak' position than in Northern marriages.

THE WEDDING: NORTHERN

The actual wedding was a complex ritual spread over three days before the decisive rite, with further rites on several following days. There is no need to describe these rites in every detail, for much of the material would be outside the scope of this book, and the interests of its readers. But something must be said about the amount of participation and responsibility borne by the various kin and members of the settlement in the wedding, and about the relations between the bride's and groom's relatives. The wedding was one of the main times at which the individual affirmed his socio-religious affiliation, and marriage was, of course, the keystone of the kinship system and the social duties and obligations which flowed from it.

The first example is the wedding of the Delanikoro Northern girl whose engagement has just been described. The first day (*telwan*) saw the construction and dedication of the 'altar' at which the wedding was to take place. This was formed by a tall bamboo post, whose erection was the scene of a separate rite, performed by the bride and the priest. In front and around the altar, on a low platform of packed earth, various symbolic objects were placed. Twice during the day the bride appeared before the altar and made obeisance, after which she was rubbed with a purificatory paste made of turmeric and oil by the young girls of her kin group in the settlement, including both agnates and maternal kin, and by friendly neighbours of different caste. During all the bride's activity at the altar the mother sat behind, with the end of her shawl on her daughter's head to symbolize her continued attachment to, and protection of, the girl (see Plate VII*a*).

Meanwhile, the men were busy with the secular side of the occasion which had kept some of them at work for several days past—

erecting a corrugated iron shelter around the altar, for it was February, and rain might fall; making rough wooden benches for the guests; cooking large meals outside for the day's helpers; and running errands for the many supplies which would be needed and which had so far been forgotten. In all, about fifteen men helped during the day: the entire group of agnates of the bride's father, which comprised an extended family of adult men; five men from a nearby Northern homestead of different caste but of close friendship with the host; and a few others from the same settlement. The same men were there that evening, being joined by a few others from the nearby homesteads, including a Southerner and the Sikh storekeeper. The main co-operative emphasis was on the kin group. Other men shared the work as friends, and as allies whose help was significant in the Delanikoro political scene, where Sundar, the bride's father, was one of the main leaders and rivals for power in the settlement.[1]

The morning of the second day (*bhatwan*) saw the girl's parents worship at the altar. During the day the bride was again rubbed with purifying turmeric; after each rubbing she held paddy in her cupped hands with a sprig of *kus* grass on top, whilst each girl filled both hands with paddy and placed them three times on her feet, knees, shoulders and head. The number of girls rubbing the bride should be uneven, and similarly the rubbing itself occurred five times—twice on each of the first two days and once on the final day.

There were fewer people at the homestead during this second day, mainly members of the extended family and their chief helpers, and these started to decorate the marriage booth around the altar. Towards evening people began to arrive from all over Delanikoro for the pre-wedding feast. Invitations had been given by the 'inviter', in this case a relative of the host, to the head of each homestead 'and his family'. The only absentees of any note were men from a Southern homestead who said they were too busy with their own affairs. No Muslims had been invited, nor a section of the settlement which was being boycotted by the rest of the inhabitants.[2] About one-third of the guests were from outside Delanikoro. Most were Northerners from the neighbouring settlement with whom Delanikoro men had become friends at the time when their settlement's store had also served the Delanikoro population. There were also some Fijians who, it was said, had not been formally invited. Everyone fed, and then there were songs from one or two men. People left at about eleven o'clock.

Next day was the wedding day (*shadi*). It was spent in preparing food, putting the finishing touches to the decorations—oranges and guavas were hung from the ceiling of the marriage booth, for the

[1] See p. 127 seq. [2] See p. 126.

69

groom and his entourage to pick if they felt hungry—and entertaining the guests who started to arrive from noon onwards. These were mainly relatives who lived at some distance. Thus, the host's sisters, his wife's parents, his mother's sister's son, his father's sister and her daughter, and the parents-in-law of his brothers all came at this time. The women went straight to their hostess, clasped her and keened loudly for a few minutes in memory of the host's mother who had died just over a year ago, and whose memory was evoked on this occasion. Then they entered the house, or the back courtyard, where they busied themselves with frying savouries, preparing materials to be used in later rites, and talking amongst themselves. The men went to the benches under the shelter, and were given tobacco and *yanggona*.

By sunset a loudspeaker had been installed and was blaring popular songs from a corner of the men's shelter—an essential part of an up-to-date wedding in Fiji. People were arriving from Delanikoro itself now, and at seven o'clock the first batch of about fifty men was given a simple meal of rice and vegetable curry. At half-past seven word arrived that the groom's party had arrived, and soon after the lights of pressure lanterns were seen across the field, nearing the homestead from the roadside. The bride's father advanced to meet them, met the boy's father with a double handclasp, and gave him money as a token of his readiness to complete the wedding.

The meeting of the bride's and groom's parties brought the convergence of what had been two similar programmes. For the groom, also, had been purified with turmeric for the past three days by the girls of his household and extended family; he, too, had erected a bamboo altar, though a less elaborate one, and had also feasted the people of his settlement on the night before. Later he had taken a last meal with four younger agnates, and had been dressed and decorated. Now he had come with an entourage of about thirty men—kin and friends in his settlement. As with the engagement party, the exact number was not known to the host beforehand, but was of a good but not overwhelming size.

The groom was received as an honoured guest in the rites which followed. The bride's father washed his feet in water and put a *tilak* on his forehead, and he went to the house and was received by the bride's mother and other ladies, in an uneven number, who in turn made the *tilak*, passed a pot of water and a flame in circle before him, and gave him a betel leaf in which there was money. Only after being thus received did the groom and his party retire to a special house set aside for them. There they were plied with tobacco, *yanggona* and cigarettes, one or two men always being on call to meet their smallest need. And well might they be! For it was almost expected that the groom's party would complain of inattention and inadequate provision for their needs. Since the groom was the stronger of the pair, this being, at least outwardly, the relation between the couple during the rest of their married life, his entourage felt that they should be placated by the bride's people; they were the 'invaders', who would later return with a bride for their settlement.

Whilst the groom's party sat and chatted in their house, and the rest of the guests talked above the sound of the loudspeaker, the bride bathed with water in which the groom had washed his hair, this having been brought in a bottle and added to water in the bride's house. Then she had her nails cut and her feet decorated with henna, and finally decked herself in a *sari* and a set of ornaments brought for her by the groom. These had been handed over to her father by the groom's brother in a ceremony supervised by the priest, who called several witnesses to vouch for the precise nature of the gifts. The groom's side also gave clothes to her mother and sister, her brother, and the factotum.

The wedding proper started at a quarter to midnight, just four hours after the arrival of the groom. It first centred around the transfer of the bride from her parents' to the groom's care (*kanyadan*—gift of the maiden). The bride's father again washed the groom's feet, tied a purificatory sash of turmeric-dyed cloth around his waist, and showered the pair with prosperity-giving paddy and rubbed their palms in *ghee* (clarified butter, also a sign of prosperity). The actual transfer was made when the bride held *kus* grass in her cupped hands; under them were the hands of her mother, then of her father and lastly, sustaining all, those of the groom. Whilst they sat thus, the bride's younger brother poured water over the hands as the priest chanted. Then the parents withdrew their hands, and the priest changed from Sanskrit to Hindi as he made a short speech to the couple, saying that by their joined hands they showed that they were to be married, and called on God to bless the union.

Now the couple moved to the wedding bench, where their feet were washed by the bride's parents, and presents given them by female relatives and friends. Each woman was purified and then gave her present to the groom, who handed it over to his factotum. In all, nineteen presents were given by kin (of which nine were from women living in the settlement); twelve gifts were from people of other kin groups inside Delanikoro and two from those outside the settlement —most being from people in the extended family with which, as has been said, the bride's father had a close alliance. No gift came from people in other cultural groups. The pattern of gift-making illustrates the obligations of kinsfolk at weddings, and the way common neighbourhood and cultural group can combine to create social obligations. Most of the gifts consisted of a *sari*, usually of

71

pink or pale blue georgette, the material for a blouse, and a glass cup and saucer with 2s. or so in the cup; that is, the bride's friends and kin did not give their main presents to be useful to the groom.

The most important rites started with the priest tying the end of the bride's *sari* to the end of the groom's yellow sash, and their circumambulation of the altar. Four times the bride went first, and three times the groom preceded her; before each round they poured parched rice into a container held by the bride's younger brother. The rite took a long time since, for modesty's sake, the bride was so enveloped in her *sari* that she had to be led by female kin (see Plate VIIIa). Then the priest asked seven questions of the couple, six of them directly addressed to the bride and calculated to set out the relation of co-operation which should exist between them, with the groom taking any final decisions.

With this, the couple changed places on the bench, the bride now sitting on the husband's left hand side—symbolically the weaker side. This change marked the religious validity of the marriage. A further rite followed, which some people maintained was of equal importance. The couple were covered, for modesty, with a large sheet, and the groom placed red powder in the bride's hair parting—the traditional sign of married status.

Next, the civil marriage was held. Previously, banns had been drawn up at the Government office in the town, and had hung in front of the office for twenty-one days, authorization for the marriage being granted after no objections had been received. Now, the priest completed the certificate of marriage, and bride and groom both signed it with two witnesses. This gave legal recognition to the marriage, whose parties were then bound by British law in such matters as divorce and maintenance.

This linking of the religious and civil marriages had been a comparatively recent event in Fiji. During the indenture period, those couples who declared that they were married when they arrived from India were registered as such; but the only marriages made in Fiji which were officially recognized were those certified by the authorities, on the payment of a fee and the publication of banns. These marriages—known to Fiji Indians as *marrit*—were infrequent, for immigrants were accustomed to the Indian situation, where correctly performed religious marriages were recognized as legally binding. They therefore preferred to marry according to Hindu or Muslim rites, but these marriages (*shadi*) were not recognized by the Government. As a result, women married by *shadi* alone had no legal claim for maintenance should their husbands desert them; but the shortage of women no doubt enabled them to make second marriages fairly easily, and so diminished the incentive to have a civil marriage.

It was not until 1928 that an Ordinance linked the civil and religious marriages, thereby in effect recognizing the latter. This was done by licensing certain priests to conduct the civil marriage, under pain of fines should they perform a religious marriage without it, and by forbidding other priests from performing religious marriages. At the same time, couples were allowed to register their purely religious marriages retroactively, and even those who did not do so were legally recognized to be married if they had intended the rite to be valid at the time. They were then able to get birth certificates for their children, a compulsory duty and one which became increasingly necessary as education spread—for children required a certificate to enter school.

In this way problems of legitimacy and inheritance were minimized in Fiji in contrast to, say, Mauritius where Indian religious marriage is officially unrecognized, and where only a small proportion of the Indian population go through a civil marriage ceremony, which is not legally required.[1] Further, the new law stopped the practice of marrying quite young children, as had been the case in India, for the priest could not complete the civil certificate for spouses under the legal marriage age.

It is significant that the certificate was completed *after* the religious ceremonies, for this shows the importance given by Fiji Indian society to the latter. If some impediment were to arise between the start of the rites and the culminating act, which would render the marriage null, it would be disastrous to have had a civil marriage beforehand, which would make the couple legally, but not socially, married.[2] This procedure was presumably copied from the English form of marriage seen in Fiji and compares with, say, the French system where, though people may regard the religious service as the 'true' marriage, the official ceremony at the municipal office has priority.

After the civil marriage, the couple entered the house of the bride. There, in traditional style, the ladies of the house played tricks on the groom, and the bride and groom gambled together (the groom should always win). The groom was mocked, often with sexual allusions, and the joking relation which he would have with his wife's sisters was started—for instance, they gave him betel leaves to eat, filled with stones instead of areca nut. By 3 a.m. the festivities were over, and the groom retired. Most of the guests had been asleep long since, not having witnessed the marriage rite.

[1] Personal communication from Dr. Burton Benedict.
[2] It is said by farmers that occasionally the civil marriage *is* held first, and that in exceptional cases the *shadi* has not eventuated. The girl then remains in her parental household, since her parents deem it irreligious to send her to her husband without a *shadi*. A divorce can, of course, be later obtained if this situation lasts.

By next morning several of the groom's party had left, and only a few close friends stayed, as well as those who had friends in Delani-koro. The groom sat quietly in his dishevelled finery of satin coat and sash, and the other guests waited patiently while the bride's people cooked a meal whose preparation had begun before dawn that morning. In all there were some fifteen men on the groom's and thirty on the bride's side. By noon the meal was ready, and the groom, his father and two brothers and his mother's brother's son sat down to eat in the wedding booth near the altar (see Plate VIII*b*). Food was brought but the groom refused it; he was given a table and chairs, but still he refused; the bride's father handed him the money collected during that morning and the preceding evening from his guests (a sum of £24); only then, did he slowly start to eat, and everyone followed him. The meal was the most elaborate of the wedding, with two kinds of curry, chutneys, and rice and fried pancakes.

The money and goods collected by the groom at this time constituted, in effect, the bride's dowry. In contrast, the ornaments, etc. which she had been given by the groom and by her relatives remained her own property. The dowry had not been arranged beforehand, and the groom could, in theory, have refused to eat until he had denuded the bride's household of all its property. But in general there was a conventional amount expected; wealthy people might give houses or blocks of freehold land, but the poorer people's main gift was the cash collected from guests—sums which were returned to them, with a slight increment, at their own subsequent weddings.

After the meal, the couple left the house to the accompaniment of weeping from the bride's womenfolk. Later, the bride was received by her female affines at her husband's house, and refused to unveil herself to them until she had been given suitable presents of cash— but since she did not want to displease her future house-mates, she did not force them to give a large sum. The money collected was her private property.

Some three days later, the bride returned to her household, and left again about a fortnight later, when she started to live with her husband, and to be a full member of her conjugal household.

The wedding described in its essentials is an example of an orthodox Northern ceremony. Differences in detail were observed on other occasions. For instance, in one wedding the seven questions asked by the priest were accompanied by seven steps by the couple, and these were marked by seven rows of paddy on the ground. Again, the two days' preliminaries for a wedding in Namboulima contained some major omissions, mainly because no priest was available and the participants were vague as to what had to be done. But there was little of the luxuriant ritual variation that exists in India between different castes and different regions.

Weddings of Northerhers belonging to the Arya Samaj were much less complicated, as became a sect dedicated to preserving the ancient, and simple, Hindu rites. The groom was welcomed, there were the circumambulations of the altar, whose centre was a fire rather than a bamboo, and the vermilion mark was placed in the bride's hair. But the entire rite took a single evening since there was no preliminary purification with turmeric, and the guests were feasted only once.

THE WEDDING: SOUTHERN

The Southern weddings attended showed certain variations from that described for Northerners. A brief outline of a wedding witnessed in Namboulima will suggest these.

This wedding also started with two days' purification with turmeric, and a feast on the evening of the second day.[1] The party of the groom left the settlement, and was greeted by the bride's father, for in this case the wedding was held at the bride's homestead, though traditionally it would have been at the groom's. But the parents of the spouses greeted each other as equals, exchanging betel, rather than with the subordination of the bride's side as symbolized in the washing of the groom's feet. The groom was welcomed by the bride's female relatives, and the rites started at midnight.

For the first hour, the place of the wedding was prepared by a party of five women, sisters and brother's wives of the groom, who had come with him on the wedding party. They ceremonially brought earth and water to the wedding booth, and placed these as directed by the priest. Then the couple emerged, were rubbed with fragrant sandalwood paste, had their feet and hands decorated, and performed a rite in which they took their wedding clothes which were spread in the booth. By dressing for the wedding at the same time, the couple's relationship differed from that of the Northerners, where the bride's dressing and ritual bath were dependent on the provision of special water by a groom who was already dressed.

The central rite of the wedding came soon after the couple had emerged again. It consisted of the tying, by the groom, of the *tali*— a thread dyed in turmeric—round the bride's neck. After this, their robes were tied and they went five times round the central altar. But when they again sat down on the wedding bench, the bride was still on the groom's right; they had not changed places, as in the Northern

[1] A Southern friend writes that three or four days before this, worship and sacrifice may be made to the lineage ancestors and goddess,

rite. In some Southern weddings they changed, however, and the variation in this custom indicates that it was less crucial for Southerners. Gifts were then given by relatives, and presents by the bride's father, and a last rite ended the wedding at 4.15 a.m.

The main differences from the Northern rite were that the parents took little part and did not ceremonially 'give away' the bride; that bride and groom took a more equal part in the rites; and that women came in the cortege of the groom, being in fact necessary for the preliminary rites. The main rite of marriage was different, but there was the same emphasis on purification, though not on the public making of marriage vows.

THE WEDDING: MUSLIM

The weddings of Muslims in Fiji were, of course, quite different from Hindu rites, as an example from Vunioki shows. The wedding was held, as is customary, at the bride's house. The day before, the groom had heard readings from the Quran, and on the day of the marriage, his sisters had stained his hands and feet with henna, this being the only preliminary rite. The cortege, of men only, assembled at noon, and was fed on meat curry and rice; they left in the late afternoon and went by taxi to the bride's homestead. In the main they were fellow Muslims of Vunioki. A few Hindus had been pressed to come by the groom's father, for without them the cortege would have been too small, and the bride's father would have been hurt at an implication of his own poverty and unimportance. Because the Muslims themselves were in many places only a small cultural group, they often needed Hindu guests to fill out the party.[1]

The groom was met at the bride's house by senior women of her family—her mother, father's sister, elder sister—who welcomed him with betel and gifts of money, and who covered him with scent, before seating him amongst the other guests. A *maulvi* from his side and one from the bride's settlement prayed, and asked him if he was prepared to marry the girl; he affirmed this three times, in front of two witnesses, both from the girl's side. The witnesses and the *maulvis* then went to the girl's apartment in the house, where she sat dressed in her wedding clothes and ornaments brought by the groom, and asked her if she were willing to marry the boy for the consideration of £6 bride-money. She agreed, the party returned to the assembly of men, the *maulvis* said a short prayer, and the wedding was over save for completing the usual civil marriage certificate. There was a feast that night, and the couple returned home on the

[1] In some settlements, of course, the Muslims were consciously Muslim and did not wish to invite those of other religions to their affairs (see Chapter VII).

next day. In theory, the girl could have refused to marry, and have demanded a higher sum of money; but in fact the amount had been predetermined by the parents. In return, the bride brought with her money and clothing of considerably more value.

It is now time to sum up the most significant features of these weddings.[1] One is that few close kin took part in the wedding rites. The parents were important in greeting the spouse and in giving away their daughter; the bride's younger brother was needed for the Northerners' circumambulation, and the bride's younger sister might also play a part; but other kin were not essential. There was, for example, no major role for the mother's brother, or for the sister's husband, both of whom were important in the Northern Hindu marriages witnessed in Central India. This fairly restricted role of kin in ritual matters will be contrasted with their importance in the secular aspects of the weddings.

Secondly, the roles within the rites were not exclusive to certain kin. The girls rubbing the spouse with purifying turmeric paste could even be, and often were, of different caste and even of different 'culture'. Again, one wedding was classed by an informant as being 'all upside down', for, he said, the groom's mother being dead, her place had been taken by the father's sister. But this was in theory impossible, since it implied an incestuous relation between the father and his sister. It was the more inexcusable since women were there who could have filled the mother's role, such as the mother's sister, for a widower can marry his wife's sister. Nevertheless, the father's sister thought she could do everything better than anybody else and took this role. When the groom's procession arrived at the bride's house, the bride's father should have greeted a man in the relation of father to the groom. The groom's mother's sister's husband was there, who could, as we have just seen, have been the groom's father. But his caste status was reputedly doubtful[2] and the bride's father refused to shake his hand. Instead, the groom's mother's brother came forward. But he could not possibly be viewed as a 'substitute father' since his relation to the real father was one of 'brother-in-law', not of 'brother'. The bride's father thereupon withdrew, and let his step-son carry out the rite. The main point about this case is not so much that these mistakes occurred, but that they did not prevent the wedding from proceeding. People might have a

[1] Not included are accounts of Sikh, Gujarati, etc. marriages which seldom occurred in the settlements.

[2] See p. 162.

77

clear idea of the categories of kin and the need to differentiate kin-ship roles to correspond to them, but they evidently did not regard this as essential.

Thirdly the father's reception of the groom in Northern weddings was as an honoured guest to whom obeisance was due, and the feelings of the groom's entourage were an extension of the 'strong' position of the groom. This point should perhaps be emphasized, for in several weddings attended by the author as a member of the groom's entourage, an atmosphere of superiority could be felt most strongly. Even people who knew members of the bride's group were rather formal with them when they arrived, and would only sit and talk to them informally after the night's ceremonies were over. An example of the relation between groom's and bride's side comes from a Delanikoro Arya Samaj wedding.

The bride's father said after the wedding: 'I expected about thirty men in the entourage, but actually sixty-five came. I had prepared Kisun's house for them, and they went there on arrival, and food and tobacco were brought to them. I couldn't go to wait on them myself, because I had to be in the wedding booth. But as soon as I could, I went there. Some were sleeping inside, others were playing cards on the grass. These I asked to come to my own house, where they would be more comfortable. They refused, saying that the night had half gone, and this would be useless. I gave them tea and food at six-thirty—they did not have to wait for breakfast until nine o'clock like some groom's parties. But they were angry at me, and said they had had no room. Some wanted to leave right away, others to have lunch too. I could do nothing, and said I would do what they wanted. But they left angry, criticizing my arrangements. What more could I do? I pleaded with them to take my house. I give them my daughter, a cow as dowry, money and clothes; all this is not a happy matter for me. Yet they can only be angry. But it is their fault, they would not co-operate with me, and they brought too many in their party.'

This atmosphere of criticism was very common among the groom's parties, whether or not any gentleman's agreement about the size of the entourage had been broken. It is interesting that the relationship did not only concern the two kin groups involved in the marriage, but also could be extended to include other settlement members in the party. Not only did the people in the groom's party feel that they represented a dominant kin group, but also a dominant settlement; and they expressed this quite explicitly. This is important because it was one of the few occasions on which any settlement *esprit de corps* was encountered.

The last point concerns the role of kin and others in the secular aspects of the wedding. Here the whole scale of the wedding depended on the availability of labour—largely drawn from the household and the extended family *within the settlement*, but also depending on friends in other kin groups and even other cultural groups. The manpower needed to make shelter and arrangements for guests, and to cook and do other jobs, was considerable. At the Delanikoro wedding described first, about seven men did almost nothing else for at least a week; and another half a dozen worked for the last two days. This is why weddings were best held in May and June, after cane planting and paddy harvests, and before the cane Gangs started work; but many people still held them in February and March, the months which are best for the agricultural calendar in India itself. Of the men who did most work at the Delanikoro wedding, only three were of the extended family. One of the others belonged to the neighbouring homestead which had a close tie of co-operation; and three others were less closely linked—one being of a different cultural group—but had personal reasons for giving so much help. For instance, one man had a wedding of his own soon, and counted on reciprocal help; another counted the bride's father as his patron, for he occasionally borrowed his money.

The scale of a wedding was thus an index of the amount of help a man could command. It was not just a question of the money he was prepared to spend, for nobody was hired for this help except, occasionally, a chief cook. Wealth was important, of course; for dowry and food expenses had to be commensurate with the scale of the wedding. But its role was less as a direct cause of a large wedding, than as creating obligations to a rich man, and thereby providing him with clients who would give up time to help at his wedding. Rich people did not need to give large weddings if they were not also ambitious for power and a following in the settlement. The richest man in Delanikoro, for example, married off his daughter with derisive simplicity, even to the extent of having the wedding in the daytime in order, it was said, to save the expense of lighting. He did not worry about people's comments, and his lack of contacts with the settlement was so marked that he had nobody to help him at the wedding,[1] and was only saved by the decision of the settlement's leaders to provide their services, so as not to let the settlement down in front of outsiders. (This being another example of the way weddings were seen as the concern of the entire settlement.) Weddings in Fiji Indian settlements, then, were indices of a man's influence in the settlement, as well as occasions when the settlement itself was represented against the 'outside' by its members.

[1] He had lent his money outside the settlement, and so had no debtors to call upon for help (see p. 57).

Ritual Activities

The death of a Hindu in a settlement set off a series of rites. There was first the funeral, carried out on the same or the following day; then followed rites on the third, and the thirteenth days; and finally, commemorative rites occurred after a year, and in theory on each anniversary thereafter. The nature of these rites, and the number and social position of the participants, can best be shown by following the funeral of a Northerner in Vunioki.

This man died at nine o'clock one morning. At about one o'clock a small group had gathered—seven men of his extended family, and eight of other kin and cultural groups. He had been old, relatively undistinguished, but with some quite influential kinsmen. Other men came later, including representatives from the houses of the settlement's leaders. Twenty-five men were present by the time the funeral took place, as well as women of nearby homesteads. His son washed and dressed the corpse, laying it on a bier covered in *kus* grass, rubbing its face with *ghee*, putting basil in its mouth, and sprinkling the shroud with camphor, talcum powder and flowers. When all was ready, the womenfolk came to have a last look at the face; the man's sister and his son's wife made loud lament, and were led away by their fellows.

The pallbearers in the procession to the cemetery included men of the dead man's kin group, his cultural group, and other cultural groups (e.g. Muslims). On arrival, the body was lowered into the grave, and the bamboo bier smashed. Then the dead man's son got into the grave, and put camphor in the four corners. A priest said a short prayer, and the son threw five handfuls of earth on to the shroud. He got out and a wooden top was placed over the body, after which everyone threw five handfuls into the grave, and earth was shovelled in.

During the time that the grave and its headstone were being made, the men of the cortege walked round the cemetery, trying to identify the headstones. It was a difficult job, since few were marked, and most were uncared for. But people could remember the position of the most recent graves, and knew their occupants. There appeared to be no division of the cemetery into plots for each kin group, however, though spouses were frequently placed close to each other. The cortege then returned to the dead man's house. Here the man's sister had prepared a fire, and invited everyone to throw a chilli in it and warm their feet. The chilli gave off an acrid smell and was supposed to drive away any spirits which might have accompanied the men from the cemetery. Only a few older men did this, most being embarrassed and rather contemptuous of this custom.

80

No food was cooked in the bereaved household, and that evening men brought dinner from two homesteads of relatives nearby. By this time collaterals had arrived from a town some thirty miles away, and about a dozen people stayed until midnight, talking quite normally, and distracting the chief mourner.

On the third day a small rite was performed. When there was a cremation this was to disperse the ashes. For thirteen days the chief mourner—here the dead man's son—did not shave, nor eat spiced foods. At the end of this time he shaved his head and performed rites of propitiation to the dead person's soul, both at the nearby river and in the homestead's compound (see Plate IX*b*). Then he gave presents to the Brahman priest who had officiated, and afterwards fed a dozen guests, mostly kin but including the priest. The Southerners had the final propitiation on the sixteenth day; until then a light burnt continuously in the house, and food was offered to the spirit and afterwards eaten by the chief mourner. On the sixteenth night, a pan of fine ash, smoothed and made airtight, was put in a closed room. Next morning it was opened, and a footprint indicated the creature into which the soul had been reincarnated.

Contrary to normal practice in India, most Fiji Hindu funerals were by burial and not by cremation. The latter was much more expensive, since wood and *ghee* were required and a much more elaborate ritual necessary; and it could be performed only after a death certificate had been obtained. This was too lengthy a process for people in remote settlements, and a priest calculated that not more than 5 per cent of funerals were by cremation. The continuity of generations provided by a cemetery was only partially fulfilled, however, since the graves were not marked nor consistently arranged.

The rites were simple and relatively inexpensive. For example, at the funeral of the wife of a cane farmer of average substance, the priest was given £1 cash, some cloth, and about £1 of foodstuffs. The total cost of the funeral was rarely more than £2–£3.

Muslim funerals were similar to the Hindu rites described. There was the laying out, the leave-taking by the women, the cortege to the cemetery, a prayer by the *maulvi* and the interment with a close agnate sprinkling scent over the corpse, the throwing of earth on the grave by the attenders, a final prayer, and the planting and watering of shrubs at each corner of the grave. There was propitiation of the spirit on the third and fortieth days.

Attendance at funerals, like that at weddings, to some extent measured a man's influence in the settlement—either that of the deceased, or of the man who was the chief mourner. But it was a much less sure guide than the number of wedding guests; for funerals happened at short notice. Some men's absences were unavoidable, and did not necessarily signify anything about their relations with the dead person's household. It was also easier for an individual to represent the men of his household, or even of his extended kin group, than at a wedding. For the most important element at a funeral was sympathetic presence or a token of this by a representative of the kin or cultural group, whereas actual physical aid was needed at a wedding from as many as could be mustered. Hence, numbers were relevant mainly for funerals of the most influential people and their close kin. Here, everyone tried to attend, and there was considerable crossing of settlement boundaries. The funeral of the daughter of an important Muslim in the next settlement was attended by at least eleven people from Vunioki, of whom seven were Hindus. In this case, many of the attenders had direct economic obligations to the bereaved kin and no substitute mourner would have been acceptable. The attendance of Hindus at Muslim funerals and *vice versa* depended on the state of communal relations at the time. In Vunioki there was a tendency for more Muslims to go to Hindu funerals than *vice versa*; in Delanikoro, on the other hand, there was practically no movement in either direction across the religious boundary.

A commemorative and propitiative rite (*sraddha*) was performed by Hindus to the dead person's spirit. This took place during two weeks of the Indian month of Bhadrapada (October–September), on the date on which the person died in either fortnight of any month. Offerings of food were made, and a priest chanted verses. Some said that the rite was a propitiation and honouring of the spirit of the dead person and his other forefathers by the eldest son, or, in his absence, by the eldest son's or daughter's son, or the eldest living agnate. Others maintained that it was an intercession with God, asking him to take care of the father's spirit, and the spirits of other ascendants, wherever they had been reincarnated. The rite took place in the morning, and was attended by members of the household only. Sometimes a dinner was given in the evening to which collateral members of the kin group were invited; these might have performed *sraddha* to their own forefathers and, by extension, to the same ascendants as their host. The gathering was never a large affair, and the expense was at most £3–£4.

Probably not more than a quarter of the men carried out this duty beyond the first year after a death. Some India-born men did not know whether their fathers were now dead; others had left an elder brother in India, charged with this duty, and did not know whether he still carried it on. In this way genuine uncertainty could be added to disinclination and make an excuse to avoid holding the rite. Nevertheless, by holding the ceremony at least once, men fulfilled

(b). The priest (left) performs the orthodox Northern marriage.

VII (a). The bride is purified with turmeric.

(b). The bridegroom consents to eat.

VIII (a). The circumambulation of the altar.

IX (*a*). Ritual shaving of the baby's hair.

(*b*). A son propitiates his father's spirit in a funerary rite.

X (*a*).   A woman worships Hanuman.

(*b*).   Curing a headache.

their obligations to their forefathers whose duty it had been to beget male offspring for this purpose.

Another category of rites was confined to the individual or the household or kin group, but was not connected with the life cycle. Some of these rites were periodic, some were not.

The two main periodic rites concerned the welfare of the descent group. Here is included the *sraddha* ceremony, in so far as it referred not only to the dead person, but also to his agnatic ascendants. For the entire agnatic line was comprehended in the rite, itself a factor in the complex of activities centring round the principle of patrilineal descent.[1]

The other rite honoured the tutelary deity of the agnatic line. The instances recorded involved the sacrifice of some animal—a cock, a goat or a pig—to assure the benevolence of the deity and the corresponding prosperity of the descent group. One such rite in Delanikoro was held at a small thatched hut, adjoining a series of homesteads occupied by an extended family of Northerners. These comprised five surviving brothers, the children and widow of a sixth, and two adult sons of a widowed sister. The main roles were taken by the youngest brother and the sixth brother's widow. The other inhabitants formed their audience; there were no outsiders.

The rite started with the widow and youngest brother sitting crosslegged in the hut and pouring *ghee* on a small fire placed amidst other material of worship (seven piles of pancakes, blocks of camphor, etc.). Then there was a short silence and the widow started to sway, her movements becoming more and more violent until she was rhythmically beating the earth in front of her with her elbows. She was possessed by the lineage's tutelary deity. Her brother-in-law asked if all was well. She answered that she had been neglected, and that they had not worshipped her adequately. The men defended themselves, but she was adamant, and they promised to do better in future. (The point of the argument was that the rite should be performed every three years, but they had delayed because of the expense of buying the pigs.) She then put some of the camphor and vermilion into an amulet which she gave to a brother's daughter, who had been unwell. Then the shakings diminished and she slowly returned to a normal state, took some water and went outside to wash her face and mouth.

The scene shifted to the ground outside the 'temple'. Two small pits had been dug, and two pigs were brought. Turmeric was sprinkled

[1] See p. 173 seq.

over them and their heads were cut off and placed beside the pits; on them the widow sprinkled turmeric and a little alcohol. They were then buried in the pits; the carcases were butchered, the hearts and livers cooked together and brought on a brass tray to the pits. Two or three pieces were placed on the ground and liquor poured on them; the rest was distributed to kinfolk. The pigs honoured the spirits of the dead brother and his lineage deity. There was a feast that night off the rest of the meat. The cost was about £3.

Not all households propitiated a tutelary deity. It was generally held to be difficult to neglect any spirit demanding periodic propitiation without incurring misfortune; but some people had become more and more lax in worship, and, feeling that they did not suffer in consequence, had left off altogether. In one instance, too, an old India-born Southerner had simply forgotten the name of his tutelary. His son said that he had written to relatives in the Nellore District of Andhra State, asking them for information, but had had no reply. In the meantime, said the son, he worshipped his wife's tutelary—an indication that in Fiji patrilineal descent, though the most important, is not the exclusive principle of allegiance, and that membership of a clan may count for little.[1]

Other periodic rites were the result of individual decisions. One Southerner, for example, had been very ill with rheumatic fever; a hospital-mate had suggested that he make a vow to a Muslim saint called Nagore Mia, and he had recovered. Every year since then he had called a *maulvi* and held a small rite in the saint's honour, and several white flags flew above his house in token of these. Again, men might take vows to appear for a certain number of years in the fire-walking rite of honour to Mariamma, the smallpox goddess. Or people might worship Lakshmi, Rama or others of the Hindu pantheon in their houses, weekly, annually or daily. Some farmers had Fijian spirits on their land, and propitiated them each year. Thus a Southerner of Vunioki told me that he had the grave of an important Fijian in his field, and that Fijians came to make offering. He had started to do so himself through a Fijian 'priest';[2] when for two years he had not done so, misfortune had occurred. His bullocks died, he lost money, and he had then resumed the worship. Several other farmers of Vunioki alleged that they had Fijian spirits on their land, and that these could understand prayers made to them in Hindi. They said that if they once started to take notice of them, they would have to stage a rite each year. But by not doing anything at all, they believed that the spirits ignored them.

Many small rites were the result of *ad hoc* decisions, and had no

[1] See the fact that many do not know their clans (p. 63).
[2] All Fijians are of course Christian, and such practitioners are unofficial.

periodic character. Of these, perhaps the most frequent were the sacred readings organized by Hindus (*katha*) and by Muslims (*kitab*). In each case, a priest was present, who offered a prayer and then read a selection of sacred writings. Many of these readings were attended by members of the household alone; but some men had them in the evening, and followed them with a dinner and perhaps the singing of hymns afterwards. In this case up to fifteen or twenty men were invited. Generally, these were from the extended family living near the host's homestead. For the reading was usually undertaken in fulfilment of a vow, made at a time of illness or misfortune, or for the maintenance of prosperity, and kin were held to be most interested in this; but they seldom came from more than, say, half a mile away. Any further audience was usually composed of neighbours, generally of the same cultural group. Similar rites were those made in honour of Hanuman, Ganesh and Surya (the sun); these were made to ask for children, for the cure of headaches, for an increase in income or in fulfilment of vows—to name a few of the many reasons. Worship to the monkey-god Hanuman was made under a bamboo pole with a red flag, and these flags could be seen in any Fiji Indian settlement, becoming paler and paler as the sun and wind weathered them, until they were at last quite white (see Plate X*a*).

Many of these rites were conducted by unregistered priests, men who were not authorized to conduct weddings and who had to content themselves with less lucrative services. Such people might also have small temples at which clients could initiate rites. There was, for instance, an old Southerner in Vunioki who had a thatched temple to Kali in his compound. He would intercede for clients if they wished it, and also had a small annual rite for which he collected money from each Hindu household. His main income came from healing, however, for he had a reputation for efficacious amulets, given to children who were thought to have the evil eye on them, to women who were subject to fits, to people suffering from migraine and so forth.

This ability to heal was possessed by many people. Some used amulets filled with spiritually powerful materials or verses; others performed simple rites. An example concerned a Muslim labourer of Namboulima, who was known as a curer of headaches. His procedure for men was to face the subject and draw his fingers across the forehead, whilst reciting verses; at the end he would blow on the forehead. For women patients he drew a pattern with ash on the ground whilst he recited, and at the end blew and made a *tilak* on the forehead (see Plate X*b*). He had learnt the verses from a book, he said; they were Muslim texts and mentioned the names of saints—for Hindu patients he simply substituted the name of the god Ganesh.

85

A more difficult method involved possession of the healer or his patient by the spirit of the disease. There were no more than one or two such experts in any settlement. Here the possession made possible the questioning of the deity as to why he afflicted the person, and what he would like done as the price of leaving the latter in peace. Often the reply was a demand for a further rite, involving the sacrifice of goats and libations of liquor, both of which were consumed by the participants afterwards. For this reason some people were sceptical about such healers, saying that they themselves fed well at the patient's expense. Seances were held in private, and only the healer, the patient and perhaps a few close friends who were also devotees would be present. There were also seances called for general advice on personal problems, at which the medium was possessed and passed on the instructions of his tutelary. Men at Vunioki said that some had Fijian spirits, such as Dengei, as tutelaries.

There is only a limited degree of social interaction based on the rites described. At the most, they cement the ties of extended family and near neighbourhood. Conversely, there is no record of a break of relations through lack of an invitation to these rites.

RITES OF THE MAJOR HINDU FESTIVALS

Several major Hindu and Muslim festivals were celebrated each year by the Fiji Indian rural community, of which the majority were observed in one or other of the three settlements.[1] Some called for settlement-wide activity, some were largely confined to a single cultural group, and yet others showed a dependence of settlements on the town.

Diwali, the festival of lights, marked the Hindu New Year[2] and fell in October–November. The worship of Lakshmi, the goddess of wealth, was especially popular on this day. Children let off fireworks, and adults cooked good food for the evening, when lights were lit in every window, pinpointing the furthest homesteads on the hillsides. These lights were said to commemorate the welcome given by the people of Ayodhya to Rama, their king, on his return from Lanka where he had vanquished the demon Ravan.[3] This was a traditional basis for Diwali; but another common custom in India, of decorating

[1] Other festivals celebrated in India were recognized elsewhere in Fiji. The Tamil New Year (Pongal), for example, was extant among Southerners, though not those of the three settlements studied.

[2] There are several eras in India, of which this is one. Hindu and Muslim calendars were rarely observed in Fiji.

[3] See p. 94.

the cattle, was not observed. A few people went into town to see the illuminations, but this was mainly a festival held within each homestead, without a complex ritual.

Christmas had no religious significance for Fiji Indians, of course, but it had become a festival because it was a public holiday, and offered an excuse for festivities. The pattern in Vunioki suggested that Christmas was an occasion for travel; people working in towns were given leave to visit their relatives in the settlement, and several young men went off by bus to see other places on the island. The hotels were crowded with Fijians, whose celebrations the Fiji Indians were glad to share. As one old man said, when asked what he had done at Christmas, 'I have done nothing at Christmas; I do not drink liquor'.

The next major festival, that of Holi, came in March. In India it is the spring festival, falling in the short season between the cold and hot seasons. In Fiji, too, it marked the start of a climatic change—from the hot season of thunder and hurricanes to the cooler part of the year. As with many spring rites, the Holi festival was traditionally a period of licence, when the poor were free to insult the rich, the women to forsake their modesty, and all classes of society to mingle and to throw red dye on each other, the sign of Holi. Freedom from normal restraint was carefully regulated in Fiji—it did not extend to women, nor to those men who did not wish to join in; but the aspect of equality was there, as expressed by one man when he said 'the importance of the red dye is that everyone looks the same when it is poured on them; it makes everyone equal, and happy'.

The Holi festival in Delanikoro started a fortnight before its climax,[1] with the singing of special songs in its honour. These songs, commonly called *chautal*, were sung by ten or a dozen men. They were accompanied by a drummer, and by cymbals played by some of the singers. The leader of the performance sang a verse; the chorus then repeated it, being divided into two groups and singing alternately. The line was repeated perhaps ten to fifteen times, the drummer varying the rhythm, and the tempo gradually increasing until both parties were singing as fast as they could. Suddenly all would stop, and the leader would sing a new verse, to repeat the procedure all over again. The songs could roughly be divided into two categories; first, there were devotional and descriptive songs, which concerned the Holi festival itself; and second, there were songs about topical events—mostly in India—which resembled calypsos.[2]

Each song lasted for about a half-hour, and between there were intervals of talk. The meetings were held after the evening meal, and

[1] For a fuller description and analysis, see Mayer 1952.
[2] See p. 192 for an example.

87

went on until around midnight. They provided an occasion for co-operation and conviviality between the younger men of the settlement, for no India-born people took part. The main participants were members of the most important faction of Delanikoro, and included both Southerners and Northerners.

On the full moon night of Phalgun month, the Holi rite was held. The centre of it was the lighting of a large bonfire, made from brush-wood collected by the men themselves. The blaze symbolized the triumph of good over evil, and the victory of true over false gods. The time of lighting, and the inaugural rite, were supervised by the settlement's priest. A large crowd had gathered, probably some three-quarters of the settlement's male population under forty.

Next day saw the play with the red-dyed water. It was started after a meeting held at the hall of the Youth Association.[1] Fifty-three of the eighty-eight men in the settlement were present. All but six were Fiji-born persons of under forty years and of these, there were twenty-eight Northerners and nineteen Southerners. In short, a good cross section of the Hindu population took part. The meeting was held to decide the route of the procession, and to emphasize that red water could only be thrown at those who were prepared to take part in the play. The Holi games had in fact been tamed because of latent hostilities within the settlement which might flare up under the provocation of a too liberal use of the red dye.

The procession of men then visited all households save those of Muslims and people whom the settlement majority was boycotting[2] (see Plate XIII*b*). They were doused by the householders including women, and received sweetmeats from them. No games were played at some of the houses in which a death had occurred during the past year; instead, the householder made a contribution towards the expenses of the Holi ritual. This visiting lasted from about 10 a.m. until 5.30 p.m., when people repaired to the Youth Association's hall, and sang *chautals* until midnight.

The Holi festival not only marked divisions in the settlement, but also provided a context in which the settlement faced other settlements as a unit, through the singing of *chautals* in competition. On these occasions the two leaders of the group and the two halves of the chorus were from competing settlements. Each leader took it in turn to initiate a verse, which could be from any epic or poem, but which had to have some relevance to the verse immediately preced-ing it. Presence of mind was therefore required of the leaders, who could never repeat themselves and who always had to have an answering verse ready; and dexterity was required of the choruses, who had to sing at high speed a verse which might be quite un-

[1] See p. 109 seq.   [2] See p. 125 seq.

familiar to them. The contest was decided when one of the leaders had no relevant verse to offer.

Teams from Delanikǫro had competed on several occasions and, thanks to the knowledge and quick wit of their leader Sundar, had been successful several times. On one occasion, Sundar said, they defeated sixteen teams and won a drum as prize. Here was an activity in which the settlement as a whole was represented, even if everyone did not take part.

The importance of Holi varied in different settlements. In Vunioki, for example, there was no procession, one or two men going to the houses of their friends to play with the dye. Similarly in Namboulima *chautals* had been sung by a few enthusiasts, but there was no procession, nor any assembly of the settlement for a single bonfire. It is possible that the greater distances between homesteads in these settlements worked against the idea of a procession; for such a group would have had to walk several miles to visit all the homesteads, whereas in Delanikoro it was a matter of hundreds of yards.

The festivals of Sivaratri and Ram's Birthday (Ram Naumi) were not occasions for any settlement-wide activities. A dozen or so devotees in Delanikoro met on the latter day at the Youth Association's hall, and had an evening of devotional reading. But in each case the festival was mainly celebrated by individual decisions to fast, or to have small rites in the homestead itself.

A major festival held in April–May in Delanikoro was the worship of Kali. This was performed on a hillock overlooking the settlement. Seven virgins and a Brahman youth sat in line, whilst an old man of the settlement performed a rite with the settlement priest's help, and then sacrificed a goat in honour of the goddess. Afterwards the girls and the youth were fed. Both Northerners and Southerners took part in the festival, but the degree to which the entire settlement participated is not clear since it did not occur during fieldwork there. Similar to it was the Kali festival in Namboulima, in which goats were sacrificed in three places, an indication of the larger size of the settlement as compared with Delanikoro.

In July, the Southerners of Delanikoro had a major religious festival honouring the goddess Mariamma. Preliminary rites were performed at a temple in the neighbouring settlement to the west, built with contributions from Southerners of the half-dozen nearby settlements and the town. The Mariamma festival given by the Delanikoro people was, however, entirely theirs; the only outsider was a Southern priest from Suva who was brought to manage the procession. Thus, the festival did not represent inter-settlement co-operation.

Proceedings were started at the temple in the early evening when twelve Southern men started to make themselves up as dancers of a drama drawn from the *Ramayana*. Their ages ranged from eighteen to thirty years; two of them portrayed women, and one was a comic, whose role consisted in making fun of the dancers. With him he had a 'stooge' who retained his everyday dress. The dance went on from about 9 p.m. to 4 a.m. accompanied by Tamil hymns sung by a chorus of six men and led by the only India-born person in the proceedings. The story, told through the medium of these hymns, was translated for the onlookers by the 'stooge', who also went through the crowd collecting money contributions, usually about 1*s.* per person, towards the expenses. The dance left the performers extremely fatigued, and this may have been a pre-condition for their subsequent ordeal.

The rites of the procession started later that day, at about 7.30 a.m. Their main end was to transfer the presence of the god and the goddess from their shrines in the temple to two pots. One, made of pottery, represented the male deity, and was borne by a dancer called Raman in the procession; the goddess's, made of brass, was held by Sundaram, a large man of about thirty years. The pots were filled with turmeric-dyed water, and had boughs of *neem* leaves and flowers on their mouths. The other result of the rites was to purify these bearers of the deities, and to install as the goddess Mariamma a man of twenty-five, of slight build, called Subramaniam. These three men, together with the man with the whip (called Lakshman) and a youth who bore the goddess's trident on which were impaled green limes, made up the heart of the procession. One or two other men joined as supernumeraries (without changing their clothes or undergoing any purification), and the Suva priest was the official leader. The chorus and drummers accompanied the procession throughout.

The procession set off, at its head Subramaniam, already exhausted but going at a feeble, jogging dance step, the two men with the deities on their heads walking normally, the singers and drummers following them with Tamil hymns. Nothing was done until the border of the settlement was crossed, and the first Delanikoro homestead reached. This, as it happened, belonged to a Southerner, and from it came his womenfolk. They sprinkled turmeric water on the feet of the principals, and touched them with their hands and sometimes their foreheads; then they circled them with an oil flame, and gave the leader a coconut to break before them. The following crowd of Southern and Northern residents of Delanikoro received offerings (*parsad*) of fruit and sugar.

Then Lakshman faced the men bearing the deities. As he stared at them, so they started to lunge forward at him, their bodies growing rigid and tense. Raman's breath started to hiss louder and louder, until Lakshman whipped him with an eight-foot lash of coconut fibre; round the waist first and then, as he stretched out one arm after the other, across the forearm (see Plate XI*b*). In some cases the whip curled round the body with its own momentum; but in others it seemed clear that the end of the lash struck with full force. When he had finished, Raman seized the whip and faced Sundaram, both holding their pots and glaring at each other; soon Sundaram's face became distorted and he started to roar before he, too, was whipped in the same way. Lakshman never whipped Sundaram—this was Raman's duty, perhaps as bearer of the male deity, and he seemed to beat much harder than did Lakshman.

The whipping over, the procession went on to the next homestead. The principals were quite composed, and even talked to the retinue; only Subramaniam, representing the goddess Mariamma, was by this time almost insensible and had to be supported under each shoulder (see Plate XI*a*). The rite varied at each place. In some no offerings were made, but only the flame passed round; in others a cock was sacrificed, and the head sprinkled with turmeric-water; at some places both men were whipped, at others only Raman. In all, the people of nineteen homesteads worshipped—seven of these being Northern and twelve Southern.

There were some apparently unforeseen incidents. During one rite a 'supernumerary' who had been dancing in an abstracted manner started to glare at the whipper, moved into the centre and was whipped three or four times. He made no sound, but just clenched his teeth and rolled his eyes, continuing to do this long after the whipping, when everybody's attention had been directed elsewhere. Later he rejoined the procession.

On another occasion, Raman was being whipped after an obeisance by the wife of an India-born Southerner, whose house lay in a field some thirty yards from the spot. As Lakshman finished there were yells from the house, then sounds of falling, then silence followed by bellowing. Three or four of the onlookers ran over, and found the Southerner lying on the floor of his front room. They raised him and he stood, shaking and yelling 'Govinda' (a name of Krishna). Suddenly he went out of the door and walked, staring unseeingly, down to the road where he fell before the goddess Mariamma (Subramaniam). The Suva priest made the four principal actors walk over his body. He got up, snorted, looked at Subramaniam, cried a little, and walked a little distance away and stood silent. Nobody took any further notice of him. Later he followed the procession without talking to anyone; when Raman was whipped his teeth clenched, but he was not possessed a second time. This possession 'at a distance' took the others by surprise; the man was known by everyone to be strict in his devotions, but nobody had thought the sight of the procession would affect him so strongly. He was said to have been possessed by his own tutelary spirit, not the deities of the procession, and this may explain this call on Krishna in what was a Sivaite procession.

Occasionally, too, Subramaniam, who walked in front of the two deities, would catch sight of the pots, and would go into a deeper trance. From being 'drowsy' and limp, his back would arch in an apparent rigor, his legs stiff and apart, his head to one side with eyes rolled upwards. He would stay like this until the Suva priest slapped his chest several times and Raman squeezed four limes (symbols connected with the goddess) over him, throwing the remains to the four points of the compass. It was said that Subramaniam, as the goddess, was especially excited by the sight of the 'female' pot—and, indeed, it was noticeable that this deeper trance was twice occasioned when he saw Sundaram, bearing the female deity, whipped.

The exit from Delanikoro was marked by a small rite, culminating in the Suva priest chopping a banana in half.[1] Then the procession returned to the temple, in which Raman and Sundaram placed their pots on the shrines amidst the loudest singing and drumming of the day, and Subramaniam was divested of his women's clothes, and whipped for the only time that day.[2] Afterwards, all the principals in the procession ate ravenously of the meal given by a local devotee, for they had fasted during the festival. They appeared exhausted by their physical ordeal of the past twenty-four hours, but neither Raman nor Sundaram showed any marks from the literally hundreds of lashes they had received in the procession. The skin of Sundaram's forearms was slightly scaly, as it might have been had someone scratched it—but there was no question of a weal.

Flagellation was basic to this festival, and was undertaken in a serious and not at all sensational way. It proved, on the one hand, the genuineness of the deities, and on the other the strength and sincerity of the worshippers' faith. Northerners had no such tests in their rites. One Northern resident of Delanikoro said this rather regretfully for, he maintained, there was no way of knowing at the time whether Northern priests and rites were completely adequate. Occasionally, it was said, Northerners had entered into the Mariamma procession; but their bodies did not withstand the whipping, and were immediately bloodstained. Although in theory anybody having

[1] It was unfortunately impossible to see whether a similar rite attended the entry into Delanikoro territory.

[2] Next day a small procession took the pots to a nearby stream and 'cooled' them by emptying their contents in the water. The pots were returned to the temple.

sufficient faith could go through the ordeal, the strength of this faith was apparently culturally induced, for nobody could well believe after seeing the procession that the whipping was artificial and that outsiders could be whipped in a different manner.

The flagellation described was not the only kind of ordeal practised by Southerners in Fiji. A more famous rite was based on fire-walking, and was held in the Mariamma temple near Suva each August.[1] It followed roughly the same pattern as for the Delanikoro worship—an all-night session of dancing, and purification in the morning before the fire-walking in the late afternoon. The men who participated did so in expiation of a vow. They became entranced before reaching the temple, skewers being stuck through their cheeks, tongues, and necks, and they then walked in procession behind a man bearing a pot similar to the one described for Delanikoro, and also representing the goddess. In front of the temple a pit about twenty feet long was prepared with live coals, and the leader and his followers walked on this and went through to the temple, where the pot was deposited and the skewers withdrawn.

Delanikoro Southerners played their part in this fire-walking rite. Some helped with the arrangements, and sold the admission tickets which raised money for temple funds. Some also took part in the procession. This is what Sundaram said about it: 'Three years ago my eyes became very bloodshot, and I could not see properly in the sunlight. I tried some medicines, but they did no good, and I promised I would go through the fire three times if the goddess would cure me. Soon afterwards, my eyes got better, and have remained all right. So a week before the rite I stopped eating fish and meat, and slept apart from my wife. In this way I became clean. Two days before, I went to Suva and met the priest of the temple. He asked me if I wanted to go through the fire, and I said I had made a vow to do so. He replied that it would be all right, that it would not hurt me, and that he would lead me through it.

'There were rites and dancing on the evening before, and the next day we bathed. They put skewers through my tongue. It hurt a bit, and those who were thinking bad thoughts and were not straight in their purpose bled. As we walked to the temple, I began to lose the great fear I had had of the fire-walking. Everything became blurred in front of my eyes, like a field shimmering in the hot sunshine. But I could see and hear things; only my body was heavy, as if a weight were on my shoulders. I did not feel any heat when I went through the pit. This year's rite is the last of the three, and I have no fear when I think of it.' It is interesting to note that Sundaram was at

[1] There had also been fire-walking rites at Nandi and Lambasa but these had not been as regular, or of such long-standing, as the Suva festival.

first afraid of his ordeal and was reassured by the priest. The fire-walking needs a leader, in fact, and instances had occurred in other places in Fiji where the procession had been started, but had come to a dead stop in front of the pit because there was no adequate leader to take the devotees through.

It should be noted that Delanikoro Southerners took part in this festival, which was outside their own boundaries, and this leads to a review of the other times at which major religious occasions linked settlements to town.

The most important of these was the Ramlila, which took place in October. The festival commemorated the triumph of Rama and his ally Hanuman over the demon king Ravan—as in the Holi, it was the triumph of good over evil. To this end the story of Rama in the epic poem *Ramayana* was read for nine consecutive days, and on the tenth the enactment of the final battle and the defeat of Ravan took place, with school children dressed up as Rama and Hanuman and as the monkeys in Hanuman's army (see Plate XII*a*). Each market town had its Ramlila, and though there is a definite date on which the festival should end, in practice each town had its own on a different week-end (thus, in 1951 the Rakiraki Ramlila was on October 29, and the Mba Ramlila on October 22). This was to enable traders and merry-go-round operators, etc. to work in each centre, for the Ramlila was a country fair as well as a religious festival, and there were several dozen stalls of sweetmeat and fancy goods sellers (see Plate XII*b*), as well as of amusements and sideshows. Almost everyone in the settlements of the town's hinterland came to the last day, and spent the time meeting friends, taking children round the stalls, and only incidentally watching the enactment of the battle and the burning of the enormous straw-filled guy of Ravan. Indeed, at a Ramlila in Mba, the burning took place at sunset, and most people had either gone or were too busy preparing to leave to watch the proceedings. The festivals were organized by committees of townspeople—the managers of the temple if the fair were held on temple ground —which financed them, from the leases paid by stall-keepers.

In May, Lambasa staged the Vishnulila. This included the procession around the town of deities from the Southern temple there, mounted in traditional style on a temple car. Many of the householders living on the route of the procession offered worship, and people from both town and countryside lay under the car as it proceeded, in expiation of vows made for cures, for children and other personal matters. There was a small fair in the temple grounds, to which a number of country people came. A smaller Vishnulila also occurred in October, at the same date as the more important Ramlila.

Such fairs could be held in settlements, too, though this was

94

apparently rare.[1] Thus the people of Namboulima had an annual Ganeshlila in August, which drew people from settlements in the interior of Vanua Levu. The festival was held in a grove donated by the people of Namb́oulima to an ascetic, and a committee of all cultural groups arranged for the rites to the elephant-god Ganesh, the location of stalls, and the supplies of firewood, etc.[2] Several storekeepers came out from the town and provided a fair. In recent years, however, the crowds had declined greatly, as had outside participation, and such rural fairs may go out of existence, as most settlements are connected to the town by road, and their inhabitants are more inclined to participate in the town fairs alone.

The religious dependence of settlement on town varied from place to place, and with individual requirements. It was strong for rites which were not performed and for purposes which could not be adequately fulfilled in the settlement. An example would be the case of Sundaram, who made a vow to take part in the Suva fire-walking, though he could also have perhaps vowed a less spectacular worship and sacrifice to the goddess at his homestead. The dependence of the people of one settlement on ritual facilities provided in another appeared to occur much less often; indeed, the link between the Delanikoro Southerners and the nearby Southern temple is the only example provided by this fieldwork.

THE MUSLIM RELIGIOUS CALENDAR

Muslims, of course, had their own religious calendar. Ramadan, the month of fasting, was observed by only a few in the settlements; as it was said, the need of hard physical labour was a valid reason for not fasting, since God would not want his children to starve for want of a harvest. The breaking of the fast at Bakr-Id was attended by a service in the mosque, followed by feasts in each homestead, or a gathering of a few nearby kin. Since neither Vunioki nor Delanikoro had mosques, any occasion requiring a service meant a visit to town, and worship with people from other places. The Namboulima Muslims had their own mosque, and one resident was literate in Arabic, so that their religious needs were met within the settlement. There is no evidence that the Namboulima mosque, a thatched hut, acted as a centre for Muslims from nearby settlements. These people, if they made a journey outside their settlements at all, went to the main mosque in the town.

[1] The Ramlila was always held in the towns, where the crowds could be controlled.
[2] See p. 132 for the connection of the festival and the settlement shrine with factions in Namboulima.

The Muslim festival which had had most impact outside the cultural group was that of Moharram. This commemorated the martyrdom of Hasan and Husein on the battlefield of Karbala, and a bamboo-and-paper mausoleum (*taziya*) was built, taken in procession, and then 'cooled' by sinking in a river or pond. In former times, the processions of these *taziyas* were occasions comparable with the present Ramlila celebrations. But the Muslim teachers who came in the 1920's reproached the orthodox Sunni Muslims for participating in a festival belonging to the Shia sect. Public Moharram processions were stopped, and the building of *taziyas* was in 1951 a purely domestic rite. In former times, many Hindus joined in the public processions, and vows were made and *taziyas* still built by Hindus in 1951. The only *taziya* built during the Moharram of October 1951 in Vunioki was in fact the work of a Hindu household (see Plate XIII*a*). Worship was conducted by an 'unregistered' *maulvi* of the settlement, and the participants included the head of the homestead and his ladies—one of whom had made the vow to celebrate the occasion—as well as a neighbouring Muslim woman. Nine male guests were invited—all northern Hindus save for one Muslim—and they sat in a hut and drank *yanggona*, not looking at the rite. No food was offered and the total cost was not above £1. It was a far cry from the *taziya* rites of former times.

CONCLUSION

This chapter has shown that both for active participants and for those who attended, the rites were both religious acts and occasions when various social roles and relations were made manifest. The latter aspect was especially significant because there were no purely secular social gatherings. Men might, of course, stop in at a homestead lying on their way home from town or from their place of work; but any less casual gathering had a religious base. In these scattered settlements there were no regular meeting-places of the kind used each evening in a village—save, to a limited extent, the store's veranda. The more socially minded men would give frequent *kathas* for the gatherings that they provided, and some such ritual concomitant was, as far as is known, always present. There was no such thing as 'a dinner party'. For some, this situation gave religious activities a wider significance than they might otherwise have had; for many others, it tended to bring out the secular elements in the gatherings. Weddings, for example, were often the excuse for a good party by men who liked to meet each other, and who might not even bother to see the rites performed; and larger occasions tended to turn into country fairs almost purely secular in character.

The account has tried to indicate that, in general, people co-operated only when it was personally convenient or advantageous to do so. There was no corporate rite of the descent group, at which attendance was enforced by members; and the congregations at weddings, funerals and life cycle rites comprised both kin and neighbours, and did not define any precise group, whose very membership depended in part on attendance. Participation in the major festivals was optional, too, and the entire population did not gather as one religious unit, though the settlement was sometimes represented to the outside by one section of its population—for instance, by the Holi song team.

The structural aspect of religious activities is therefore best seen in terms of individual obligations rather than of the maintenance of groups. One aspect has only been touched upon; it is that men vied for prestige and leadership through religious contexts. The size and composition of the wedding feast or groom's party could show the extent of a man's following; to organize the Holi procession might be in part a symbol of a leader's authority in other matters. Associations inaugurated to hold weekly readings of the sacred *Ramayana* could become weapons in the hands of factions. This aspect of the religious sphere is best considered in an account of the political organization of the settlements.

V

CONTEXTS OF POLITICAL ACTIVITY

Politics are generally considered to concern those who make and maintain the laws of the country, and who take care of its external relations and defence. As such, they refer to formal legislative bodies and the leaders and parties which make them up, as well as to the various arms of civil and military force.

Looked at from this viewpoint, it is doubtful whether the activities to be described could be characterized as political. Yet, within the microcosm of the settlement, they filled many of the same functions as more conventional political factors. The School Committee and the cane harvesting Gang elected officers to run these important concerns, and had constitutions to which all members had to adhere; the informal councils called to decide disputes exerted pressure towards conformity to norms of behaviour, if not an adherence to a formal legal code. The rivalry between settlement leaders for power in these fields was analogous to similar competition at a higher level. In this sense, what follows concerns politics in the settlements.

An account must first be given of the composition and operation of the various political associations in the settlements, as well as of the support given to politicians outside the settlement. Not only will this show the degree to which settlements were separate political entities, and the degree to which they were linked to regional and Fiji-wide political organizations; it will also provide a picture of the various contexts in which political rivalries could exist, and the associational bases on which leaders could develop their influence.

THE CANE HARVESTING GANG: ITS OPERATION

Sugar cane was harvested by the co-operative efforts of growers, efforts which had social as well as economic implications. Their basis was the Growers' Harvesting Agreement, sponsored by the CSR Company to ensure an efficient harvest and an even flow of cane to their mills. The Agreement was signed each year by all the farmers who had normally already signed the Memorandum of Purchase, defining the price and condition of the cane to be harvested.[1]

The paragraphs of the Agreement set out the important aspects of the Gang's work. The first stipulated that each signatory provide one member of the Gang for each six acres (or an equivalent weight of cane to be cut). The second bound each member of the Gang to obey the orders of the head of the Gang (the *sardar* or, in the Company's terms, the Ganger) 'selected by whatever method is agreed upon'. The *sardar* thus had the power to direct members of the Gang; the method of his selection was an important issue.[2]

The following two paragraphs set out rates of pay for the Gang members. The cutters received payment proportional to the amount and type of cane they cut. On a good field, with cane running at twenty tons per acre or more, the cutter would earn 1*s*. 3*d*. per ton. For a field with less yield the rate rose, since more work was required to cut the same weight of cane; thus, a ton cut in a field of only eight or nine tons per acre would earn the cutter 2*s*. 2*d*. Further, any man cutting more than two tons a day earned a 50 per cent bonus on the additional wage; and there was also a bonus for cutting fallen cane.

The cutters filled trucks brought by 'linemen' on a portable track from the CSR Company's permanent railway line (see Plate VI*a*). These linemen were paid a fixed daily wage, this being 4*s*. in Vunioki in 1951. There was a water-boy, paid 3*s*. 6*d*., and the *sardar* got a daily wage of 5*s*. in Vunioki and 4*s*. 10*d*. in Namboulima, the amounts being fixed by the Gangs themselves. This latter wage ran counter to the terms of the Agreement, which stipulated that payment to the *sardar* be made on the basis of the amount of cane cut by his Gang each week. It is interesting to note that *sardar's* wage did not, in comparison to that of the water-boy, reflect the responsibilities which his position carried. The rates laid down in the Agreement would have had the *sardar* of the Namboulima Gang earn about 7*s*. 6*d*. per day, instead of the 4*s*. 10*d*. he actually got. It is as if the feeling in the Gangs was an egalitarian one, which had successfully circumvented the proposition that the *sardar* should be rewarded according to the work done by other members. It indicated a feeling against people becoming 'too big' which was reflected in the opposition to leaders in other spheres of activity.[3]

The next paragraph laid down that the grower should provide bullocks to draw the trucks containing his cane to the permanent way. Usually the owners of the field did not do this and animals were

---

[1] See pp. 38–9. The Harvesting Agreement set out by Shephard (1945: 53–4) is analysed. Later Agreements have differed in details but not essentials.

[2] See p. 103.

[3] See p. 136.

hired at 5s. per pair per day (1951 rate) from several members of the Gang who were quite willing to gain this extra income.

The fifth paragraph laid down that the CSR Company would decide the order in which the fields of cane should be cut. This was an important duty of the European Field Officer in charge of the sub-sector, for there was a period towards the start of the harvest during which the cane was heaviest, when all the farmers wanted to have their cane cut.[1] Further, the rattoons of the fields which were first cut would frequently have a longer period of growth before they were cut in the following year, since the same rota was not always followed. Again, towards the end of the harvesting season the hornets nested in the cane; cutters sometimes burnt it to destroy them, and this resulted in a reduction of the price paid by the CSR Company to the growers.[2] Moreover, the best workers would have gone away by the end of the season and slower workers sent up the harvesting costs, to the detriment of the grower. Lastly, the weather started to break by the end of the harvest season (in early November) and rains could make transport difficult. For these reasons, the order of cutting would have been the source of serious quarrels, had it not been taken out of the hands of the Gang, and made the responsibility of the Field Officer.

The next two paragraphs dealt with the security given by each member of the Gang. Members allowed the CSR Company to keep back from the money due to them for the sale of their cane a proportionate bond to ensure their fulfilment of the Agreement. This was released to them when they had completed their work as Gang members.

The Agreement mentioned that all charges involved in cutting a member's cane should be subtracted from the proceeds of the sale of that cane. These charges included the cost of the cutters, linemen, *sardar*, bullocks, etc. for as long as they worked on the member's land. Such expenses varied considerably according to the accessibility of the fields and the density of the cane. The Agreement did not specifically mention, but it was expected in both Namboulima and Vunioki Gangs, that each member should put in through his labour or the hire of his animals as much as he took out through the Gang's

---

[1] Under a price agreement negotiated in June 1950 payment was made per ton of cane cut, and on the mean percentage of sugar extracted by the mill (assessed at the end of the crushing season), and on the overseas selling price, and size of total output.

[2] The juice of burnt cane took three or four times as long to crystallize as that of good cane, and the mill's operation was impeded; hence, a lower price was paid. Also, burnt cane, if left on the ground for more than about four days, was spoilt by fermentation; and there was always a risk that heavy rains would stop the harvest for this length of time.

labour on his fields. If he fell short of this contribution of labour at the end of the season, he could be assessed a penalty, at rates decided on by the Gang as a whole. This system differed somewhat from that set out in the Agreement, which assumed a full attendance from all members throughout the season. The former system provided an incentive to harvest quickly, and to retire from the Gang when the 'ingoing' and 'outgoing' accounts were equalized; the latter would have had the growers on good blocks with low harvest expenses working purely for the sake of the other members for at least part of the season. The former took perhaps a more realistic view of the situation, and laid down the convention that the work should only equal the obligations incurred. Hard workers met their obligations soonest, and it has been noted that the Gang tended to become slack at the end of the harvest, being composed of the weaker and lazier members.

Namboulima and Vunioki both had Gangs, whereas Delanikoro growers had a very different harvesting arrangement. Seventeen men growing cane on CSR land joined a Gang operated privately by the CSR Company without a *sardar*. A further eight growers with Fijian leases received wagons from the CSR Company, but did not organize themselves into a Gang. Instead, they agreed amongst themselves as to how many wagons each would have, and made arrangements to cut themselves, or through day labourers. No Gang existed in Delanikoro because the size of the blocks was small and the numbers were too few to justify an elaborate organization.

The size of the Gang and the scale of its operations varied. Vunioki had thirty-seven men in the 1951 Gang. Namboulima, on the other hand, had a large Gang of eighty-seven members. Vunioki's 410 acres of cane land produced 5,118 tons of cane in 1940 and 3,627 tons in 1950, in contrast to the approximately 8,000 tons cut in 1951 from Namboulima's 820 acres.

The extent of the CSR sub-sector within which cane farmers formed a Gang had been decided by the CSR Company partly as the result of historical circumstances (e.g. the Vunioki Gang was formed on the basis of the plantation, which the Company took over in 1939); partly as the result of topography, for cane lands lay mainly in valleys and it was easy to create a Gang in a single valley; and partly, perhaps, quite arbitrarily, as when a boundary had been drawn to bisect a valley in order to have two Gangs of reasonable size. However, the sub-sector tended to comprise the cane farmers of a single settlement—and, indeed, to go far in defining that settlement too. In Vunioki, a few farmers of a nearby settlement had been included since they were too few to form a Gang; but they were a small minority of growers. The social concomitants of the Gang's work were thus significantly centred on a single settlement. The two most important of these were, the hiring of alternates, and the election of the *sardar*. Both took place shortly before the harvest.

THE CANE HARVESTING GANG: ROLE OF THE ALTERNATE

Growers who did not want to work in the Gang could arrange for someone else to act as their alternate. The latter had no voice in Gang affairs, nor did he sign the Agreement. But he was hired for the whole harvest season, and was closely linked to the Gang through his interest in the number of days he would have to work to clear his employer's expenses. Each alternate was paid a seasonal bonus. Its size varied in different Gangs; in Vunioki it was £33 in 1950 and £36–£38 in 1951, whereas in Namboulima it was only £20 in 1951. The latter place was further from the town, where the chance of work in the mill during the harvest caused bonuses to rise considerably.[1]

The size of his bonus was out of proportion to the daily wage earned by the alternate. For his mere attendance at the field each morning an alternate in Namboulima earned about 4s.; if he cut a ton of cane his total wage would be, say, 5s. 6d.; but if he worked twice as hard and managed to cut and load two tons, he would only earn 7s. For this reason the alternate was not very much interested in his output. He cut a 'reasonable' amount, which varied, through a process of implicit agreement in each settlement, from 1·2 tons in Namboulima to 1·8 tons in Vunioki and was said by Field Officers to exceed two tons in some Gangs. It is possible that there would have been less variation had the output reflected the alternate's wage. As several outsiders stressed, the system of alternates slowed up the work of the Gang.

The growers realized this, and in Namboulima supported a proposal by the Field Officer that bonuses should be abolished, and a higher rate paid per ton of cane cut. The alternates opposed the measure, of course, and they were powerful enough to defeat it.[2] This was partly because they formed from one-third to one-quarter of the Gang in Namboulima and Vunioki; a strike of alternates would have meant that this proportion of the growers would either have had to cut cane themselves or would have had to hire alternates from a distance at perhaps greater expense. Some of the growers were old men, who could not do the work themselves, and others were men

[1] There is no record of men being hired from other settlements as alternates in Namboulima or Vunioki; a few Vunioki men had gone to the neighbouring settlement of Wailevu in the past.

[2] The incident illustrates the existence of an economic interest group, cutting across other social alignments, as is mentioned on p. 59.

who reckoned that they benefited economically by being free of harvesting chores. Thus, one farmer said he had paid £20 for an alternate, but had made £35 on beans which he had thereby been able to cultivate.

People did not choose alternates on a cultural or kinship basis, but rather made arrangements with people whom they thought were good workers, as the table shows:

TABLE 1

| | No. Alternates | |
Category	Vunioki	Namboulima
Grower and alternate; same cultural and kin group	5	5
Grower and alternate; same cultural, different kin group	2	4
Grower and alternate; different cultural group	5	7
Total	12	16

An effect of the alternates was to reduce the average age of the Gang, which comprised few men over thirty-five years. The operating Gang, in fact, represented the youth of the settlement; its formal membership was restricted to the growers, who were older. It was this formal membership which selected the *sardar* and made the Gang an instrument of settlement politics.

THE CANE HARVESTING GANG: ELECTION OF 'SARDAR'

The Gang in Vunioki was formed in 1939, when the CSR Company took over the plantation, and in the following twelve years there had been ten *sardars*. Eight of these years had seen the rule of three *sardars* from the Arya Samaj group of Northerners, and there had also been two Muslims and five Southerners.[1] A greater continuity of leadership had existed in Namboulima. The Gang there reached back twenty-five years or more, to the time when the land had first been converted into peasant farmers' blocks shortly after indenture. For a long time after this the *sardar* had been a Muslim who had also held that post in the indenture system. It was only when he had become too old that a new man, a Southerner, had taken his place. He had served for seven or eight years, and in 1950 had resigned because he wanted more time to manage his own affairs. Another Southerner had become *sardar*, and he retained his post during the 1951 season.

Most elections of the *sardar* had resulted in unanimous decisions.

[1] On three occasions there were two *sardars* during a single year.

103

In fact, in some twenty elections only one open vote was recorded. Votes were disliked because the minority party feared later discrimination by the *sardar* for having voted against him. It was also considered bad to 'form parties' and people thought that decisions should always be taken unanimously, at least on the surface. This unanimity, however, frequently masked serious disagreements. It was preceded by intense canvassing of all the Gang members, to find out where their support lay, and if possible to convert opponents. By the time of the election, the candidates could reckon the size of their support, and would withdraw if this were not enough. The only vote recorded was fourteen to eleven—close enough for each of the rivals to think he had a chance of success. Another way of evading an open election was to ask the Field Officer to select the new *sardar* and thereby act as a neutral party and a scapegoat for a losing side. This had been done in both changes in Namboulima, though people maintained that the outgoing *sardar* had advised the Field Officer over the second.

The *sardar*'s position carried prestige and authority, which in part explains the rivalry that could arise over it. *Sardars* were popularly supposed to have a hand in planning the order of cutting cane—though in fact this was the Field Officer's duty—and in this way were held to have economic power. Also, the daily administration of the Gang was a responsible and skilful job, on which the welfare of many people depended. *Sardars* had to plan the efficient use of the Gang's time and compose disputes among Gang members. They also had to learn how to manage accounts, for they noted the amount earned and the expenses incurred by cane growers, and thereby became qualified to lead in other activities, such as the School Committee.

Yet the sometimes intense rivalry which developed over the *sardar*'s post cannot be entirely explained by these attributes of the position. To some extent it must be seen as an index of wider rivalries in the settlement, and an analysis of factions shows how the post of *sardar* was used as a context of competition.[1] The power gained from control of the Gang was made more important by the lack of any positions of statutory authority in the settlements. There was no settlement headmanship to which a man might aspire, so he tried to control a faction, and through it the leadership of the Gang.

THE SCHOOL COMMITTEE

There were various ways in which schools were organized in 1951. A minority were under the control of the Government, and of mis-

[1] See p. 123 seq. and p. 134 for the significance of *sardar* elections in Vunioki and Namboulima respectively.

sions and other educational societies. By far the largest number were operated by non-denominational committees in the settlements. A committee was formed by the inhabitants, which obtained buildings and started running a school. After a few months it was inspected by members of the Education Department;[1] if it met their standards, it was officially recognized, and teachers were posted there on Government strength.

Committee schools were ultimately the responsibility of the Education Department. The curriculum was approved by the Department, and the teachers were directly under the Department and could be transferred according to the Director of Education's orders. Inspection of the school was carried out periodically by the Inspector of Schools in the district, and the Organizing Teachers under him. If these men submitted unfavourable reports, the school could have its recognition withheld.

The School Committee also had vital responsibilities, however. Though the Education Department contributed 75 per cent of the staff's salaries, the remainder was found by the Committee, which levied a £3 contribution from all parents and supporters, and extra fees from parents of children in the two top classes. The Committee was also responsible for housing the masters, and for the construction and maintenance of the school buildings. More intangible, the Committee shouldered the burden of maintaining public support of the school and of education as such, as well as that of relations with the masters. Without the work of the Committee, then, the school would have foundered just as surely as if the Department had withdrawn its staff or its financial support.

The official policy was to have no two schools within three miles of each other. Consequently, the School Committees in each of the areas studied were composed of men from several settlements. People in Delanikoro and Namboulima shared schools situated in neighbouring settlements. The Vunioki people were luckier; the school was situated in the middle of their settlement, and drew children from parts of settlements to the south, east and north. All these schools were primary establishments. They accepted children of five years and upwards during the initial two weeks of the academic year. These could pass through eight standards, the maximum permissible age being fifteen years. Hindi was the language of instruction in all these schools until the fifth standard, after which English replaced it. Provision could be made for the substitution of regional tongues (Tamil, Telugu, Urdu, Gujarati, etc.) as the initial medium of instruction. This was rare and depended on the recommendation of the

[1] The Education Department of the Fiji Government, started in 1916, was reorganized in 1929 under a Director and a Board of Education.

School Committee, the availability of qualified teachers, and the desire of a viable group of parents.[1] Thus, in a school near Vunioki composed entirely of Southern children, only 14 per cent elected to learn in the regional language, rather than in Hindi.

The Vunioki school's 1951 enrolment was about 200, of which 102 were nominally on the rolls from Vunioki settlement itself. These included 66 boys and 36 girls, compared with 24 boys and 31 girls who were of school-going age but were not registered as pupils. The rolls did not represent a steady attendance. Numbers varied both with the weather—since smaller children could not ford the streams during the rainy season—and with the agricultural cycle—for older children were called away to help with cane planting or paddy harvesting, etc. There was a good proportion of girls in the lower classes, but this steadily decreased. By the time a girl was ten years old, she was needed at home to help in the housework and to look after the smaller children; and by the time she was twelve it was considered wrong for her to be in contact with older boys outside her immediate family. Besides, education was seen mainly as an economic advantage, and there was little use in educating girls since they were lost to their parents at marriage.

Just as their children were in the majority over those of any other settlement, so Vunioki men tended to dominate the School Committee. The three top positions were Manager, Secretary and Treasurer, and the first two had always been occupied by Vunioki men until 1950, when a Manager from Wailevu was elected. The Secretary remained a resident of Vunioki, and the Treasurer came from the neighbouring settlement of Korovou. The Committee itself consisted of no fewer than twenty-seven men.[2] Not all of these came to meetings, however, and the working group consisted of seven or eight men, mostly from nearby homesteads in Vunioki.

The school to which Delanikoro children went was operated by the Methodist Mission, and there was no controlling Committee on which Delanikoro parents were represented. The school was easily reached, children going each day on foot along the road, and a few travelling by the bus which passed near the school. In all, 54 of the 90 school-age children went to school. The operation of the school played no part in Delanikoro's political activities.

The school available for Namboulima children lay about one mile

[1] An increasing number of Vunioki Muslim boys were attending a recently opened Urdu school in the town, since the Committee in Vunioki had rejected their request for Urdu teaching there.

[2] This reflects the tendency in India to nominate every person of real or potential influence to a committee, to carry on the traditional pattern in which anybody could speak to an issue, and there was no exclusive membership. (See Mayer 1960: 116 seq.)

to the north of the nearest parts of the settlement, and considerably further from other wards. Many children were therefore unable to go there, especially the younger ones. In twenty-nine homesteads scattered among all wards 36 of the 69 children were going to school —a similar proportion to that in Delanikoro but a much lower one than in Vunioki. In addition, a Namboulima resident had been running an unofficial school for the past two years, in which he taught Tamil (not offered by the Committee school) as well as other subjects to about 20 pupils. Such schools existed elsewhere, too, in 1951, but their attendance was limited, and most pupils took only a few years' instruction there. Parents who were keen to educate their children saw to it that these attended schools from which they could take examinations to qualify them for further education in the secondary schools open to Fiji Indians, or for clerical work in the towns.

The Committee which ran the Namboulima school had the CSR Company's Field Officer as Manager[1] (this was a not unique instance of enlisting the help of the Field Officer). A man from the next settlement was Secretary, and one of the Namboulima leaders, a man called Ramnath, was Treasurer. Other Namboulima parents were on the Committee, but were not in the same position of dominance as were, say, the Vunioki men on their Committee. Few of them took the trouble to attend meetings, and most were satisfied to use the school, whatever differences there might be over its management.

Disputes of varying degrees of seriousness had occurred on each of the Committees. One, for instance, was over the situation of the Vunioki school. Originally the buildings had stood in Korovou; but there had been difficulty in providing drinking water there, and the site was in any case at one end of the school area. Vunioki people had therefore started to press for the move to a central position in Vunioki itself. The Committee divided on the issue and deadlock ensued; the Vunioki members had numbers on their side, but the Korovou people had the actual possession of the buildings. A solution came in dramatic fashion. One night a number of Vunioki men went to the school and were said to have actually dismantled the main building, taken it to their site in Vunioki, and rebuilt it before the morning. The Korovou members had to accept this as a *fait accompli*, and the dispute was ended, though feeling between the two sides continued to colour other business of the Committee.

This is an example of the rivalry *between* settlements in a multi-settlement Committee. But the Committee's work was also affected

[1] The CSR Company had given the school building in 1942: it had been a Field Officer's bungalow, no longer needed when Namboulima and the neighbouring Gang were merged into one sector.

107

by factional alignments *within* settlements. Thus, the Manager of the Vunioki school was for several years one of Vunioki's main leaders, a man named Hardayal Singh; but people in a faction opposing him pressed so strongly for another Manager that finally a new man was chosen in 1949, a 'neutral' from Wailevu. Factions within the settlement proved stronger than settlement pride in possessing the Manager.

Differences might also arise over matters of administrative policy. For instance, all the fees of the Namboulima Committee had always been collected by the Headmaster, contrary to the practice in some other School Committees, where the amounts had been deducted from the cane farmers' accounts with the CSR Company and only parents without cane had paid directly to the Committee. In 1951 a dispute arose between the Treasurer and the Headmaster, the former alleging that the latter had not handed over to him all the monies that had been collected. In the Committee meeting held to consider the position, the Manager recommended that the cane farmers should pay through their CSR accounts, and the Headmaster supported him; but the Treasurer wished to have the existing arrangement continue. In the end a compromise was reached by appointing an Assistant Treasurer, who lived near the Headmaster, to whom the latter could at once pay the funds he collected from parents through the children, and so lessen his responsibility. The enmity between the Headmaster and the Treasurer illustrates another factor in disputes, namely the relations of the teaching staff to the School Committee. Teachers usually came from other settlements, if not other districts of the Colony; but at the same time, they were usually members of cultural groups existing in the settlement. They might thus identify themselves, or become identified, with their own cultural group—or indeed with any faction in the settlement. If this identification became linked to disputes between members of the Committee, the Committee's work might suffer. For the masters—and especially the Headmaster—played a key part in the general administration of the school.

There were many ways in which the master's relations with the parents could deteriorate. A common one was through children who told tales out of school to their parents. A master, for example, might cuff a recalcitrant pupil; but by the time the latter reached home, this would have been magnified into a thrashing sufficient to excite the parents' anger. Another·stemmed from the practical side of the curriculum. Pupils were made to grow vegetables, cut the grass in the school compound, etc., as training for their future careers as farmers. The parents in rural settlements on the whole disapproved of this, saying that they did not send their children to school for activities, which could be very easily taught at home. From such generalized discontent it was easy to start saying that the masters were using the pupils' 'forced labour' to cultivate their own vegetable patches, etc.

These examples show that a master could make enemies, through no fault of his own, often because he symbolized an educational process of which many farmers were suspicious. As one man said, 'Yes, I am sending my son to school; it will either make him into a good man, or into a devil'. On the other hand, the master might himself start to take sides in settlement politics as well as the disputes within the School Committee. His activities could not become too disruptive, of course, because the Education Department would simply transfer him to another settlement; but they could affect the work of the School Committee, just as they could also be a stabilizing influence, and might even keep a foundering School Committee temporarily afloat.

Disputes within the School Committee might provide ammunition for canvassing before School Committee elections. As in the Gang, there were few elections at which a vote was actually taken; most occasions resulted in unanimous decisions on lines decided beforehand. Although some people might doubt the value of education, and maintain that it turned their children into people who were no longer satisfied with being farmers, yet were often not qualified to do anything else, most Fiji Indians desired their children, especially their sons, to go to school. It was this desire which kept the School Committees functioning in spite of disputes.

THE YOUTH ASSOCIATION AND RAMAYANA SOCIETY

The two associations described above were devoted to ends which could not be satisfied in other ways. It would have been impossible (as far as is known) for a cane grower to sell his crop without joining the Gang and signing the Harvesting Agreement. Similarly, the Education Department would not recognize a school unless there were a responsible School Committee behind it.

Other associations were, on the contrary, 'voluntary' associations. Their ends—settlement of disputes, celebration of festivals—could be attained without becoming a member; for disputants could go to the Courts, and anybody could observe a religious festival at his house or any public temple. The stability of these associations was of a different order, and qualities of leadership and action had also to suit the different context.

There was no voluntary association in Vunioki in 1951. In Namboulima there had been one, called the Temple Committee; but this had become ineffective by that year. In Delanikoro alone did one exist, known as the Youth Association. It was the second of the kind in the settlement; the first had functioned for only two years in 1939–40 before dissension between its officers had broken it up. It appears to have attempted arbitration in one or two cases, and to have organized the Holi festival. The second Association had been founded in 1947. It was open to all inhabitants of the settlement, though mainly patronized by men under forty years. The India-born said that they were content to leave such bodies to those who 'know the Fiji ways' and could run them; and older Fiji-born men, some of whom were involved in the ill-fated first association, took no interest in a body which had been started by younger people.

One of the main aims of the Youth Association was to arbitrate in disputes which would otherwise have resulted in expensive litigation, or which might have led to physical violence between the participants. One case, for example, occurred when a farmer dug a canal through his land, and wished to pass it along the boundaries of his neighbour's property, to reach a larger drainage canal. The neighbour objected, tempers were inflamed, and there were one or two brawls. The canal-digger had the fate of his cane crop at stake, since cane will not grow in inadequately drained land, whereas his neighbour had planted paddy, which would have been spoilt by drainage. The Youth Association held a meeting, heard the views of both sides, and told them to accept the *status quo*. This was effective, and the quarrels ceased.

Another case in which the Association was less successful concerned a dispute over property. A widow had a Fijian lease, and a marriageable daughter. The latter had proved difficult to match, and when a suitor came who offered to marry the girl and support the widow in return for the transfer of the lease, the widow rashly accepted. No sooner had the transfer been made, and the marriage certificate signed, than the son-in-law told the widow to go away. She resisted, and appealed to the Youth Association; this body was partially successful, for it managed to get her a small house site and garden to live on. But it could not make the son-in-law give her full maintenance, as he had promised.

A third case completely resisted the Association's efforts at solution. Two India-born men had bought a piece of freehold land in partnership, but the stronger of the two withheld the other's share of the proceeds. There were constant quarrels over this, and the Association stepped in, extracting a promise from the weaker man that he would leave if he was paid a sum of money as compensation for relinquishing his share. The stronger, however, refused both the invitation to attend the meeting of arbitration, and the decision of the Association. He was said to have boasted that no bunch of youths could stop him doing what he wanted. The weaker man left the settlement, and may later have brought a case in the law courts. The Association's reply to the offender was to boycott him from the functions of its members.

These examples show the degree to which the Association was capable of arbitration. It solved a dispute in which no wrong had actually been committed—for the canal-digger had not encroached on his neighbour's land—and which was still in the formative stage. It alleviated a dispute in which the stronger party did not actually lose any of his advantages, for the house site given to the widow still belonged to the son-in-law. But it was quite unsuccessful when pitted against a matter with important economic concomitants in which one party refused to recognize the competence of the Association to consider the matter at all.

The role of the Association in religious affairs was usually less controversial. This was because people did not have to participate in its activities, as long as they were known to approve tacitly, and occasionally to subscribe to the expenses of major festivals. Men refusing to pay such subscriptions were boycotted by the Association's members, but most people would give a small cash contribution towards the purchase of goats for the Kali worship, or would entertain the Holi procession, etc. They were not required to come themselves to the Kali sacrifice, however, or to sing *chautals*: nor were they asked to attend the regular readings of the *Ramayana*, or the other occasions observed by the Ramayana Society (Rama's birthday, Sivaratri, etc.). These latter were technically not the business of the Youth Association, it is true; but in fact the men who were selected as officers of the Ramayana Society were elected at a meeting of the Youth Association, and it would be true to regard the former as the religious branch of the latter. Most social gatherings took place on religious occasions,[1] and the same was true of many Associational activities. Plans were made, and Association policies discussed, during the intervals of reading the *Ramayana* at the weekly gatherings.

The officers of the Youth Association consisted of a President, Secretary and Treasurer, as well as a small committee of three or four men. All of these were elected annually, at a general meeting to which the two dozen or so active Association members came.[2] Meetings were held in a hut, purchased by the Association for £50, and situated on a patch of leasehold land donated by an India-born Northerner. There was talk of an annual subscription of 2s. 6d., but no figures were produced to show how regularly or widely this was collected. In addition, the Association's officials took up a collection when

[1] See p. 96.
[2] There were fourteen active members of the Ramayana Society.

there was need for extra funds such as for purchase of the hut. This rarely happened, largely due to the money raised by the Association's stall at the town's Ramlila; £14 were raised in 1949, largely on games of skill or chance. The accounting for this money appears to have been a perpetual source of friction within the Association.

The election of officials followed the pattern noted for the Gang and the School Committee. Elections were, wherever possible, unanimous expressions of support for candidates already selected through pre-election canvass. Into this canvassing entered the pressures of dispute and faction, just as they did into the preliminaries for the other elections. The main difference was that the voluntary Association could either cease to exist, if differences were too irreconcilable, or could go into a state of suspense until they had been resolved. The Gang and School Committee, on the other hand, *had* to have leaders with power to make and enforce decisions, or else the work for which they had been constituted would simply not have been possible. In addition, the Gang had to have an election of the *sardar* each year.

An example of the ability to postpone elections in a voluntary Association was provided when the Youth Association ran into difficulties during 1951. The minority faction presented a strong enough challenge to make it doubtful whether there could be a clear-cut unanimous election since the parties were evenly enough matched to be unwilling to succumb without an open show of strength. Even if one party had been elected, the other might have been unwilling to support it in the Association's work. Though the leaders had talked of an election at the end of 1950 an actual date was never given, and the delay lasted throughout 1951.

The turning point probably came at a meeting one evening, convened to discuss a quite unrelated matter. Some fifteen men were present, including the rivals from each party. When the challenger had left, the talk veered to the subject of elections, and why nobody was willing to put forward his name. The rank and file members tried to convince the incumbents that they should again stand; one man even made a public declaration that he would stand for any of the offices, and challenged everyone else to do the same. He was answered by Sundar, the most important man of the party in power. In an impassioned oration, he begged to be excused for any sins of omission or commission during his period of office, and said that he, rather than the ordinary members, would run the risk of violent attack if he were elected. All those present assured him that his fears were without foundation, and that they would in any case back him up if it came to an open fight. Nothing was then decided; but Sundar must have thought that this public declaration of support was sufficient, and he allowed his name to go forward. The other party presumably recog-

112

nized that Sundar had the upper hand, and he was unanimously elected early in 1952. Threats of violence, incidentally, are not to be taken as completely irrelevant; for there had been cases where disappointed rivals had beaten up the victorious candidates.

Something must be said about the boycotts made by the Association. These had occurred because the Association considered that it represented the interests of the entire settlement. Its leaders maintained that they were acting for the good of the settlement, even when their actions might not please or benefit some of its residents. In theory, then, every loyal settlement inhabitant should bow to the Association's decisions, at least in public.[1] This is what some members had, in fact, done; for they opposed the Association's leaders in private only. Such people created rival factions, but their activities took place within a formal framework of settlement unity. Other people, on the other hand, had not accepted the claim of the Association to regulate the settlement's affairs. They simply declined to put their case before Association meetings, or disregarded the verdict when it was unfavourable to them. In such cases, the Association had instructed its members to boycott the offenders. The boycotted people were given no services by others, and the two sides did not recognize each other nor attend each other's functions. They did not speak if they met as guests at some mutual relative's or friend's house outside the settlement.

Delanikoro had had two boycotts, and it is worth noting that the principals involved were economically and socially self-contained. They did not require labour drawn from the settlement, they were not cane farmers, their children went to the Mission school, their purchases were made in the town, and for domestic rites they invited outsiders. In each case, too, they lived on the periphery of the settlement, and did not even need to go past the unfriendly homesteads.

It is at least theoretically possible that a boycotted party could eventually swell in numbers to form a majority of the settlement, and so turn the tables on the Association. No examples existed in the three settlements; in Namboulima, however, there had been a similar but less clear-cut process, consisting in the gradual attrition of an association and its leader's influence rather than its division through boycotts.[2]

This discussion has shown two features of settlement structure. First, there was no single matter in which a person or group in the

---

[1] This ran counter to egalitarian values also held. It may well have stemmed from the desire to emulate other power structures in the Colony—the official hierarchy, the Fijian system of chiefly rule—whose parallel was conspicuously absent in the Fiji Indian community.

[2] See p. 129 seq. and especially p. 134.

settlement had statutory authority over the entire population—there was, for example, no headman with minor judicial powers or with the authority to collect taxes and organize limited public works. Hence, no decision could be made by any inhabitant or group of inhabitants which was binding on all members. Second, it was possible for people to sever all contacts with others in the settlement, and yet to carry on a normal existence except for education and cane harvesting. That is, in a settlement without a Gang or School Committee (like Delanikoro) there was no matter over which co-operation *had* to take place—and no great disadvantages need exist if there were no voluntary associational contacts. The situation was a reflection of the 'atomistic' aspect of Fiji Indian settlement and society.

THE LAW COURTS

The Youth Association was active in the general field of social control, where any issue producing a dispute was held to be a matter for the Association's arbiters. But this provided only one of the alternatives for the disputants, who could also turn to an *ad hoc* body of arbiters (*panchayat*), or to the law courts in the towns.

Sessions of Magistrates' Courts were held in the towns of the Colony, being graded according to the severity and scope of the cases they were entitled to handle. Serious cases were sent to the Supreme Court in Suva, which also heard cases sent on appeal. There were several lawyers in each town, both Fiji Indian and European, and many people in the settlements had had something to do with the courts, either as plaintiff, defendant or witness. A large proportion of twenty-three cases brought to the courts during the decade 1940-50 from Vunioki and Delanikoro about which information was gathered were in connection with assault of one kind or another. In at least eight cases the suit was brought as a direct result of fighting, sometimes with dangerous weapons like knives or guns and at other times with fists and sticks. In two further cases the subject of the case —theft, and recovery of a loan—was attended by fights in the settlements. The other cases heard included illicit distillation, possession of Indian hemp, resisting the Police when drunk, and more mundane affairs such as a petition for maintenance by a wife, a wartime sale of paddy at more than the controlled price, and recovery of debts of storekeepers and others.

In addition, the Police were called in to investigate cases of theft, rape and assault, which they dismissed for lack of evidence. There were, of course, many disputes which did not go to the courts, some being referred instead to the *panchayat*, and others never reaching the stage of adjudication. Most of the *panchayat* cases were about

114

XI (*a*). The goddess during the Mariamma procession.

(*b*). Flagellation at the Mariamma procession.

XII (a). 'Rama's army' at the Ramlila festival.

(b). A sweetmeat stall at the Ramlila fair.

civil matters, and most of the minor disputes which were never taken up concerned petty thefts and damage done by straying livestock.

Many cases taken to the courts are almost meaningless without the factional background of the disputants. Taken at their surface value, most cases of assault started with at least one party being the worse for drink, and insulting the other party. However, words uttered by a drunken person were treated as if they had been said by someone fully conscious of what he was doing. Both parties then made formal statements to the Police—for the plaintiff's report encouraged his opponent to make a counter-statement or counter-charge to defend himself. Unless the charge were a grave one, the disputants were often bound over to keep the peace for a determined period. Three of the main protagonists of Vunioki factions were bound over during 1951. Others, in both Vunioki and Delanikoro, had been fined for their part in fights.

Below this surface evidence, however, these fights centred around settlement factions comprising either men of different kin groups and cultural groups or the opposed sides within kin groups which had often been formed during quarrels connected with the partition of a joint household. These two kinds of enmity could supplement each other, of course.

An experienced European lawyer in one town maintained that Fiji Indians were less inclined to go to court than they had been, realizing the heavy costs of litigation; but he asserted that the number of cases over what he termed 'useless' assaults still formed the largest category of major cases.[1] He realized that the assault was often not itself the reason for the case and held that, as far as the court was concerned, most of these cases were time-consuming and unlikely to produce the true story of what had happened. He said that he and other lawyers had put up their fees for such briefs, hoping, unsuccessfully, to dissuade people.

The courts provided one way of defeating one's enemy, by having him bound over. The possibility of an unfavourable decision might be weighed against other advantages, too. A man who severely injured an opponent might himself be fined or bound over, for example, if he could not show he was the innocent party. He would have lost the case and allowed his opponent to triumph in the court, but this would be measured against the latter's broken leg or injured arm. Conversely, the suffering of injuries might be thought worth a victory in the court.

It is not suggested that people invariably calculated about the courts in this conscious way. Cases often started because of hasty

[1] Figures for 1951 confirm that assaults were only exceeded by such items as traffic offences (H.M.S.O. 1953: 47).

recourse to the Police which might later be regretted. On Christmas Day of 1950, for instance, a fight occurred between men of a Vunioki Muslim extended family. One of the principals was said to have drawn a knife and cut his opponent in the leg. The latter immediately made a report to the Police, who instituted a case. When the hearings started, a few months later, everyone was rather ashamed, and wished that the matter could have been settled out of court. They admitted that it was especially bad for agnates to quarrel, for such kinsmen should present a united front to the outside world. Both sides, in fact, were willing to settle among themselves and were far from wishing to 'use' the judicial process; but the knife wound had made the offence a cognizable one, and a trial was mandatory.

The courts, then, besides being places to decide cases for maintenance, non-payment of debt, etc., were also places in which the standing of faction leaders was affected. They did not, of course, provide contexts for the exercise of leadership by men of the settlement. This was seen rather in the informal councils of arbitration, the *panchayats*.

THE *PANCHAYAT*

The *panchayat* was said in theory to be formed by the selection of two men by each disputant, who then chose a fifth man as their 'head'. These heard any evidence each side presented, asked what questions they wished of the disputants and witnesses, deliberated, and handed down a unanimous decision. This was bound to be accepted, since it had been one of the conditions on which the *panchayat* had been formed—and the decision was in any case supported by the nominees of each disputant. The *panchayat* met at the house of the plaintiff, who was responsible for its entertainment.

Actual *panchayats* might differ in several details from this ideal picture. In the first place, there were not always five men. Small disputes between kin might be judged by one or two respected men of the cultural group, and issues of interest to all in the settlement might have more than five men as arbiters. Again, the method of choice was not always strictly followed; frequently both disputants would agree on the choice of the councillors. Further, though the decision was presented as a unanimous one, it might be clearly recognized that the councillors were themselves split over the right line to be taken. In the same way as everyone knew that there were parties backing different candidates to be *sardar* of the Gang, or Manager of the School Committee, although the elections were uncontested, so the *panchayat's* decision might only mask a divergence of opinion. The significant thing is that it was thought necessary to do so.

A *panchayat* was required to do its utmost to reach a decision, and

116

was almost always successful in this. People did not like their disputes to drag on after an attempt to arbitrate, as the following example shows. It concerned two Muslim brothers in Vunioki, who had a quarrel and decided to call in as arbitrator the younger brother's wife's brother. He heard both sides, but said he could not decide who was in the right. The elder brother was angry at this, and split his household from that of the younger brother, though they continued to live in the same homestead. For seven months the brothers were at loggerheads. The elder was especially angry with the arbitrator; whenever the latter came to talk and gamble at his sister's husband's house, the elder brother imagined that they 'were making a gang' to torment him. Finally, the matter was again brought up at a sacred reading given by another member of the cultural group. The arbitrator was headmaster of the Urdu school in the town. His judgment blamed both the elder brother for having falsely thought the others were ganging up on him, and the arbitrator for not having given a decision. Both men were pleased that the other had been blamed, they shook hands, and the brothers were thenceforth on speaking terms, though they did not reunite their households.

This example shows other features of the *panchayat*. For instance, it was unnecessary to have a special meeting to hear a case—this could be combined with socio-religious gatherings, as long as both parties were present. Secondly, the arbitrator should be, if not educated, then authoritative and experienced enough to make a satisfactory judgment. Lastly, both parties accepted the decision of the *panchayat*, as they were ideally required to do.[1] In fact, no case of open defiance of a *panchayat's* decision was found. It was in any case only worth making such a gesture when a fine was imposed; otherwise, decisions could be eventually circumvented, and rivalries which might have been ostensibly ended through a *panchayat's* decision could always continue in other contexts.

Fourteen *panchayats* were noted in the three settlements during the five or six years before 1951—fewest in Delanikoro where the Youth Association had tried to take over the *panchayat's* duties, and most in Vunioki. Only two of these *panchayats* concerned fights of the kind described in court cases, and only one of these, in turn, was connected with factions—the other was an isolated quarrel between men in a cane field. The rest centred around a variety of civil cases. Four of them were attempts to collect damages of various sorts. One concerned the crop eaten by straying horses; another was about an alleged breach of contract by a man who was said to have agreed to sell a horse to one man and then sold it to another; a third centred

---

[1] The *panchayat* does not appear to have considered the original dispute, and this would make acceptance easier.

117

around injuries received by bulls leased to the Gang, through the alleged negligence of a lineman who was driving them when they were hurt by a cane truck. Three cases arose out of the different habits of cultural groups in the settlement. Thus, some Muslims in Namboulima killed a cow on their land, but too near a Hindu homestead for the liking of its inhabitants; similarly, pigs were sacrificed near Muslim dwellings. There were also cases on a number of other topics. One concerned the exact demarcation of a boundary between the fields of brothers who had recently divided their joint leasehold. This constituted one of the three *panchayats* held about quarrels within a single kin group.

The sentences passed by the *panchayats* consisted of fines, to be paid to the winner as damages, or simply the condemnation of the guilty party and the order to apologize. The loser accepted the sentence, as we have seen, but the defeat often rankled and led to attempts to avenge himself which might lead to the recruitment of factions. A dissatisfied loser could, of course, always take the case to the courts. None of the cases cited were appealed in this way; but rural leaders said that the judge took into account the sentence of the *panchayat*.

On one occasion a sentence was more severe than those above, since it was an invitation for the rest of the settlement to ostracize the offender completely. It occurred in a settlement near Vunioki, and concerned a man judged to have committed incest with his daughter. After consideration, the *panchayat* decided that the girl should be married off as quickly as possible, and that the settlement should ostracize the father. This was at first successful. Then, little by little, people started to visit his homestead when he invited them, and after a few years only the stricter people would not do so. The attempt to resolve the boycott issue in Namboulima by means of *panchayats* was also ultimately unsuccessful.[1]

People recognized, in fact, that *panchayat* decisions had no force unless both accusers and offenders accepted them. One reason for this was that *panchayats* were only *ad hoc* bodies; having passed their decisions, they had no officers with power to enforce them. They therefore depended entirely on the force of public opinion. This contrasted with the boycotts demanded by the Youth Association, which, as a permanent body, could try to maintain its decisions. This is the reason why the decisions to boycott produced complete social ruptures within Delanikoro, whereas similar decisions by *panchayats* in other settlements produced only temporary splits at the most. The force of public opinion should not be minimized, however; the very fact that a man had been condemned by influential men of the settle-

[1] See pp. 131–2.

118

ment, and had been shown to have committed a heinous act, resulted in public disapproval—and this was the major force making it usual for the culprit to pay the fine or present the apology demanded by the *panchayat*. It was only later that the misdemeanour was forgotten, or minimized, and normal relations resumed with those judged by the *panchayat*. *Panchayat* decisions, then, were maintained as far as they were partly by the moral norms of the community, and partly by the prestige of the councillors giving judgment.

How were these councillors recruited? Of the seventeen men who had served on the *panchayats* recorded in Vunioki, eight were residents of the settlement, five were of neighbouring settlements, and four came from the town. In fact, only eight men had served on more than one *panchayat*; five of these were Vunioki men, two being India-born, and three came from two neighbouring settlements. The most popular men were the *sardar* of Wailevu settlement (the School Committee Manager), and Hardayal Singh of Vunioki, who was frequently *sardar* there. Next to them came Govind, the richest man in the settlement to the north of Vunioki, and a major money-lender. *Panchayats* were essentially rural councils, in distinction to the urban background of the courts. Their recruitment of men from outside a settlement was mainly of those who already had some sort of economic or associational interests there. Their leaders were experienced in positions of authority (often being *sardars*) and of a commanding temperament, for other wealthy men were never chosen, nor were several more highly educated men in nearby settlements. A man needed a 'hot' disposition to be successful in a *panchayat*. He had to have the courage of his convictions, and the authority and oratory to persuade his fellow councillors into taking a unanimous decision.[1]

It was said that *panchayats* had been more frequent and more influential in former times. Stories were told of men who had completely dominated entire settlements, to whom every dispute had been brought, and from whose decisions there had been only rare appeals to the courts. Such men had sometimes been supported by Government officials and encouraged to fill the role of leader in their settlements.[2]

One eminent Fiji Indian maintained that a system of '*panchayat* rule' might have been inaugurated in settlements up to about 1925,

---

[1] See p. 137 for a general discussion of leadership in the settlements.

[2] A stronger reason than the existence of capable arbitrators may have been a general fear of the courts, induced by the large number of charges, and high proportion of convictions, under the indentured labour laws. In 1901, for example, no fewer than 2,468 charges were brought (for failure to fulfil tasks, absence, etc.), and out of these 2,202 convictions resulted, with fines or gaol terms for all but 63 of these. (Indian Immigration Report for 1901—Fiji Legislative Council Paper 20 of 1902—quoted in Gillion 1958.)

had this been officially planned as a system of nominated *panchayat* leaders with statutory powers of local government. There seem to have been contradictory attitudes held by Fiji Indians towards authority up to that time. On the one hand, people thought that nobody had the right to a pre-eminent status; on the other, the tradition of hereditary status had not been entirely lost. In the event, the former won the day. In 1951, said this informant, such traditional forms of social control as the *panchayat* were being further weakened by new influences coming from the towns, such as the idea of an elective system of government, and the notion that formal education was superior to personal intelligence as a qualification for positions of authority. It is indeed true that the three settlements produced fewer recent cases in the *panchayats* than in the law courts, and that the subject matter of the former was less serious to most people than that of the latter. Any future structure of elected local government bodies will presumably accentuate this trend.

IMPACT OF WIDER POLITICAL ASSOCIATIONS

What was the influence of outside associations on the politics of the settlement? 1951 saw no functioning local branches of cane growers' unions in the settlements studied. In each settlement there were one or two men who were recognized as the main supporters of a particular union. They convened no meetings of their followers *as union members*, however, nor did they take decisions as union supporters. Their actions were seen rather to be those of faction leaders within the settlement, one of whose bases of power was the adherence to a union.[1] Similarly, a cultural group in a settlement might support a union *en bloc*; for example, the Southerners often backed the Maha Sangh, the Arya Samajis the Kisan Sangh. But this was seen as one of several social concomitants of the cultural group and not as a separate factor; that is, the links formed by membership of the union reinforced the ties members had towards each other as people of a cultural group *within* a settlement, rather than the ties to other members of the same union *outside* the settlement.

There were no political parties in Fiji in 1951. Leaders might ally themselves in coalitions to fight elections, and several of these alliances had lasted for years. But there was no formal organization, perhaps because, with only three Fiji Indian seats, the party member in the Legislative Council would have often been a single individual. Some of the socio-religious associations[2] came close to acting as party organizations. Thus, the Central Organization in the Suva area supported Pandit Vishnu Deo, the senior Indian politician, and its

---

[1] See p. 140, for example.　　　　　　[2] See p. 10.

branches performed a supporting role similar to those of a political party, though centring on a single leader. Again, though politicians might differ on specific issues, their differences were not crystallized in political programmes of a formal kind.

The loyalty to political leaders was either based on the issues of the moment or on a personal support which was maintained irrespective of the political situation, and which might be based on common religious or cultural beliefs, on favours done by the leader to the settlement, or on the fact that an opposing faction in the settlement supported the rival leader. Both kinds of loyalty existed in the three settlements. On the one hand, the men of Delanikoro had always supported a particular leader, voting for him in the Legislative Council elections, and siding with the policies of the unions with which he was linked. One of the reasons for a boycott by the Youth Association was that the culprit had supported the opposing candidate in a Legislative Council election.

On the other hand, Vunioki offered an example of shifting allegiances, based on the issues of the moment. A majority of voters supported the successful candidate in the 1950 Legislative Council election, at least ostensibly on the issue that he was a Fiji-born man opposed to an India-born candidate. A few months later, Vunioki farmers disregarded the policy of the cane growers' union which their candidate advised them to support. This union did not want farmers to sign the Memorandum of Purchase of Cane, which was then up for renewal, maintaining that it gave the grower too small a share. Union enthusiasts tried to convince the Vunioki growers that it was against their interests to sign, and that they should even refuse to plant their cane unless they had a suitable contract. But the campaign was a complete failure in the settlement, and a man who was said to be the main supporter of this union and who had voted for the candidate allied with it, was among the first to sign the new contract.

VI

POLITICAL PATTERNS IN THE SETTLEMENT

THE associations just described have been characterized as contexts in which men aspired to leadership in the settlement. It is now time to focus on these men, and to show the ways in which they extended their influence through their membership of the cane-harvesting Gang, etc., as well as through their formally 'non-political' affiliations to a kin and cultural group. A few leaders were at the centre of each settlement's political configuration, and their rivalries and alliances created groups of adherents. People supported them for various reasons, and remained with them for different lengths of time. The groups they formed will be called factions, and what follows deals mainly with the factions in each settlement. Over what issues were factions formed and maintained, what proportion of the settlement's population was involved, and what were the social and personal characteristics of the leaders? Answers to these questions will indicate the structural significance of factions, and the importance of political activity as a way of gaining prestige.

FACTIONS IN VUNIOKI

Factions in Vunioki can be approached through divisions within the Southern cultural group. The extended kin group of eleven Southern households, territorially discrete from the rest of the settlement, and comprising all but two of the cultural group's homesteads, had by 1951 become divided into the two factions shown in the diagram below.

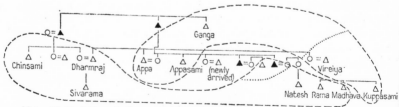

Note: Dotted lines indicate people who kept aloof but whose feelings were with the faction in which they are included.

122

The series of disputes from which these Southern factions stemmed started between the brothers Dharmraj and Appa, and concerned the management of the Fijian lease held jointly by them. After several years of discord over the division of the crop and the contributions of labour, the lease was divided. In this, Appa's part was taken by Appasami and Ganga, close relatives of Appa's wife; Dharmraj was supported by his wife's brother Chinsami. Personal dislikes were also involved, for both Chinsami and Appasami were domineering men.

The quarrels during 1950 centred mainly on one large field at the river side, through whose centre a boundary was marked with stones, which each side accused the other of moving when ploughing. During the year, a *panchayat* was held over this boundary dispute. The three *panchayat* members came from nearby Wailevu and were distant kin of both parties. They decided that Dharmraj's family were guilty of encroachment and ordered them to move back the boundary markers. This was a defeat for Chinsami, who tried to avenge himself by arranging a Police raid on an illegal liquor still of Ganga's. The case was dismissed by the magistrate for want of evidence, and Chinsami was again defeated.

The conflict within the Southern cultural group existed concurrently in a context of settlement-wide importance—the control of the Gang. This had occurred through the intervention in Southern factions of an outsider called Hardayal Singh. He was an Arya Samaj Northerner, a substantial cane farmer and a man of *sardar's* calibre since he was sufficiently educated and with experience of Gang work. Soon after his arrival in Vunioki in 1940, Hardayal Singh had become linked to Appasami, borrowing his money and calling him brother. By 1950, Hardayal and Appasami were ranged together against Chinsami and his faction. The Southern conflict was thus expressed in the elections of the Gang, for the election of Hardayal Singh as *sardar* was regarded by Chinsami as a defeat for his faction, both in the Gang and in the context of the Southern group's rivalry.

The history of recent Gang elections had therefore been one of attempts by Chinsami to have his candidates elected, and of resistance by Hardayal Singh and Appasami. Chinsami had been mainly unsuccessful in recent years, because his candidates when elected proved less capable than Hardayal Singh. The work of the Gang, and hence the prosperity of its members, suffered under their administration, and this was more important to most growers than any factional consideration. Chinsami was further handicapped because he was not a cane farmer, and so could not attend the Gang election meeting, having instead to work through allies. Nevertheless, in 1949 he had managed to have Dharmraj elected. He proved incapable, as was the head lineman, Madhava, another in Chinsami's faction, and it was clear that they could not win another election. Chinsami therefore threw his support behind a compromise candidate—Mokub Singh, Hardayal Singh's brother's son. But Hardayal Singh refused this appearance of bowing to Chinsami's will. He ordered Mokub Singh to defer to him as a senior kinsman, and was himself elected, appointing as head lineman one of his Muslim supporters.

Neither side had enough votes to win automatically (Hardayal Singh having thirteen, and Chinsami five sure votes in 1951) and the balance was held by men who had no consistent voting pattern. Thus, the men of the Muslim cultural group supported Chinsami's candidate in 1949, but voted for Hardayal Singh next year. Their leader Abdul himself had ideas of being *sardar*, and tried to keep his kinsmen's votes uncommitted until the last moment, in case he might be chosen as a compromise candidate. Other farmers formed no *bloc*, but voted as their own interests dictated, being influenced by expectations of favour from the candidate they supported or by the criterion of fitness for the job.

The days of canvassing before the Gang elections therefore saw Chinsami and Hardayal Singh trying to influence this floating vote, partly by accusations of partiality on the part of the rival candidate in the order of cutting cane, etc., and partly veiled threats against the property of the voter. For it is easy to fire a man's cane when the Gang is working at the other end of the sub-sector, and cannot therefore salvage it before it goes bad. The fact that Chinsami was less often successful meant both that technical proficiency was a main consideration for the *sardar*, and that the favours which Chinsami could dispense, were his candidate elected, were not enough to counterbalance this need for efficiency and that fears of damage were discounted. This suggests that political stakes were low, favours were few and minor, and that there could thus be a large floating vote, fairly unconcerned with the results of the election as long as the Gang continued to function satisfactorily.

It has already been said that to win the Gang election mattered more for personal and factional prestige than for the tangible benefits that resulted. To win this election became a point of factional competition far more than to become the Manager of the School Committee. This was perhaps because the Committee was less in the public eye, having fewer economic connotations than the Gang. It is also possible that the presence of men of other settlements on the School Committee softened the rivalries between Vunioki men, by interposing a greater number of neutrals who had little interest in these manœuvrings. Finally, it must be admitted that, as in the Gang, the faction led by Chinsami did not have leaders of the calibre required to operate the School Committee.

Nevertheless, Hardayal Singh, who had been Manager of the school for some years before 1951, did not resign his post until he was forced to do so by lack of public confidence. This resulted partly from a deterioration of conditions within the school and its staff, the responsibility for which could be laid at his door, partly because of lobbying against him by Chinsami and the Manager whom he had displaced. The new Manager was Narain, the *sardar* of Wailevu and, as an outsider, an uncontroversial figure in Vunioki. But had Chinsami's faction possessed a capable candidate, the School Committee might have provided as fertile a field for disputes within the settlement as it did in other places.

Unlike the situation in the other two settlements, allegiance to outside politicians and union leaders was not a factor in Vunioki's rivalries. For the cane farmers there acted according to what they thought were their interests of the moment, and individual assessments might or might not coincide with factional alignments.

Comparatively few people were overtly partisan in all disputes of the factions, some eight for Hardayal Singh and seven for Chinsami. Besides these, seventeen and three men were in homesteads of growers who generally, but not invariably, supported Hardayal Singh and Chinsami respectively in Gang elections. A further sixteen men could not be counted on by either side. Many others in the settlement had never been compelled to make a choice. Mixed farmers, for example, did not join the Gang and were not forced to attend School Committee elections. It is estimated that some twenty men supported one or other of the school Managers, and a further twenty-two were without overt interest in any of these factional contexts. Such men could live almost entirely insulated from the settlement's political activities.

FACTIONS IN DELANIKORO

Disputes in Delanikoro had resulted in either a boycott of the minority by the majority, or a division into factions of the kind described for Vunioki.

One boycotted group consisted of people in the single homestead of the man who refused to accept the Youth Association's arbitration in the dispute with his partner over some freehold land. He was an India-born Sikh who had his main contacts with co-religionists in the town, and openly asserted that he did not need the aid of any Fiji-born people, whom he characterized as soft and lazy.

The second boycotted group occupied a ward at the southern end of the settlement; it was made up of six homesteads of orthodox Northerners related by kinship, and two further Northern and one Muslim homestead. Two men stood out in the group: Baburam who

125

had been in the settlement for many years, and Sahdeo, whose sister had married Baburam's son and who was a more recent arrival, having settled in the last decade like most others in the ward.

The boycott had occurred some three years before the fieldwork, and was the climax of Baburam's relations with the rest of the settlement. Factional seeds were sown, as in Vunioki, in a series of disputes between Baburam and his close kin. Since the latter were at the same time neighbours and close allies of Lakhan and Sundar, the founders of the Youth Association, Baburam also incurred their hostility and the disapproval of the Association. He was in any case dissatisfied with the Association's leaders. For, since he had been one of the officers of the previous short-lived Settlement Association, he expected to be given an executive or at least an advisory place in the new Association. Instead, he was asked to join as an ordinary member. People said that he did, in fact, join and paid his initial dues of 2s. 6d., but refused to give £1 10s. as contribution towards the purchase of the Association's hall. Baburam himself maintained that he had never joined the Association, since he could look after his own affairs much better, and did not, in any case, agree with all of the Association's policies. He thought it had been wrong to boycott the Sikh, for example.

At this stage, the relations between Baburam and the rest of the settlement illustrate the point already made, that there was no social context in which all people of a settlement *had* to unite. These relations might have evolved into a permanent though informal division, but for the efforts of the Association to impose specific courses of action on the entire settlement.

Its first step was to proclaim publicly Delanikoro's allegiance to one of the candidates in the 1947 Legislative Council elections. This estranged Sahdeo, who was one of the small number in the settlement to support the other candidate, partly because his employer in the town had told him to do so under pain of dismissal. The Association then demanded a boycott of a Muslim of the next settlement, who was alleged to have made insulting remarks when drinking on the public road in Delanikoro. But Baburam, and especially his son, were friendly with this man and had no intention of breaking with him because of an order from a group of people with whom they had quarrelled, and whose authority they regarded as dubious and unnecessary. It is significant, too, that Baburam's was among the nearest of the Delanikoro homesteads to this nearby settlement, and that when the boycott was complete, Baburam occasionally got helpers from there. Ties at the periphery of the settlement could be as close with the next settlement as with the one in which the homestead was formally situated.

The final break was made when Association leaders asked new settlers in Baburam's ward of Delanikoro not to have any contact with him or with Sahdeo, but to become members of the Association and boycott them. The new settlers, even though not Baburam's kin, were unable to obey this order, for they could not afford to have unfriendly relations with their nearest neighbours. Some regretted their position; as one settler of a year's standing said, 'I am in the wrong part of the settlement. I want everyone to know that I am friendly, want to be included in invitations and to have friends. But I am not invited. Even if I were, I should have to refuse, because I cannot anger my neighbours, it is them I must live with and not the others.'

The consequent boycott of such people, with whom there had been no history of quarrels, made the division in Delanikoro take on a different complexion. It became a split of territorially defined factions to which people subscribed merely by settling in either area.

Distinct from these complete ruptures of social relations were the divisions in the majority population, expressed through factions inside the Youth Association. The deadlock which existed during the early part of 1951[1] was due to factions which were evenly enough matched to prevent a unanimous election, and hostile enough to make secession a possibility if one party's leaders were re-elected. The supporters of the reigning party, led by the Northerners Sundar and Lakhan, were more numerous, for the opposing faction, led by an India-born Southerner called Kanni and his son Gopal, contained only seven close supporters—five members of a Southern kin group and two Northerners (one being a close friend of Kanni's son-in-law, and the other a man who worked near Gopal in the town, both related to leaders in the other faction). Lakhan and Sundar, on the other hand, had ten close and eight committed supporters from their own kin groups, their Northern neighbours, and a few Southerner homesteads. But thirteen others, known to be interested in the Association, were men who might support Kanni and make the parties evenly matched. This explains the hesitation of the Northerners. The crucial meeting has been described, in which Sundar was convinced that he had sufficient supporters to make it unlikely that Kanni's faction would openly challenge him. In fact his election in 1952 was unanimous.

These factions had evolved over various issues. A major one was Kanni's charge, made as a Southerner, that the Northern leaders had been biased in favour of their own cultural group when settling disputes. Another was his allegation that the Association's accounts

[1] See p. 112.

were being mismanaged. Indeed, though the officers continued to say throughout the period of fieldwork that they would produce the documents, they were in fact never placed before the members, and this charge may have had some truth in it.

Lastly, Kanni opposed the very principle which we have seen to be the Association's most significant structural feature. That is, he criticized it for wanting to act on behalf of the entire settlement, whether people wished it to or not, and to boycott everyone who questioned its decisions. He would have made of the Association a body confining itself to the organization of festivals, entering the field of arbitration only when both parties asked it to—as did the *panchayat*.

Kanni's criticism of the Association was therefore based both on alleged misdemeanours of its officers and on the whole conception of the Association's role. It was a criticism that could not be openly contained in the Association, since it cut too deeply against both the leaders and their programme.

These leaders, of course, had counter-charges against Kanni. They maintained that neither he nor his son Gopal played their full part in such Association activities as the preparations for festivals.[1] They added that Kanni had tried to set the Association against the Muslims.[2] For if everyone were against them save Kanni, the latter could act as their friend and gain favours from them. Finally, they alleged that Kanni had inveigled them, and other Northerners, to take his part in the quarrels he had had before the start of the Association with Virasami, a fellow Southerner but no kinsman of Kanni's. These quarrels had centred around a £40 debt which Virasami refused to repay to Kanni; but, they said, Kanni had linked this to alleged maltreatment given by Virasami to his daughter-in-law, and by so doing had enlisted sympathizers for his side. Ill feeling between the two men and their respective kin had been heightened by a series of small disputes until finally the sons of Kanni and Virasami had come to blows during a football match, and their fight had spread to sympathizers and had resulted in several injuries. Sundar and Lakhan had supported Kanni over this, but they were now on Virasami's side, and maintained that they should always have been there.

These charges and counter-charges over incidents inside and outside the Association outlined a trend in which Sundar and his friends

---

[1] But both men had regular work in the town, and could not take entire days off to help in Association work, as could the leaders and others who were farmers and so masters of their time.

[2] Indeed, something like a boycott existed against some of the Muslim homesteads, though this was said by both sides to be revocable, and did not take in all Association members.

had at first supported Kanni, when he had arrived in Delanikoro some fifteen years before, but had then withdrawn when they found that he and his son Gopal were becoming serious competitors for influence in the settlement. Their competition was channelled through the Association, and this was especially irksome to Sundar and Lakhan who, as founders of that body, felt that it was their special preserve. A follower of Sundar said that when Sundar had left Delanikoro for a year recently, he and Lakhan had arranged to make Gopal the Secretary with Lakhan as President, to quieten his criticism and show him how difficult it was to administer the Association properly.[1] But now they felt that Gopal was acting with undue authority, without acknowledging his debt to Lakhan and Sundar for being an officer of the Association at all.

'I do not like the tone in which Gopal reads the *Ramayana*,' said this informant, 'for Sundar taught him all he knows about reading in public, and also started the *Ramayana* Society.' The protégé, if ever he had been one, now refused to play his subordinate part; and the possibility that he might obtain power without Sundar's sponsorship doubtless lay behind the postponement of the election.[2]

The numerical position of factions in Delanikoro was similar to that in Vunioki, in that both Sundar and Kanni depended on uncommitted Association members to give them victory. At the same time, it was less easy to stay completely aloof from settlement politics than in Vunioki. Only four men could be said to show no overt interest; and twenty others, though managing to keep out of the Association's rivalry, nevertheless supported the boycotts of the Sikh and Baburam. This difference was in part the result of the Association's policy of speaking for the entire settlement, and in part a function of the greater density of population, which forced people into more repeated social contacts and made it difficult for them to keep entirely to themselves.

FACTIONS IN NAMBOULIMA

The 1951 pattern of factions in Namboulima can be said to have started from fifteen years before, when a man called Dayal had come to the settlement to open a store. Previously, political power in the settlement had been in the hands of a man named Ramnath. He had been both the chief arbitrator of disputes, the settlement's spokesman with the authorities, and the head of the only association in the

---

[1] Another reason may, of course, have been because Gopal had sufficient followers to render his elevation necessary to prevent a division.

[2] Kanni himself did not stand for election. He had been active in the first short-lived Association; but the second body was very definitely for the Fiji-born, and he would not have had any chance as an India-born person.

settlement, the Temple Committee. This had been formed when a Southerner named Venkatasami had leased a plot of land to the settlement on which to build a small temple. The Temple Committee managed the land around the temple—and had planted a pleasant grove of mango trees there—and it also conducted the annual Ganeshlila fair, an event which brought farmers and traders from outside Namboulima, and for which were enlisted the services of all men in the settlement. It did not, however, benefit from the renting out of stalls at the fair; for the land had been leased on condition that all rents from it reverted to Venkatasami.

By profession, Ramnath had been a salaried employee of Narain, the settlement's only storekeeper. At that time, stores in rural settlements flourished, and Narain's, as the only establishment in a large settlement, must have been a prosperous venture. It was perhaps this feature which encouraged Dayal to settle in Namboulima and start trading. His decision not only presented a threat to the prosperity of Narain and Ramnath, but carried implications for Ramnath's influence in the settlement; for, as Narain's right-hand man, Ramnath was concerned in the amounts of credit given to customers and this economic power undoubtedly buttressed his authority in other spheres of settlement activity. The existence of another store would give Narain's customers a bargaining weapon and thereby diminish the control held by Ramnath.

The enmity of Ramnath and Dayal was basically commercial in origin. But the competition between them brought in religion, cultural divisions and allegiance to wider political alignments in the town. From the economic sphere, the rivalry between them broadened until it was Ramnath's leadership of the settlement which was challenged.

The main attack on Dayal's emerging position occurred at the time of an ascetic's visit to Namboulima, some eight years after the storekeeper had arrived, and attempted to use his affiliation to the nonconformist Arya Samaj sect to discredit him. Perhaps it is best if the story is told from notes of an account given by a Northerner, inclined towards Ramnath, but by no means his close follower. Any supplementary or contradictory information is put in brackets.

'The ascetic,' he said, 'gave a talk at the temple, and said he could answer any question. Southerners, Muslims, all were assembled but none asked a question, and the ascetic called them goats. Then Dayal asked him how he came to Fiji and when, and what work he did here, was he a field labourer or did he come even in indenture as an ascetic. [Dayal elaborated this by saying that the ascetic implied that the spirits of Hanuman, Gandhi and others were in him; so he asked him how he came to Fiji—by boat or by himself flying through the air—

knowing that if he lied he could be checked, and if he told the truth his pretensions would be exposed.] The ascetic was angry and threatened to leave Namboulima. Ramnath saw his chance and said that Dayal should rather be evicted for his lack of faith and reverence. All the people clapped their hands in agreement, but the ascetic spoke for him and the meeting finished.

'Afterwards Dayal sent Ramnath a letter, saying that he should be told what his error had been in asking this question; if he had made none, then Ramnath's suggestion was wrong, and a *panchayat* should sit to decide this. [Ramnath apparently did not reply to this note, so Dayal himself called a *panchayat* to justify his action.] At the time set by Dayal for the *panchayat* only he and two others were present —Ramnath's sister's husband [who had been hostile to Ramnath for many years] and a Muslim labourer from near this man's homestead; all the rest of the settlement were with Ramnath.

'Ramnath now saw the success of his policy [the English word "line" was used], and tried to join this religious matter to a commercial boycott [thinking that the people would follow him in this economic matter too]. He and the Temple Committee decided to fine anyone who ate and drank at Dayal's. People still went to Dayal to trade [Dayal said he told his customers—most of whom had credit accounts with him—that he would claim full repayment from the first man to trade elsewhere] and as Dayal offered them *yanggona*, or even whisky, it was hard to refuse and some drank with him. So people were fined by the Temple Committee, the money going towards temple maintenance and the cost of offerings. [The people fined were fairly unimportant in the settlement in 1951, and it may have been that Ramnath did not wish to penalize the larger fish who may nevertheless have swum into Dayal's net: it is noteworthy that the culprits acknowledged Ramnath's power at least enough to pay their fines.] But trade still went on, and Ramnath suggested to several people that, since they were liable to eat or drink at Dayal's if they went there, would it not be better to stop trading with him altogether. He did not say this in public, and later maintained that he had been misunderstood, but it is true.

'Dayal again called a *panchayat*, with many big men from outside Namboulima. [These included the head of the Arya Samaj in the town, and the local member of the Legislative Council.] He said the fault must be decided. Ramnath replied that it was not a decision between Dayal and himself, but rather between Dayal and the people who had clapped their hands at Ramnath's suggestion to evict Dayal —in fact the whole of Namboulima. So he did not come, and the *panchayat* achieved nothing. Then the Temple Committee had a meeting, to which Dayal came. This was greatly for Ramnath, and since Dayal had only his two followers, he could not talk well and was defeated. He agreed to apologize to the ascetic, to shake hands with Ramnath, and to beg everyone's pardon. Two conditions, however, he did not carry out because he was an Arya Samaji—these were to read ceremonially the *Ramayana* in his house, and to have a *katha*. [Arya Samajis do not consider the *Ramayana* to be an infallible sacred book as do the orthodox Hindus and they have a fire rite rather than a *katha*. Ramnath well knew this, and probably made these conditions so as to maintain feeling against Dayal.] Because of this, the boycott of Dayal went on, until Dayal arranged for a meeting with the District Commissioner. Both sides stated their case, and the Commissioner said that religious affairs were their own business, but that all must be able to trade where they wished. [Dayal maintained that the Commissioner also warned Ramnath against trying to force a man to hear a *katha*, saying that there was freedom of religious belief in Fiji.] Thus Ramnath's effort failed, for when the economic boycott was decided the religious difference which depended on it also stopped. Dayal has never yet heard a *katha*, but there is no boycott now.'

Commercial rivalry was linked to cultural difference through a peripheral event—the visit to Namboulima of an ascetic from Viti Levu. It was also linked through the Ganeshlila, a central feature of settlement co-operation and, through the control which he exercised over it, a major source of Ramnath's influence. Here, Ramnath blocked Dayal's application for a stall—and a share of the considerable trade which occurred at the festival—on the grounds that Dayal, as an Arya Samaji, did not subscribe to the temple.

The end has been reached of what could be called the 'boycott period' in this rivalry. In it Ramnath had overtly emerged as the stronger party; he had forced Dayal to apologize to the settlement on the ascetic issue, and had further prevented him from trading at the Ganeshlila. Yet, in reality, Ramnath had lost his position of leadership in the settlement. For the economic boycott, though never openly declared, was a failure, because Dayal would not accept it. Here, Ramnath had no way of enforcing his will on the settlement, and had to be content with the appearance of victory and the maintenance of his formal position at the head of the Temple Committee.

The second stage, during the five years or so before 1951, could be called the 'divisive period'. In it, the balance of power between Dayal and Ramnath changed in various contexts. One was simply the continued expansion of Dayal's trade in the settlement. Here he was helped by Narain's death. The store was taken over by his widow, and a host of relatives descended upon her, all taking a hand in the management and all being maintained off profits which should have gone into the purchase of more stock. As a result, the credit facilities of the store suffered, and so did the range of stock available. More people therefore went to shop at Dayal's, either to supplement their purchases at Ramnath's or as permanent customers with credit accounts. Dayal's was still in 1951 the smaller establishment, but the gap had lessened in the last few years. Dayal said he had one hundred credit accounts of which twenty-five or so were small ones for day labourers; Ramnath maintained that he had nearly two hundred accounts of which over half were substantial—but in Narain's day there were said to have been three hundred. This meant that more people were indebted to Dayal and so were unwilling to go against him in any conflict.

Dayal's growth had not only come about through Narain's decline. He had several influential relatives in the town, one of them an important storekeeper and importer. These people gave him good credit terms and tided him over the difficult months before cane payments were made. Commercial rivalry was, however, only one aspect of the new phase of the conflict between the two men. For it had by now shifted into a considerable dependence on outside political factors.

Vanua Levu had at first been relatively untouched by the cross currents of cane union policies and electoral alliances which had become normal in Vitu Levu in the dozen or so years before 1951. Until 1950 there was only one cane union, the Maha Sangh, which also existed in Viti Levu. In the latter island the Maha Sangh was known to be the union of the Southerners, particularly in the 'dry' zone, but in Vanua Levu all cane growers joined it, and it represented the farmers of all cultural groups in Namboulima. Elections for the Legislative Council occasioned rivalries, but these do not at first seem to have been closely linked to those of Viti Levu.

In 1950, however, a second cane growers' union was formed, which supported Viti Levu's Kisan Sangh and rivalled the Maha Sangh. This affected the relations of Dayal and Ramnath in Namboulima. The former supported the new cane union and the politicians who were behind it; the latter remained with the old union, and was a strong supporter of the sitting member of the Legislative Council who was also connected with this union. The disagreement between these unions over whether to sign the new contract offered to cane growers by the CSR Company has already been mentioned in the affairs of Vunioki.[1] In Namboulima, it provided a vehicle for the rivalry of Ramnath and Dayal; for, though neither was a cane grower, their views were well known. Ramnath agreed with the Maha Sangh that the contract should be signed, and Dayal opposed him. Those who followed either were assumed to be their supporters.

[1] See p. 121.

When the growers met to sign the 1951 Harvesting Agreement and thereby constitute the Gang, sixteen growers who followed the new union had not yet signed the contract for the purchase of their cane. All of these were either Muslims, or Dayal's fellow Arya Samajis. The Field Officer said that they announced to the meeting that they did not intend to join the Gang, since it had been rumoured that their cane would not in any case be cut. They only joined the Gang after he had assured them that the CSR Company would make every effort to cut their cane as well as that of the men who had signed the contract. In the end, the campaign against signing failed, as it did in Vunioki. Ramnath thereby gained at the expense of Dayal; nevertheless, the incident showed that some members of the Gang were prepared to support the new union, and had thereby left Ramnath's orbit.

This change was made even clearer in the process of selecting the *sardar* in that same year. There were disagreements over candidates, and two groups met to decide on their nominees. One, which contained Ramnath's supporters, assembled at the temple; the other refused to go there since it was not neutral ground, and gathered at the end of the road leading into the settlement. Ramnath's group put up two Northerners and a Southerner; the other group suggested the leading Muslim and another Southerner. Apparently because they were unable to meet together and discuss a common candidate, the two groups then sent their nominees to the Field Officer, who selected the Southerner nominated by Ramnath, who had been *sardar* during the previous year.

Dayal once said, 'When I came to Namboulima, everyone listened to Ramnath, and did what he advised. There was only one committee, and Ramnath was its head. Now, what do you see? Everyone has his own committee, and none of them listens to Ramnath.' This statement typifies the process characterized as the 'divisive' stage of the rivalry. The allegiances to different unions and politicians, and conflicting opinions about the *sardar*, marked a division of the settlement in which the minority cultural groups of Arya Samajis and Muslims had gone their own way. True, Ramnath was left with most of the Northerners and Southerners, but few of these gave him such unquestioned primacy as he had had. Thus, the Southerners were now said to have a local branch of the Sangam, their socio-political association, and to settle their own affairs within it. The Arya Samajis were, of course, completely allied to Dayal; and the Muslims had inaugurated a branch of the Muslim League which was in close touch with the office in the town. Because of the steady attrition of its supporters, the Temple Committee executive was left high and dry, with Ramnath and seven or eight staunch collaborators, Dayal having two or three. Further, Ramnath had some twenty, and Dayal about ten, overt but less close supporters. The rest of the settlement was neutral; people often traded at both stores, and tried to keep themselves uncommitted.

This account has shown how factions spread outside what might be thought of as the political sides of rural life. Not only the Gang, the Youth Association, and the union, but also the kin and cultural group were contexts for competition. How were men recruited to follow leaders in such a wide variety of situations?

An important reason for supporting a man in a dispute or series of disputes was that of individual benefit, expressed in the repayment of obligations or the support given in anticipation of favours. In Delanikoro, for example, a single Northerner sided with Virasami in his early disputes with Kanni and the rest of the Northern cultural group. This man had been thrown out of the household by his father when a boy, finding a home with Virasami. This kindness he repaid with his support. The anticipation of favours was suggested in the case of the Sikh's dispute over freehold land, where it was alleged that the leaders of the Youth Association supported the plaintiff because he had promised them small portions of the land if he won.

Another common reason for joining a faction was that of ties of kin group or cultural group. People said that they supported leaders belonging to these groups in order to preserve their unity. Where factions had not created breaches within the cultural or kin group, such unity could be upheld. But where cleavages existed, support was given for the more prosaic reason that there were social obligations to be repaid to certain kin, or that these kinsmen could offer aid in case of attack if they were living nearby. Friendly kin were also useful for making small loans, co-operating in farm work and so forth.

There were, in fact, several benefits to be derived from support of a leader, and a person had to balance these against the disadvantages which would accrue from the hostility of the other faction. The number of neutrals provides an index to the importance of co-operating with kin or neighbours of whatever faction, and to the degree to which people were self-sufficient in their homesteads.

Past or future benefits did not provide the only factors behind the support of a leader. A number of men might also be influenced by the rights and wrongs of the disputes over which factions had been formed. It may be, for example, that Dayal's blunt questions to the ascetic at the Namboulima meeting shocked some of his hearers into supporting Ramnath. But the recruiting power of the subject matter of a dispute, though considerable at any particular time, was less lasting than motives of benefit. For instance, the rivalry between Ramnath and Dayal recruited followers on several issues—about the trade monopoly; about the status of Arya Samajis; about the policy followed by cane unions over the 1951 contract. But a man who had supported Ramnath over the insult to the ascetic, as a matter of principle, might have felt lukewarm in the later dispute about whether to sign the cane contract or not; if the subject matter had been the only reason for his adherence, he might well have withdrawn as an active supporter. The more constant members of each faction were therefore usually tied to the leaders for reasons of personal benefit or obligation, though they could also be fully convinced that they were right in the issues over which they were quarrelling at the time.

A general attitude towards factions was the idea that factions of all kinds were wrong, because they destroyed the unity of the settlement. People knew very well that there were parties within the Gang; but their trials of strength rarely came into the open, and the *sardar* was elected without overt opposition. In the same way, people in a *panchayat* might have different ideas about the judgment, but were in theory won over by the view of the majority or of the most commanding member, and the verdict was announced without dissent. It was often said that other affairs of the settlement should also run like this. The faction broke this real or overt unity and this was both morally and materially bad; it bred quarrels and distrust, and it could lead to fights, the burning of opponents' cane and other material losses.

But the idea of the unity of the cultural group or the kin group also existed; and adherence to unity here tended to make people join factions, rather than stay away from them. To this was added a man's fear that unless he was a member of a group of this kind, and showed his loyalty to it in times of dispute, nobody would help him if he, in turn, became involved in disputes which could not be amicably settled.

There were thus two forces influencing a man in his political relations. The first provided him with reasons for remaining neutral in rivalries regarded as morally wrong. This was supported by the pattern of settlement, for a person in the average homestead would find it fairly easy to avoid contact with even his close neighbours, and only in Delanikoro were any large number of homesteads placed close enough to each other for there to be unavoidable contacts. The force was also strengthened by what appear to be egalitarian values in Fiji. Many men said that a feeling of equality was strongly felt by Fiji Indians. It may perhaps have started in the indenture period as a reaction from the strongly hierarchical caste society which the immigrants had known, but in 1951 it took the form of jealousy felt for anyone who tried to make himself a leader. Disagreement with factions *per se*, or with the policy of a leader was thus not the only reason for neutrality. As one man said, 'In Fiji nobody rises without everyone wanting to pull him down, for nobody likes to see men greater than himself.' The process of 'pulling down' could be through organizing an opposing faction, of course. But an equally effective way was simply not to support anyone who tried to mobilize opinion and supporters. This second way was favoured, for it resulted in a calm life, in which a person did his job and was not bothered with difficult personal relationships nor the risks of fights and damage to his property or reputation.

The other force pulled in an opposite direction, by presenting the advantages of supporting a leader, and taking an interest in the patterns of power in the settlement. Such support ensured physical and perhaps financial protection, as well as reciprocal aid in a number of social contexts (e.g. weddings). For in some cases the maintenance of mutual friendship depended on giving support to a comrade's attempts to become a public figure. The size of factions and the intensity of their rivalry varied in the settlements with the relative weight of these forces.

CRITERIA OF LEADERSHIP

Several features emerge from a survey of the characteristics of those prominent in public life in the settlements, and especially of the eight main leaders at the time of research—Hardayal Singh, Mokub Singh and Chinsami in Vunioki, Sundar, Lakhan and Kanni in Delanikoro, and Ramnath and Dayal in Namboulima. Together, they build up a picture of the 'average' settlement leader, though this is, of course, based on only a tiny number of men.

All those mentioned were Fiji-born, save Kanni. In general, the India-born took little part in public life. Their values and those of the Fiji-born frequently conflicted,[1] and many Fiji-born ridiculed the India-born as old-fashioned and unsuited to the modern world, despite their sentimental regard for India. India-born might be called in to arbitrate affairs of the kin group, for this was considered to be a subject for which they were well qualified by their life in India. But the operation of associations was essentially an activity started in Fiji, and the India-born themselves said that they were content to have Fiji-born men in control, who 'know the new ways of work'.

Leaders were fairly young, the majority being between thirty-five and forty years old. But this may simply have been because most of

[1] See p. 187.

137

the older men had hitherto been India-born and thereby ineligible. Only when the leaders of 1951 have grown into their fifties and sixties will the optimum age for leadership be clearly seen. It is worth noting that Kanni, the single India-born leader, was only about fifty years old, but had come from India as a small child. He illustrated a type which was transient in Fiji Indian rural society, and did not actually attend sessions of the Youth Association, but worked through his son Gopal.

These leaders came from every cultural group except the Muslim,[1] though men of the minority cultural groups tended to have smaller followings. Besides the tendency for men to draw support mainly from followers of the same kin and culture, these minority groups laboured under technical disadvantages. A Muslim leader, for example, was not expected to organize adequately Hindu festivals like the Holi. Similarly, Southerners were said to talk Hindi with accents, even if they were Fiji-born,[2] which, in situations where oratory was most important, was clearly a drawback. Indeed, Kanni may well have missed being a powerful leader simply because his speeches in Hindi, though delivered with force and fluency, had a strong Southern accent which made everyone laugh.

The disadvantages of belonging to a minority cultural group showed themselves mainly in voluntary associations, for the leader of the Gang or the School Committee was chosen for his ability irrespective of his cultural group. The Namboulima Gang had been headed by a Muslim and two Southerners for example; and there had been a capable Muslim *sardar* in Vunioki in 1940. Leadership of the Gang was, of course, not entirely decided on capability—but even Southerners in Vunioki admitted that some of the inadequate candidates elected at Chinsami's urging had to be changed. The tendency towards cultural group solidarity was weaker in these associations than elsewhere, and it enabled men from all groups to gain positions of power.

All the leaders were said to belong to upper castes.[3] The caste affiliations people had in Fiji were not necessarily those which their forebears possessed in India. But the very fact that some people had thought it worthwhile to change their caste affiliations shows that caste was important for status in some circumstances, particularly

[1] This omission is partly merely because there was no important Muslim leader at the time of fieldwork, though there had been before. Partly, it may reflect a withdrawal of some Muslims from the public life of the settlement (see p. 152 seq.).

[2] One highly educated Northerner maintained that he could pick out a Southerner talking Hindi even if this man had never talked a southern language in his life.

[3] By this is meant the traditional 'twice born' division of Hindu society.

those of leadership, though it had only a part of the force it still possesses in Indian society. There was little positive attention drawn to their caste by leaders. One or two were very conscious of their higher caste status—thus, Mokub Singh was a Rajput and maintained in private that this made him more reliable and fearless than some other men of the settlement. But such sentiments were not voiced as appeals for public support.

The size of a leader's kin group had little to do with his political power. In the first place, a man could recruit allies by other means. Though a person like Sundar had brothers who helped him in public affairs, a leader like Dayal had been none the less successful for not having had any kin in Namboulima. In the second place, his kin might as easily oppose a man or remain neutral as support him. Some factions started within kin groups and drew in men from the other cultural groups, such as the quarrel between Chinsami and Appasami and Hardayal Singh. It was better, of course, for a leader to have a large and united kin group behind him, but it was not a necessity.

All the leaders were literate in Hindi, and half also knew some English. Illiteracy was a handicap and was in any case disparaged. When a bridegroom was not able to sign the marriage certificate, for example, the guests remarked that it was a matter of shame for a Fiji-born person to put his thumb-print on a document. The only times when literacy was not needed were during the deliberations of the *panchayats*, for in all other associations there were accounts to be kept, rules to be studied, and sometimes letters to be written. The Gang and the School Committee were the most demanding, and here it was an advantage, if not a necessity, to know English. Mokub Singh and Hardayal Singh, the most successful *sardars* in Vunioki, both knew English, whereas Chinsami's unsuccessful candidates had not done so.

Education was often useful in providing a leader with outside contacts. Lakhan, for instance, knew politicians through writing to their newspapers about the Youth Association's work, and about the Fiji-wide political situation. He would not have been chosen to sit on a *panchayat*, for he did not have the authoritative manner described under the category of 'oratory'; but he was elected head of the Youth Association, largely on the criteria of education and outside contacts.

The aid given to leaders by outside contacts was of two kinds. On the one hand, people in the settlements (especially the younger men) admired town life, and would have liked to take more part in it themselves than the visit every Saturday. They liked the easy way in which people could gather after work, and have a drink of beer or of pineapple juice together. They liked the cinema and the town clothes which they themselves only wore on their weekly visits. One of the ideals of these men was to 'wander around', mostly in towns. Hence the leaders who had the time to do this won their approval. Lakhan, for example, spent a lot of time in town and Chinsami was a lorry driver and had travelled widely.

The other kind of outside link was one with a powerful man in the town, who could render services to the people of the settlement and thereby buttress the power of the settlement leader. Thus, Lakhan made much of the fact that he could ask favours from the one or two politicians whom he knew—to put pressure on the relevant department to repair the Delanikoro road, for example. Hardayal Singh had at one time been in the inner councils of a cane union, and also had relatives influential in the educational and political circles of the Arya Samaj. He was in a position to get favours of several kinds for people—entrance into schools, introductions to solicitors and so forth. In Namboulima, Ramnath had the support of the sitting member of the Legislative Council and the Maha Sangh union leaders, and Dayal was allied to the rival candidate and the other union. The fortunes of the two men depended to quite a large extent on the fortunes of these friends in town. In addition, Dayal's contact with traders in the town provided the basis for his growing commercial power; his contacts were partly with kin, but also went through them to others in business circles.

Some contacts which are normal in other peasant societies were of little or no significance in Fiji Indian settlements. It must be remembered, for example, that because the CSR Company bought the whole of the major crop in some settlements, there were no important ties with crop-brokers in the town. Again, because land was nearly always leased from the CSR Company or from the Native Land Trust Board, there were few ties between farmers and landlords who might live in the towns. Nevertheless, influence outside the settlement was an asset to leaders, and it was increasing with the growth in the settlement of political and occupational associations which extended throughout a district or the whole country. Any official scheme for local government would provide yet another outside channel of significance for settlement leadership.

The richest men of each settlement kept out of public life as far as possible. Some of them were India-born, and a withdrawal was thereby made easy. Others lent their money in other settlements, and were either ostensibly neutral or so withdrawn from settlement matters that their voices were never considered. They may have been rich precisely because they devoted themselves wholeheartedly to increasing their wealth, and were not sidetracked into disputes. For this they were criticized by those who thought that public spirit was more desirable than neutrality, at least for men of their wealth.

The leaders were not poor men, however. Hardayal Singh, Mokub Singh and Chinsami's widowed mother had fertile blocks of cane, Sundar and Kanni both had small plots of land and the latter was also an urban wage-earner, Dayal and Ramnath were traders, and only Lakhan had no very visible means of support save the labour of his mother. Leaders thus had enough money to pay for adequate ceremonies in their households and to be able to entertain visitors with liquor or food when the occasion demanded. One might say that they were men whose desire for power and whose energies had turned into the political, rather than the economic sphere; for none of them apparently tried very hard to make money. Only for Ramnath and Dayal did wealth mean anything, since on it depended the status of their stores and of their rivalry. The correlation between economic status and leadership may thus be a negative one, for greater wealth appeared to make a man more cautious in his dealings with others in the settlement.

The remaining attributes of leaders were the personal ones needed to gather a following and keep it in the changing contexts of disputes. Besides ambition, and perhaps the dislike of an opponent, these characteristics included a mind easily made up, a self-confidence which would persuade the speaker that he had, in fact, made up his mind rightly, and a temperament volatile enough to enable him to speak with passion, yet not so 'hot' as to make him lose his discretion and his control of his hearers. All these qualities were shown on the frequent occasions when the leader had to assert his position with oratory—in meetings of the Youth Association, in the private canvassing for the leadership of the Gang and in *panchayats* of all kinds. Many people judged the weight of a man's cause by the way in which he spoke in its defence. Thus, a Namboulima resident, in speaking of the Temple Committee meeting at which Dayal was made to apologize, asserted, 'Dayal said only two words in his defence, and could speak no more. Everyone said that he was in the wrong, and that God had closed his mouth.'

Not all leaders were orators to the same degree. Perhaps the best were Ramnath and Sundar. The former was extremely fluent and forceful; the latter sometimes stammered in his fervour, but this only added an extra tension to what he was saying. At the other end of the scale were men like Dayal and Chinsami, who had no great fluency, but who spoke quietly, with shafts of telling sarcasm or understatement which their hearers' knowledge of their power made the more emphatic.

The motives for becoming a leader were two in number, both well known in other societies. One was the belief in a principle. This made a man take a stand on a specific issue, and try to get others to do so. Thus, Ramnath said that Dayal had insulted the ascetic, and asked everyone to make him apologize and hear a *katha*. A principle of Fiji Indian life—that one did not insult holy men—had been transgressed and expiation should be made in a similarly religious idiom, by hearing a sacred reading. Similarly, the notion existed that settlements, in fact, any gatherings, should be united. It was this which led Sundar and Lakhan to found the Youth Association, and it was this which made them try to squash any opposition or keep it underground, so that the settlement would remain united, or at least that part of it which was recognized by the Association. Their efforts may have resulted in more divisions than would otherwise have occurred—as their opponents alleged over their boycotts—but the principle behind their actions was consistent.

The other motive was individual ambition, which could turn into personal rivalry and was shown in the reluctance of leaders to give up any position of power. Hardayal Singh, for example, could easily have ended the rivalry which rent the Gang in Vunioki; for Mokub Singh, his nephew, was an acceptable compromise for Chinsami's faction and he could well have accepted him without loss of face, saying that he wished to pass on the post to a younger man of his kin group. Instead, he insisted that Mokub Singh defer to his senior position as uncle, and campaigned against Chinsami and his group. Similarly, Sundar and Lakhan preferred to risk strangling the Youth Association by postponing indefinitely the elections, rather than run the risk of Gopal's victory therein.

The two motives did not remain distinct, of course. Ramnath's attitude over Dayal's insult to the ascetic was caused as much from personal rivalry as from a matter of religious principle; and Sundar's rivalry with Gopal was cloaked in the principle of settlement unity within the Association. If, however, they can be distinguished as parts of the reason why men strove for leadership, they complement the reasons already given for people following leaders. For factions were joined either for personal gain, or to support a strong leader for unity's sake over some issue about which he was felt to be in the right.

To be a leader, and to have a faction of followers, gave a man prestige in a society in which most successes were of individuals, rather than of groups, and in which primacy was achieved rather than ascribed by birth. In rural settlements there was little differentiation of wealth and education, and to excel in these counted for comparatively little, for rich men were not respected unless they were also leaders. Men therefore competed for political power, and the idiom of their competition was a factionalism over shifting issues and with varying support. In particular, they competed for control of the Gang, either directly or through their allies, since the Gang formed the clearest socio-economic interest group. Any development of local government in these settlements would perhaps widen the membership of the factions. In 1951, large numbers of people remained uncommitted to factions. But with the introduction of statutory bodies concerned with the welfare of every inhabitant, it would be less easy, and less profitable, to remain uncommitted. The introduction of a system of local government might also shift the emphasis of factions, and political activities generally, from personalities to programmes, thereby making the membership of opposed groups more stable and more closely based on relatively unchanging issues rather than on a volatile recruitment over disputes and personal clashes.

VII

CULTURE, CASTE AND KINSHIP

FIJI Indians were influenced by cultural and kinship affiliations in several important ways. Economically, kin were likely to co-operate (or dispute) with one another; religious rites were culturally distinct and often took place within the kin group; and in political activities kinship and culture were significant as sources of conflict or recruitment for factions. In addition, caste membership could affect a man's relations with his fellows. To what extent could people be said to form groups based on culture, caste and kinship, and what were the relations between these groups?

THE CULTURAL GROUP

The term 'cultural group' can justifiably be used to anaiyse Fiji Indian society on the basis of broad cultural variations, consisting of different language, rules of marriage, religious rites, diet, names, etc. Some of these differences were mutually irreconcilable, such as the different religions of Muslims and Hindus; others could in theory be bridged, as when a person became bilingual. In practice, stereotyped views were held about cultural groups, however much assimilation there had in fact been. An example would be the observation that Southerners talked Hindi badly, however fluently they might in fact speak.

THE CULTURAL GROUP: RELATIONS BETWEEN NORTHERN AND SOUTHERN HINDUS

The main factor keeping Northern and Southern Hindus apart was the almost total absence of inter-marriage. Everyone knew of one or two mixed households, either with a Southern or a Northern bride; but these were said to be extremely rare, and no examples were found in the three settlements. Thus the two cultural groups were physically separated in the sense that there were almost no homesteads in which people of both were found.

144

The main bar to inter-marriage was most commonly said to be the difference in language. Northerners came from the Hindi-speaking parts of India, whereas Southerners stemmed from Tamil-, Telugu- and Malayalam-speaking areas whose tongues were quite unintelligible to Northerners. Though Hindi was the *lingua franca* of Fiji Indians, Southern languages were still spoken in some homes, as the 1956 Census figures show:

TABLE 1

Language	Households in which Spoken as Main language
Hindi and Hindustani	20,808
Tamil	1,498
Urdu	1,223
Gujarati	830
Telugu	797
Punjabi	468
Malayalam	134
Other	90
Total	25,848

Northerners maintained that a girl would feel uncomfortable in a house where her affines might speak in an incomprehensible tongue, and where she might not know that she was being insulted or mocked. This argument, however, only applied to Northern girls in Southern homes. For most Southern girls knew some Hindi, and could therefore marry into Hindi-speaking households with little or no trouble. It is in any case by no means certain that Southern languages were spoken in all households of the Southern cultural group. The proportion of Southern language-speaking households in Table 1 is about 10 per cent; and, unless these households contained many more people than the Northern households, this percentage did not represent all those who had come from South India.[1] Thus, there were probably many Southern households where Hindi was spoken as the main language, and where there could be inter-marriage of Southern boys with Northern girls.

[1] There are no exact figures for the present division of the Fiji Indian population on lines of origin in India. But 45,833 indentured people came from Calcutta and 15,132 from Madras (Gillion 1956: 139) and this represents approximately the proportion in 1951. Again, Coulter (1942: 81) estimated that in 1935 64 per cent of the population stemmed from the North, 29 per cent from the South, and 7 per cent from other areas.

The language question involved more than a reluctance to inter-marry. Many Northerners felt uncomfortable when in the company of Southerners talking Tamil or Telugu. One Northerner described these languages as sounding like 'peas shaken in a cup' and main-tained that Southerners refused to teach them to Northerners so that they could have a secret language among themselves. But this argu-ment runs against the fact that younger Southerners were by no means agreed that it was a good thing to learn their traditional mother-tongue. It was mainly the India-born who tried to maintain Tamil and Telugu, and who started schools which taught in these languages from the earliest classes.

The younger people often had ambivalent feelings towards their traditional language. These were expressed, for example, by a South-ern school-teacher qualified to teach Telugu. At one stage he main-tained that it was important to teach this language, and that he was proud of his Southern cultural traditions and did not wish to forget them. But later he said that it was not fair to burden Southern chil-dren with a third language—Hindi and English being essentials for any Fiji Indian who wished to have an urban career—when Northern children had only English to learn. Young Southerners frequently felt self-conscious of speaking a different language, and might even refuse to talk it to their India-born parents, though they understood it well enough. Language, in fact, was seen as a symbol of cultural difference, and was often held both by Southerners and Northerners to be a greater differentiating factor than was actually the case.

When this latter point was made to a Northerner in reply to his talk about the linguistic barrier to inter-marriage, the argument usu-ally turned into an enumeration of other Southern customs which would make inter-marriage hazardous even for the younger genera-tions. These customs were seen by Northerners as distinctive, if not unnecessary, ridiculous or even immoral.

One concerned diet. It was said, with justification, that Southern curries were much hotter than Northern dishes, sometimes even to the point of being inedible by the uninitiated. This is not such a minor point as might be thought, for a Northern bride would be reminded of it three times a day in a Southern household. Another had to do with the rites of the cultural groups. In Delanikoro, for example, the annual procession of the goddess Mariamma with its flagellation was exclusive to Southerners: and there were also variations in the smaller rites of the kin group. The climax of the Northern wedding, for ex-ample, was the ceremony of the seven circumambulations of the sacred fire and the reddening of the bride's hair parting by the groom. The equivalent in the Southern wedding was the tying of the *tali* thread round the bride's neck by the groom. A social difference con-

XIII (*a*).   A Hindu family worships at a *taziya*.

(*b*).   The Holi procession arrives at a homestead.

XIV (*a*). Fijian woman and Fiji Indians at a store in town.

(*b*). The weekly market in town.

cerned the place at which the wedding was held. Among Southerners this could be either the groom's or the bride's house. But Northern weddings were only held at the bride's; for the groom's was the 'stronger' party, and to marry at his house would imply that he allowed his bride and her relatives to impose on him. Northerners frequently mocked Southerners for what they regarded as weakness on the part of the husband and his relatives; and many young Southern men did not wish to get married in their own households.

Finally, there was an important difference whereby Southerners allowed cross-cousin marriage (i.e. the marriage of a man to his mother's brother's daughter or father's sister's daughter) whereas these two people were considered by Northerners as brother and sister, between whom marriage would be incestuous.[1] Southern informants asserted that such marriages were getting rarer, the participants feeling self-conscious in making a match of which the majority cultural group disapproved. Indeed, they might even defy their parents' wishes, and refuse to marry in this way.

The differences between the two cultural groups were shown in the stereotypes set up by each side. That held by Northerners about Southerners contained the elements noted above, and expressed the feeling that Southerners were slightly strange, and therefore sometimes unpredictable if not unreliable in their reactions. Such cultural characteristics were not generally talked about except when hostility existed—that is, when the Southerner's behaviour did not conform to what the Northerner would have wished. People never talked of the fact that a man was a good worker and kept out of trouble because he was a Southerner; but they would say that he was a rascal and had injured them because he was a Southerner, and would assert that nothing could be expected of people who ate nothing but chillies and married their sisters.

The stereotype of the Northerner seen by the Southerner had fewer characteristics. This may be because there were so many more Northerners that it was harder for Southerners to see them in the abstract. It may also have been because Northerners had always been the socially dominant cultural group. Southerners were the last to be indentured, and during the twentieth century provided most of the population in the estate lines. Any cleavage between indentured and free therefore drew in the difference between Southerner and Northerner. The Southerners can thus be seen as the 'weaker' cultural group, and

[1] This difference had considerable structural importance in India, for repeated cross-cousin marriages linked lineages in a way which was not possible in the North. In Fiji, however, Southerners were too new a population to have had repeated marriages of this kind.

the Northerners as the 'stronger',[1] in the sense that it was the Southerners who adopted Northern customs and not *vice versa*. One would expect Southerners not to distinguish themselves so clearly from Northerners, therefore, since to some extent they were themselves tending to become like Northerners. Thus, no Southerner said that the Northerner was a man who did *not* marry his cross-cousin—because the fact that the Southerner could do so was not to be advertised. Southerners sometimes said that Northerners were more close-fisted, and that they tended to settle disputes by councils of arbitration rather than factional fighting. These are stereotypical generalizations, and may not always be true, though.

Members of the Arya Samaj sect were Northerners by origin. Their general behaviour conformed to Northern patterns and there was inter-marriage between Arya Samajis and orthodox people. It was therefore not surprising that the attitude of others towards Arya Samajis was very similar to their attitude towards Northerners in general, and no very clear stereotype of the Arya Samaji emerged. Some people looked upon their simplified rites as being a truncated Hinduism—as opposed to the Arya Samaj's assertion that they were the pure rites, free from the overlay of later practices. The relatively short Arya Samaj wedding, with its single day of rites instead of the orthodox three days, was taken as a sign of parsimony, too. A man in Delanikoro, for example, decided, under criticism from his orthodox neighbours, to give both of the wedding feasts. Only when there was considerable hostility between them would a man characterize his Arya Samaji opponent as a 'heretic' (e.g. Ramnath and Dayal).

Another factor influencing relations between these cultural groups was the distribution of their homesteads. Each cultural group tended to occupy a separate part of the settlement. The definition of cultural neighbourhoods was clearest in Vunioki, but all three places show main centres for each cultural group. It seems natural enough that people with similar customs would have tended to settle together, and these clusters of cultural groups were in 1951 backed by ties of kinship between their members even though the original settlers might have been single men. Naturally enough, too, mutual help of an economic or social kind was more likely to occur between nearby homesteads, and this helped to distinguish the cultural group population.

Political leaders of the Fiji Indian community tended to be supported by one or other of the settlement's cultural groups. Thus, an important leader, who was closely connected with the Arya Samaj, was supported in an election to the Fiji Legislative Council by the

[1] There was no physical dominance involved, of course.

148

leaders of the Sunni Muslims controlling the Muslim League and hence by the Sunni Muslims in Namboulima. Sometimes, cane growers' unions were supported by different cultural groups, too. It will be recalled, for example, that the Maha Sangh on Viti Levu was a Southerners' union; and that a new union organized on Vanua Levu recruited members from the Arya Samaj and Muslim cultural groups alone in Namboulima.

Not all settlements had a clear cultural cleavage between members of different unions, or supporters of different political leaders. In some places the people's support of one side or the other was implicit, since no branch or representative of the union existed to promote its policies. Even where such a union organization existed, it was rare to find pressure put on people who did not conform. Crisis situations had occurred where cane growers had gone on strike at the behest of a union and had burned the crops of those who refused to strike with them. But usually no open sanctions were exerted on members holding different views from the majority, although many conformed less out of conviction than from a feeling that it was less controversial to do so, and to their interest to maintain ties of friendship with the rest of the cultural group.

THE CULTURAL GROUP: RELATIONS BETWEEN HINDUS AND MUSLIMS

Superficially, perhaps, differences between Hindus and Muslims were similar to those between the Hindu cultural groups. There was in 1951 no inter-marriage, Muslims had their own rules of marriage and other social behaviour, different ritual calendars, different diets and so forth. These traits were again made into stereotypes, which were brought forward in similar situations and with the same derogatory purpose. But the basis for these differences was that of the two socio-religious systems of Hinduism and Islam, and Hindu-Muslim relations can be distinguished from relations between cultural groups within the Hindu fold. The former will be called 'communal' relations, in accord with common Indian usage.

There were two aspects to these communal relations. One had its basis in the co-operation which evolved in the daily contacts of neighbours in a settlement, and in the work of the Gang (in which no communal distinctions were made) and beyond that, in the attitudes formed and relations made during the indenture period and the period in India before indenture.

Many Muslims and Hindus coming to Fiji had known of co-operation in India with people of the other religion. They had attended each other's festivals, had asked favours of each other's

149

saints, had provided economic services for each other, and sometimes had shared authority in the village as fellow headmen. This kind of relationship continues to this day, and can be seen in Central India. The conditions of indenture and early settlement supported and often strengthened the closeness of these communal ties. People of both religions were housed in the same barracks, and worked in the same fields. Many of them, illiterate and without spiritual leaders, performed impartially any rites of either religion which they imagined would be beneficial. And, a most lasting effect, the small numbers of women caused inter-marriage between Hindu and Muslim.

One Muslim, for example, said that he came to Fiji alone from India. He was a good worker, and in the favour of the overseer, who told him one day that there was an unattached Hindu woman to whom he should get married. He objected, but after a while, he said, the overseer persuaded him that he should have a wife, and they went to the authorities and got a certificate of civil marriage. At first he did not like the woman and used to beat her. But after a while he got used to the idea of having her as his wife, and decided to keep her. Not recognizing the civil certificate as constituting a valid marriage, he persuaded a fellow Muslim in the lines to act as her father, and to answer on her behalf in the orthodox Muslim marriage rite. He now considered his wife's 'father's' children as brothers-in-law.

In this case the couple underwent both the civil and religious marriage; in other cases either or both were omitted, but the couples lived together and may do so to this day. Eight inter-religious matches were recorded,[1] and in two cases women had had Hindu and Muslim husbands in turn. The emergence of a new generation born in these mixed households was significant for communal relations in the settlements. Indeed, there may well have been more marriages between Northern Hindus and Muslims than between Northern Hindus and Southern Hindus. There are no statistics to support this suggestion, but there are good reasons why it should be true. Almost all Muslims came from the same parts of northern India as did Northern Hindus, and thus spoke the same language and had the same provincial backgrounds. They were also in the indenture lines at the same time, where many of these mixed marriages took place. Southern Hindus, on the other hand, had great cultural differences from other Hindus, and formed the bulk of the indentured population when the others had left for their own homesteads.

Many differences between Hindus and Muslims remained, of course. The limits of exogamy were radically different, for Muslims not only allowed cross-cousin marriage, but also the matches of

[1] These were both of Muslim men to Hindu women and *vice versa* (three matches to five respectively).

parallel cousins. Diets differed in the banning of pork by Muslims and beef by Hindus. A completely different cycle of religious rites existed for each group, not only in festivals but in the rites of the individual's life cycle—for instance Muslims were circumcised.

Nevertheless, a large amount of borrowing and common participation had taken place across these communal barriers. Hindus are alleged to have formed the majority of attenders at the Muslim festival of Moharram, for example, and many built *taziyas*. Muslims in their turn had played with the red dye at the Holi festival and had come to Hindu sacred readings, drinking the milk and eating the sweetmeats first offered to the gods and then distributed amongst those present. Such overlays from one religion to another, though fewer than before, could still be found in 1951. In Vunioki, for instance, it will be recalled that a Southerner sacrificed a goat each year to a Muslim saint who had interceded for him during a recent illness; and in Namboulima a Muslim, who cured headaches by songs of praise and by prayers to both Hindu and Muslim saints impartially, was patronized by all.

The histories of the settlements studied indicate that conversion was not an important factor. Only two cases were recorded—and here is meant conversion of a man to Islam, for a wife took her husband's religion upon her marriage, with little apparent reaction from the rest of her cultural group. Each case concerned a man who was unable to marry a Muslim woman without becoming a Muslim himself. Evidently these women had relatives or other supporters sufficiently powerful to forbid the marriage unless there were a conversion. In neither instance does it appear that the man had any religious reasons for becoming a Muslim. One man, for instance, when he found that he could not get respectable Muslim spouses for his children, returned to the Hindu fold by holding a sacred reading.

A second aspect of communal relations was a differentiation which seems to have started with growing education and the consequent awareness of theological and historical differences. Hindus and Muslims who came to Fiji shortly after the end of the indenture system brought ideas of communal separation which did not fit into the Fiji situation. There was a period of public discussion and of pamphleteering, during which communal differences became clear-cut, and sometimes antagonistic. This time may have seen the end of inter-marriage.

Besides this, political developments in the subcontinent during the last thirty years had also powerfully affected Fiji. The rising communal friction there, and finally the creation of Pakistan, crystallized the Muslim feeling of being a separate entity within Fiji society. An increasing number of schools taught Urdu instead of Hindi, which although similar in its spoken form had an entirely different script, and demands were made for Muslim personal law to supersede British law, and for separate electoral rolls for Muslims, who were on a joint roll with all other Fiji Indians. This general trend had led towards a more self-conscious attitude to mixing in the settlements. For most social activities had a religious basis, and the religious aspect of communal relations was given added importance in a society in which there were few purely secular occasions for mixing in one another's houses.

Either of these two aspects could be uppermost in a settlement at a given time. The pattern of communal relations in Namboulima is an illustration of this.

The Hindus and Muslims of Namboulima had formerly attended each other's functions much more than they did in 1951. The reason for the present trend was put in this way by a Hindu. 'The Muslims,' he said, 'say they cannot eat meat at our houses unless it is killed by a Muslim with the prayer (*halal*). But the knives they use to kill are the same as we use. If they refuse to eat meat at our houses, why should we eat meat with them? We refuse to do so. If we received vegetarian food at their functions (and if they agreed to eat vegetarian food with us) this meat question would not come up. But they say that it is too difficult to cook two diets. And they also want meat if they come to our houses, for without meat they say that a feast is no good. But our custom is never to have meat at *kathas*, marriages and so on [meat is eaten at some feasts, of course—e.g. the goat or pig sacrifice]. So vegetarian food is not possible [as a basis for inter-communal feasting]. The result is that we do not go to them, nor they come to us.'

On the one hand, then, the Muslims were less eager to attend Hindu functions, since no meat was served—and even if it had been, they would not have been able to eat it, since it had not been ritually slaughtered. On the other hand, Hindus objected to the expense of providing meat for Muslims at their feasts, since they themselves only ate vegetarian food at most of them; and in any case they did not want to kill their meat according to Muslim rites.

This estrangement had taken place over the last few years, it was said. Another account mentioned this issue of meat-eating, but added other details. This was given by a Muslim, who said, 'Muslims used to go to Hindu feasts. Then about four years ago, Hamidullah's son was offered meat at Gupta's. He knew it had not been killed properly, and refused it like a true Muslim. Gupta was affronted, and his wife told him not to give any more Muslims food. A week later came the Holi festival. A Hindu threw red dye over Hamidullah without his permission, and Hamidullah got angry and hit him. The

Hindus had a meeting that night, and drew up a pledge not to eat at Muslim houses nor to invite Muslims to their functions; there were about forty signatures on it, though a few people retracted their names later. After this, Hindus continued to come to Muslim functions. They drank tea or *yanggona*, but refused to eat. So Muslims finally decided to stop inviting them.'

In this account the issue of meat-eating was again the initial difference; perhaps because a Muslim was telling it, Hindus were put in the wrong in the Holi incident,[1] and the breach was formalized by the pledge-signing. Another (Hindu) account gave a different cause for the breach, though it again centred around the taking of food at feasts.

It was said that when the Muslims decided to build a mosque in the settlement, the Hindus came and helped them. This was in return for Muslim co-operation at the Ganeshlila where, it may be remembered, all people of the settlement contributed labour and advice. The Muslim League leader in the town was said to have heard of this co-operation, and to have told the Namboulima Muslims not to take any such contribution from Hindus. When a feast was held to celebrate the completion of the mosque, Hindus were offered food, but not asked for contributions towards the feast nor for help in its management. They were offended at this, but continued to come to Muslim rites until the petition was signed, and a break was formally recognized.

These accounts differ from each other. It is possible that each gives only one aspect of the complete history of communal relations in Namboulima, and that there is some exaggeration, or inaccuracy (the suggestion that Hindu farmers were angry because they were *not* asked for contributions seems suspect!). But the underlying reasons for the breach are of interest.

These reasons—the difficulty over meat-eating or the impropriety of extra-communal contributions—should, in theory, have called forth sanctions many years before the time to which the accounts referred. But the informants gave no indication that such difficulties were of long-standing, and productive of estrangements from time to time. Instead, the accounts suggested that this was the first time they had occurred—and this may well be true. Until about four years before 1951, Muslims had eaten the meat of goats sacrificed to Hindu tutelary deities without any objection, and the two communities had co-operated in the religious occasions of each. The change since 1947 was coincidental with the establishment of Pakistan, and it is interesting that the Muslim League apparently advised Namboulima

---

[1] The description of the Holi for Delanikoro shows how much care is taken not to douse anybody who does not wish it, lest there be quarrels (Mayer 1952: 9).

Muslims over the mosque affair—and that shortly afterwards a branch of the Muslim League was started in the settlement itself. All this supports the view that the communities had started to drift apart in earnest only in the last few years, though it must not be forgotten that the socio-religious differences on which such a drift could be based had always been present.

Besides the divisive factors, however, the accounts suggest that there were forces linking the two communities. Thus, it was said that only forty of the Hindus in the settlement signed the resolution, and that some of these retracted their names later. The split was clearly by no means a complete one, for two reasons.

One was simply that Namboulima was a large settlement, and the decisions made by Hindus living near the main Muslim neighbourhood did not necessarily affect those at the other end of the settlement. The solitary homestead of Muslims living in the extreme north-west was not included in the ban by Hindus living near it; and these Hindus were therefore unwilling to observe a ban on other Muslims. Just as Baburam's neighbours in Delanikoro refused to boycott him at the request of the Youth Association, so in Namboulima the ties of neighbourhood were accounted more important than those of settlement membership. The main resolution-signers lived on each side of the largest Muslim nucleus in Namboulima; and it may be recalled that there had occasionally been other disputes of a communal kind there.[1] These complaints would not have applied to the other Muslim homesteads, which were at some distance from their neighbours. The size and scatter of the settlements thus rendered a decision of the kind taken in the resolution difficult to apply over the whole area. An unquestioned leader of the settlement might have asked for boycotts of any Hindus disregarding the resolution, but nobody had this kind of authority during the period of these events.

Distance from the nucleus of Muslim homesteads was not the only reason, however; another was presented by a few Hindus living close to this Muslim neighbourhood, who had had ambivalent reactions towards the resolution, and had continued to visit Muslim houses, and to invite the few Muslims who were willing to come. It is surely no coincidence that some of these men had been members of mixed households, as shown by the diagrams opposite:

The three brothers Ali, Ahmad and Asgar continued to attend Hindu functions during 1951. Ali, in fact, went as part of the entourage of a Hindu boy when his engagement rite was performed at a nearby settlement. Similarly Siv, though a Hindu, had until shortly before fieldwork gone to the functions of the Muslim cultural group, with which he was so closely linked. The disapproval of both the

[1] See p. 118.

stauncher Hindus and Muslims had fallen on these men. Siv had heeded this, and no longer attended rites at his half-brother's. The three Muslim brothers had also been warned, but continued to go to Hindu rites. There was some talk of boycotting them, but as yet no test case had been established, to see if they would change their minds under this threat. Their half-brother Ramcharan was in no need of rebuke. He was one of the leaders of the Hindus, and had helped to write the resolution against inviting Muslims. It is interesting to note that two of the four men who retracted their signatures from this document were Siv and Sukhu, both related in some way to Muslims; the other two were Arya Samajis whose leading politician had made an alliance with Sunni Muslim politicians. The influence of previous

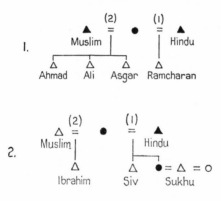

N.B. ▲ and ● = deceased person

inter-marriage and tolerance between members of the two religions remained, though it was weakening under the new forces of division.

To sum up, all cultural groups—Northerners, Southerners and Muslims—had 'cultural' differences which gave their members the feeling of belonging to a separate group. Besides this, they were often spatially separated in a way which facilitated social division, and confined petty neighbourly disputes within the cultural group. Lastly, they might be influenced by the outside in a way which heightened the feeling of group membership.

Nevertheless, the people of a cultural group did not always act as a local unit, and reasons for divisions have already been cited, such as quarrels over land, or over debts, etc. In addition, structural features underlay these disputes and divisions. These were, the unity of a kin group in opposition to others, the solidarity of a homestead, and feelings of caste difference within the cultural group.

THE CASTE GROUP

One of the questions most frequently asked about the Fiji Indian community concerns the presence or absence of caste. This section shows in what form caste had 'survived' in Fiji, and what part it played in the activities of the settlement.

As soon as caste in Fiji is considered, the problem arises of how detailed an account of caste in India should be given. It is assumed that readers are primarily interested in Fiji, and that comparisons with India should be made only to amplify Fiji conditions and not to discuss the general position of the caste system in India as well. Only a very brief and necessarily over-simplified account is given of the salient characteristics of caste in the Indian society from which the immigrants came.

All Hindus were born into a caste and, with few exceptions, could marry only the members of that caste.[1] The caste was therefore a 'closed' unit and it had a rank in what was a hierarchy of castes. This rank was to a large extent based on ritual purity, which was lessened—or polluted—by certain kinds of contact with lower castes. It was, for example, impossible for members of higher castes to touch the lowest castes, and it was equally forbidden to take food which lower castes had cooked, or to smoke the same cigarette or pipe with them. Purity was also lessened by certain kinds of behaviour hereditarily allowed to caste members. To eat certain kinds of food (e.g. some or all meats, eggs or fish), or to do any work which was connected with death or body substances (e.g. tanning, barbering) gave the caste a low hierarchical status.

The highest caste was the Brahman, whose members were traditionally priests and whose habits were the most exclusive of all castes. The lowest were the Tanners and Sweepers, who disposed of dead animals and human excreta, and whose habits were the least exclusive since they could, for example, eat from the hearths of almost all other castes. However exclusive, the caste's rules of behaviour were strictly enforced, and anyone who broke them was judged by a council of caste mates. This council might be under the control of a hereditary caste headman, or be simply a gathering of influential caste elders. It imposed fines and, in the severest cases, ostracized a man until he had made penance and purified himself sufficiently to associate with his caste fellows again. These social sanctions were supported by the Hindu doctrine of reincarnation, in which obedience to the rules governing a man's station in life was a major factor in his acquiring merit and a resultant rebirth into a higher caste.

[1] In India the sub-caste was usually the endogamous unit, but such internal divisions appeared to have no relevance in the Fiji Indian settlements studied.

The points to be stressed here are—that membership of a caste was given by birth and was immutable; that castes were ranked in a hierarchy, according to certain generally accepted standards of behaviour; that the people of the caste itself disciplined any member who disobeyed these rules, and that the caste group, rather than the individual, acted as the unit and was the object of change within the system, for by adopting 'higher' habits a local group of caste mates might raise their status.

The first weakening of the caste system came even before the immigrants had reached Fiji. It took the form of a disregard for the rules of purity. Just how soon this occurred in the immigrant's progress from his village to the Fiji sugar estate is not certain. One would imagine that caste rules were observed in the houses of the recruiter and the sub-agent; for these lived near the place where the person had been recruited, and their disregard would have led to additional resistance to indenture from the populace. The depots in Calcutta and Madras contained recruits of many castes, some of whom might stay there for weeks whilst sufficient numbers were gathered for a shipload, or until transport was available. It is possible that during this time their food was cooked by Brahmans, from whom all could eat without compromising their caste status. But it does not appear that untouchables lived in separate quarters,[1] as would be necessary if customary practice were to be followed.

Whatever the situation on Indian soil, caste restrictions did not survive the journey from India to Fiji. In the first place, the high caste people were defiled by crossing the ocean. This act put them out of their caste groups, to whose punishments they would have had to submit were they to have returned to their villages. Secondly, life on board the immigrant ships was inconsistent with caste rules. The handbook issued for the Surgeons-Superintendent of the immigration vessels advises that Brahmans could be put in the galley as cooks if they appeared to be genuinely incapable of eating the food provided by other hands;[2] but it adds that these prejudices usually disappeared after a short time at sea. There could be no rigid spatial segregation in the holds of such vessels and people who had lost caste by coming aboard were less inclined to stick to their rules of diet.

India-born people in Fiji dramatized the change which took place. One old woman told how she had set sail from Calcutta, and all on board had started to cook dinner, each caste with its own hearth.

---

[1] There were, for instance, numerous protests by people who objected to eating with untouchables (Marwari Association Reports, Calcutta 1913–16) as Dr. Gillion points out in a letter.

[2] J. M. Lang, *Handbook for Surgeons-Superintendent of the Coolie Emigration Service* (India Office J. & P. 565/1889), quoted in Gillion 1958.

Suddenly a wave rocked the ship, and all the cauldrons of food over-turned on to the deck together. It was a choice of eating food which had been mixed and so polluted, or of going hungry. From that time restrictions on food had ended, she said. No Fiji Indian informant could recall any attempt to re-introduce restrictions of food or drink after the immigrants had arrived in Fiji; and only one case was cited where a high caste leader in a settlement near Vunioki had unsuc-cessfully tried to re-introduce the segregation of 'untouchables'.

One of the main props—that of purity through diet and touch—had been knocked from under the caste hierarchy. The other im-portant upholder of both caste separateness and caste rank had been occupation. Not only were occupations graded as to purity, and thereby made indices of caste rank in the hierarchy; the fact that most were exclusive to the members of a single caste was a jealously guarded economic right. These occupations were interdependent—the priest depending on the barber as much as the barber on the priest—and only one major occupation overlay these distinctions. For all but the highest castes could engage in agriculture without loss of status, and indeed, agriculture acted as the 'safety valve' for any caste whose numbers grew too large for its traditional work.

On their arrival in Fiji, the Indians were despatched to the sugar cane estates, and there everyone did the same work. This was not in itself always damaging to caste status, since the work was agricultural. But it effectively destroyed status differentiation on the basis of occupation and the economic interdependence of one caste on an-other for services. When the immigrants had fulfilled their indenture contracts on the estates, and moved to their own homesteads as free men, the earlier pattern did not return. In the first place, there was no need for many of the old occupations. People did not use pots made by the potter, but instead bought metal pots imported from Australia; ploughs and other agricultural implements were made of iron so that there was no need for full-time carpenters. Then, too, most farmers became used to doing their own odd jobs. They mended their own equipment, repaired their own houses and so forth; and work which would have been too polluting for them to attempt in India was quite normal in Fiji. A bullock was struck by lightning in Delanikoro, for example; that afternoon, the owner gathered five of his neighbours, who dug a pit, rolled the carcase into it and covered it up, which would normally have been done by members of a low caste in India.

A reason for this lack of specialization might also have been that the necessary specialists were not available in a settlement: possibly because none had emigrated; or possibly because such specialists were few and far between in Fiji, or were unwilling to practise their traditional occupation. Homesteads were scattered and in some cases the number of customers was too small to support a full-time specialist. The population was highly mobile, too, with the danger that a debtor could easily abscond without paying his bills. In any case, the fact remains that few men carried on non-agricultural work as a living in the settlements.[1] Even when they did, their work was not necessarily their traditional caste calling. Thus, the barber-inviter in Vunioki was not of the Barber caste. The only hereditary occupation was that of priest, for those conducting major Hindu rites continued to be Brahmans by caste.

The ending of these economic and social relations between castes meant that the hierarchy which had existed in India could not be maintained in the same detail. In addition, two other important features of the caste system were greatly affected by immigration.

In the first place, the voyage between India and Fiji dealt a blow to the notion that a man's caste was given him by birth, and could not be changed. For immigrants could change their caste *as individuals*. They could give a false caste name to the recruiter; or they could give their true caste name to him, but later change it and say that they had been forced to give a false name in order to be accepted for immigration. In either case, they had taken on a new caste status in a manner which would have been impossible in India, save by going to a completely different part of the country where the change could not be detected, in effect by immigrating within India. The fact that these changes were possible had made caste status highly flexible in 1951.

Secondly, no informant could recall the existence of any caste council which could have penalized people who broke rules of eating or smoking, or who performed 'low' work, or who changed their caste names. There are several probable reasons for this lack. One is that there were often too few men of the same caste in an area at any one time to provide a council. Another is that any men of the same caste would in any case almost always have come from different villages and districts of India. They would not have known each other before immigration, and no single man would have been in a position of acknowledged leadership.[2] Again, since most of the immigrants

[1] The towns, of course, contained specialists (blacksmiths, carpenters, etc.), but these were not usually recruited by caste in 1951. The removal of night-soil was apparently still reserved for low caste workers, but higher caste men could work as, say, butchers, though this might count against them when they contracted marriages for their children. Men of the three settlements did work in the town which was not traditional to their caste. A Delanikoro man who worked in a tailor's shop was not from the Tailor caste, for example.

[2] It is, of course, possible that *sardars* in the lines used the authority gained under the indenture system to settle caste problems (see p. 5).

were young men, there were few elders on whose shoulders the operation of caste councils had traditionally fallen, and who would have been qualified to re-start them. Powerful individuals may have maintained caste rules within their homesteads and perhaps their circle of near neighbours or kin, but caste control stretched no wider than this.

Despite these undermining factors, the influence of caste was, in three ways, still apparent in 1951. In the first place, marriage was based on the endogamy of castes. People gave no very clear reasons for wanting to marry their children within the caste. Some said that different castes had different ways of life, and that a girl going into a strange household would not be able to adapt herself. But few such differences appeared to exist. In the traditional system, it is true, fundamental differences of custom often distinguished castes. One caste, for example, might consist of vegetarians; another might allow its members to eat goat and mutton, and a third might permit the consumption of game as well. These differences were important because varying degrees of purity were associated with these diets, and inter-marriage was therefore impossible. But in Fiji the differences were as much *between individuals* as between castes; a traditionally low-caste group in Vunioki contained both meat-eaters and vegetarians, both drinkers and teetotallers. The preference for caste endogamy appeared to be founded on feelings of difference, therefore, rather than actual difference, feelings which might well have stemmed from the initial desire of India-born parents to order marriages as they had done in India, though the customs which had supported the former marriage patterns might have changed or disappeared. Continuance of caste endogamy by the Fiji-born could thus be seen as the wish to follow established practice and to avoid being classed as an unorthodox person.

Though caste endogamy was desired, and though a majority of marriages undoubtedly took place within the caste, a significant number of inter-caste matches had been made. Fourteen such cases were recorded in the three settlements. Many of these could not have been avoided, and concerned people without eligible partners of their own caste in Fiji—or at least in the surrounding settlements. Not all mixed marriages could be ascribed to demographic causes, however. A Rajput boy had married an Ahir (Dairyman) girl, although both castes were well enough represented for each to have found spouses in their caste. In some cases economic gain was the reason behind such matches; in others, the personal characteristics of the spouses or their families made it hard for them to find matches within their own caste and they had to look elsewhere. Most of these marriages were hypergamous—that is, they involved marriages of higher caste men with lower caste women. In this, they followed traditional practice in India, where certain castes were allowed to marry outside in this way. Hypogamous marriages—in which upper caste women went to lower caste men—were far rarer. Only two such matches were recorded—those of a Kumhar (Potter) boy and a Rajput girl, and of a Rajput boy and a Brahman girl. Hypergamy was preferred because the children belonged to the father's caste and so had higher status, whereas in the hypogamous match they were lower than one of their parents. The largely endogamous nature of Fiji Indian castes kept these alive as separate social units and through hypergamy a measure of their former rank was maintained.

In the second place, caste could be a factor in situations of hostility. Here, a man's caste was used as a kind of scapegoat, and as a reason for the enmity. Thus, one man in quarrelling with his brother's sons over land boundaries, accused them of being too friendly with Chamar (Tanner) neighbours, and of thus being morally below him. From this it was but a short step to say that such people would, of course, try to trick their relatives over issues concerning money or property. To justify this theory, however, the speaker had to paint Chamars in dark colours too—saying that their women were loose and that they themselves were cowards. Again, a man who had had quarrels with some fellow residents of the settlement said that they were not Rajputs, as he was, and so could not be relied upon. Conflicts produced the view that if the caste of an opponent was lower in rank than a man's own, then he was craven, probably immoral and so unreliable and in the wrong; if he was of a higher caste, then he was hot-tempered, arrogant, and so unreliable and in the wrong. Only Brahmans were often singled out as having a specific stereotype—this being of addiction to comfort, of sloth, and of a tendency to over-estimate the financial worth of their ritual services. Other castes were seen purely as 'high' or 'low' by any speaker. Sometimes, however, members of a single caste group also constituted the entire cultural group of a settlement; on those occasions the cultural group's stereotype was added to the comments about caste. In Vunioki, for example, the Arya Samajis were all Rajputs, and some of the opponents of Hardayal Singh and Mokub Singh were loud in both their condemnation of Arya Samaj unorthodoxy and of Rajput pride and stubbornness. As with the cultural groups, the caste stereotypes were only unfavourable and were used in situations of hostility. A non-Rajput never commented on Rajput bravery, for instance, but only on the caste's foolhardiness and tendency to pick fights.

Thirdly, it has been noted that conditions of immigration had made it easy for individuals to assume a caste status which had not been theirs by birth, and this flexibility continued after the abolition of indenture, and existed during 1951. A man in Delanikoro, for instance, had insisted on an investiture with the sacred thread before his marriage, although it was popularly held that he was far from being a member of a 'twice-born' upper caste, whose members alone had the right to wear it, and the officiating priest was later reprimanded by his fellows. Similarly there was an instance of a father who had started to call his sons 'Singh' and to say that they were Rajputs, although he had previously made no pretension to be of that caste. In both cases there had been some comment by others in the settlement, but nobody had moved to penalize the people, by boycotting their functions, for example.

This ease with which people were able to change their caste was due in part to the inter-caste marriages in the community, which weakened the exclusive nature of caste membership; it was also due to the fact that people raised their status as individuals or, at the most, with the concurrence of their near kin, rather than as members of a local caste group ruled by a council. The smaller the number of people who changed status, the less liable were they to be noticed by others[1] and the more flexible would one expect the system to be. It was also comparatively easy to change caste, because there were few customs exclusive to any single caste, or to the upper ranks. A man wanting to be accepted as a Rajput, for instance, could be a vegetarian or a meat eater, for both habits were acceptable to those already classed as Rajputs. He did not have to change his dress, nor his domestic customs, nor the way he celebrated rites. Hence, change could be asserted with the minimum of personal adaptation, and without the danger that a social solecism would betray a lower origin.

The most difficult caste to enter was the Brahman. There had been no examples of the adoption of Brahman status in recent years, and in Fiji, as in India, the Brahman was regarded as the highest caste, and was made separate in several ways (e.g. none but Brahmans performed marriages or sacred readings). It may seem paradoxical, then, that in spite of this pre-eminence, the Brahman caste provided an aid to flexibility and the diminution of caste's importance, rather than a buttress of caste values and caste rank. The reason comes from the circumstances of Brahman emigration to Fiji. Recruiters were not anxious to enlist those Brahmans who were thought to be bad manual workers;[2] hence, some Brahmans who wished to go to Fiji were in-

---

[1] This assumes that these others would object to a large number of caste changes, which might well not be the case.

[2] Government of India, Emigration Proceedings, August 1883, A. 9–15 (quoted in Gillion 1958).

dentured under assumed names of different castes. Later, when their term of indenture had expired, they again took their Brahman names. But this temporary change of outward caste status provided the opportunity for some to claim Brahman status in Fiji who had never had it in India.

Many present Brahmans were believed by everyone to be genuine; but others were suspected of having become Brahmans by using this method. Indeed, it was a common joke to say that there were few true Brahmans in Fiji. The place of the Brahman caste as the cornerstone of the hierarchy was therefore less secure, and people took much less notice of what Brahmans might show by word or example. More than this, the fact that the membership of the top caste was itself suspect made people less strict about membership in general, and more willing to accept changes of status by others.

Caste was important in the three settlements mainly because people remembered its central position in Indian society and continued to regard some castes as higher and others as lower. Though there was no distinction of occupation, diet, dress, housing, etc. to set off a Chamar from a Rajput in Fiji, people in the settlements nevertheless maintained that Chamars were of a low status, and it was considered tactless, if not worse, to refer to their caste in their presence. To some extent this continuation of traditional usage was based on the priority maintained by Brahmans in the settlements, though this had its weaknesses, as has just been suggested.

At the same time, caste distinctions were not important enough to make everyone wish to overcome them. In a situation where it was easy to join a higher caste, it is significant that some people did *not* do so and were content to remain of low caste, even if they did not like to be reminded of this in public. Such people preferred the slight stigma of low caste status to the charge that they were not 'true' members of the caste into which they had risen. The *parvenu* origins of a Chamar who became a Rajput would be known for at least the next generation, and he would only be able to marry his children to Rajputs of similar status. No overt discrimination would exist, nor were there sanctions to make him renounce his new status; but it was often felt better to be genuine, though lower, than to be insecurely higher, since the social cost of being lower was small. Only for leaders did this not appear to be true; for such men always took on higher status—perhaps a consequence of the leadership by higher castes in India.

It is tempting to see caste in Fiji as an example of 'cultural lag' and to find in the cultural groups the same clear-cut social divisions as castes had provided in India. For cultural groups were almost entirely endogamous, with clear differences of religious and secular behaviour, and sometimes political cohesion. But this is not to say that the cultural group had 'taken the place' of caste. Relations between cultural groups had none of the ritual basis of inter-caste relations, and the hierarchical structure which was part of the caste system was largely lacking between cultural groups. Furthermore, cultural groups were only effective bodies of social control when they were allied to unions or other associations which enforced rules of behaviour on their members. One might say that cultural groups had become more important social divisions in the relative absence of castes, but not that they had become caste-like bodies, or were true substitutes for a weakened and transformed caste system.

KINSHIP

Just as many settlement cultural groups consisted of extended families, so most caste populations were at the same time groups of kin. These kin were either members of the same homestead, or lived more or less scattered.

KINSHIP IN THE HOMESTEAD

The composition of homesteads has been outlined in Chapter II. It will be recalled that some 63 per cent comprised simple households, and the rest, containing a majority of the population (53 per cent), were in a more complex organization of joint households or house groups.

The composition of joint households was never very extensive. In most cases it consisted of a father and between one to three of his adult sons, or several brothers of a dead father; sometimes affines were included. Settlement in Fiji had been too recent to allow large households of distant collaterals to grow up. Lack of land had in any case forced men to leave the household; so had quarrels, and the violation of certain patterns of behaviour between members of the household.

The basic household relationship was, of course, that of a man and his wife. This was one of public dissociation, both ideally and usually in practice. Spouses seldom showed any emotion towards each other, and addressed each other in the third person. Though outwardly the husband had complete control, this by no means always represented the actual balance of power between spouses. Wives might have considerable influence over their husbands, though women took no part in public associations or in factions, and though men arranged all important transactions with outsiders. In most households the women were given care of the money, hiding it in some place about the house, and giving their menfolk the amounts they asked for. This was because women stayed at home more than men, and so could watch the family treasure more effectively. But women in some households also controlled the amounts of money spent, and over-rode their husbands on matters of economic policy. In one or two of these households the women did not attempt to hide their dominance, and argued with their menfolk in front of visitors. If a marriage broke up—because of a wife's fading charms or too open a domination of her husband, or the lack of children, for example—both partners could remarry according to civil law, but only the man was able to make a second religious marriage too. Figures for the frequency of divorce in the three settlements were too few to be significant, but cases existed in each place. A divorce was said to cost about £25, and a suit could be brought for adultery, or at the end of a three-year separation. Children went with the mother if very young, and by the direction of the Court with either parent if older. No maintenance was payable to the wife if she had deserted her husband and refused to return to him; but the Courts enforced alimony if she could show that she had been cast out by her husband. An India-born man bewailed the increased power of the wife because of the Government's connection of the civil and religious marriages. For, he said, when religious marriages were officially unrecognized, and were generally unaccompanied by a civil ceremony, the husband was under no obligation to pay alimony if he sent his wife home and refused to live with her.

In all three settlements examples existed of couples living together with neither a religious nor a civil marriage, frequently having spouses whom they had deserted. Public opinion allowed this as long as the couples followed accepted rules of conduct, and this liberal attitude may be connected with the extremely informal conjugal relations of the indenture period, at which time some respectable couples had 'married' without any civil or religious ceremony. The children of these unions could have their births registered as natural issue, and were entitled to maintenance until they were sixteen years old. Neither they nor their mother had any claim on the estate of the father, however. Since British law applied in Fiji, polygamy was forbidden, though Muslims had in 1951 been pressing for this provision of their personal law for some years without success.

Respect was shown by children to their parents, as part of a general deference to the ascending generation. Sons did not challenge their father's opinions, at least in his presence, and did not have any over-familiar conversation or jokes with him. The few occasions on which a son openly contradicted his father presaged divisions of the household. When sons themselves became fathers and men with some power over their own families the father, unless he was exceptionally able, started to retire into the background. He might act as adviser, but would be cautious in applying his seniority lest his sons should leave him to set up their own homesteads, and thereby withdraw their economic support in his old age. Men having grown sons living with them were in fact often those who had wealth of their own or a lease in their name; the tables were then turned, for the sons deferred to them lest they lose their share. Men had informal and friendly relations with their grandchildren, and frequently acted as mediators between them and their parents.

The mother also commanded respect from her children and had considerable authority over the sons' wives. But as the latter grew older and produced children of their own, so the mother-in-law would retire, though again these relations depended on the characters of the people concerned, as well as their economic power.

The relationship between brothers and sisters, and between those who were in the classificatory relation of brother and sister, such as the children of brothers in joint households, was ideally a relation of friendship and mutual trust, in which the two persons supported each other in quarrels with people outside the household. They could joke together, but without insulting behaviour or sexual allusions. This ideal pattern was not always maintained, of course. Brothers might quarrel over the division of their dead father's assets, for example; or the younger brother might resent an elder brother's assumption that he must be obeyed—for the principle that superior age carried authority extended to men of the same generation as well as those of different generations. Relations with sisters were less liable to such disruption, for the sister usually left the household at marriage, and did not claim any share of the family property.

A woman who had married into a joint household or house group had to avoid her husband's elder brother (*barka*) and father. Such women were often seen crossing the compound with their shawls pulled over that side of the face which would be visible to the *barka*. The two people were not supposed to talk together, and the younger brother's wife (*chotki*) even tried to arrange for someone else to serve the *barka* his food. In one settlement, the bus driver used to collect the fares from his passengers. His *chotki*, when travelling, would give her money to someone else to pay or, with averted head, would leave the fare on the running board for him to pick up later.[1]

In contrast to this was the relation between a woman and her husband's younger brother (*dewar*). Here there was no question of

[1] Southerners did not have this restriction, but some were adopting it as part of the trend towards Northern behaviour.

avoidance. In fact, jokes were allowed between the two, and a certain amount of physical contact. The two could splash each other at the Holi festival, for example, and the *dewar* might pull his elder brother's wife's (*bhauji*) plaits. The informality of the relation appeared to have an underlying sexual aspect, for jokes were made on the theme that the *bhauji* was the property of all the *dewar*, since the latter could marry a widowed *bhauji*. Some informants denied this side of the relation; they saw in it and in the *barka-chotki* relation, a buttress to the authority of the older members of the household. The elder brother was the actual or potential leader of the household, they said, and he must never be placed in a position where he would suffer accusations from his younger brother. If he were allowed free relations with his *chotki*, a situation might arise where the younger brother could with reason be jealous of him, and this might break the joint household. The freedom of men with their *bhauji* was quite permissible, on the other hand, because the younger brother could be disciplined by the elder if he became too free with his *bhauji*.

A similarly informal relation existed between the women who had married into the household and their husbands' sisters. These could talk informally and joke together, and the young bride was often teased by her sisters-in-law. Usually, however, the sisters left the household on their marriage, for couples generally lived in the husband's settlement. But in some cases both spouses came from the same settlement, and in any case it was not thought wrong to settle in the wife's settlement. Eighteen men had done this, though having paternal and maternal relatives in other parts of Fiji. Further, half these men were actually living in the wife's parents' homestead. These men were in a weak position, however, for their presence in their wife's household was a contradiction of the 'strong' position of the groom. They tended to become the butts of jokes about husbands henpecked by their wives and ruled by their mothers-in-law; and they were, of course, to a large extent under the control of their affines. Ideally, their relations with these should have been ones of great formality, almost avoidance, towards the wife's father and mother, and a joking relation with their wife's brothers and sisters. In fact, the exigencies of life in the same homestead meant that the father-in-law was treated with much less formality, though with respect, and the mother-in-law could not wholly be avoided.

The rules of behaviour just summarized were followed both by kin in the same household and by those living in different homesteads. Contravention in joint households of their underlying principles—of respect for age, co-operation between siblings, avoidance, etc.— generally resulted in the division of such households.

KINSHIP: DIVISION OF JOINT HOUSEHOLDS

Details of thirteen divisions were recorded in Vunioki and Delani-koro. Some of the reasons given recurred in several cases. Four divisions, for example, were said to have stemmed from economic causes such as disputes over a father's will. A further three divisions concerned jealousies based on accusations that household members were doing unequal work or receiving unequal benefits from the income of the household. Detailed data exist for a household which came near to dividing on this issue.

In this case, the household consisted of two brothers and their father. The elder brother was literate, but physically weaker, and it was thus natural for him to supervise purchases from the market town, and for the younger brother to do more of such heavy work as ploughing. But the younger brother's wife felt that she and her husband were being imposed upon. She and the elder brother's wife took it in turns to cook the meals and one day, when the latter would not give food to one of the younger brother's children, saying that it was bad to eat between meals, the younger brother's wife made a scene and asserted that her sister-in-law had no right to say this since her husband did nothing to earn the food in question. Henceforth, the two women cooked separately, their children played separately, and there was restraint between the two brothers. The household was still joint—the income was pooled and stores given to each wife as she needed them—but it was severely strained, and matters did not change during fieldwork. Only the attitude of the India-born father, who said that divisions were a disgrace in India and that he would disinherit his sons if one occurred in his household, prevented an immediate split.

As it happened, a forty-eight-day calendar of this household's work was being compiled at the time, and the explosion came towards its middle. The table on p. 169 indicates the degree to which the younger brother's wife was justified in her accusations.

It is clear from this tabulation that the younger brother *had* been doing more work than had the elder. If a difference of five days in seven weeks be thought too slight to provoke a household division, one must note the considerable variations between the brothers' shares in cane and paddy cultivation. The elder brother was, at this time of year, principally engaged in weeding paddy—an arduous and boring job, but not very taxing physically. The younger, on the other hand, was mainly in the cane fields where he was ploughing and preparing the land for sowing, exhausting work with heavy equipment at the hottest time of year. Added to this was the fact that the younger brother's main leisure activity consisted in what has been called 'rest'

168

TABLE 2

Occupation	Elder brother	Days * Younger brother	Total
Cane cultivation	7½	18½	26
Paddy cultivation	13	4	17
Cattle herding, etc.	3½	5½	9
Work for Fijian landlords †	1½	2½	4
Total 'work'	25½	30½	56
Marketing	10	½	10½
Visits to relatives	1½	1	2½
Attending weddings, etc.	5½	5	10½
Rest	5½	11	16½
Total 'leisure'	22½	17½	40

* The compilation was made by asking each of the brothers what he had done in the morning and afternoon. It is thus not exact to the nearest hour.

† The household's land was leased from Fijians, and some paddy land was ploughed near the Fijian village. This appeared to be the total extent of work done for Fijians; it had not always been an annual task, and may have been done in return for Fijian support over the lease's renewal.

—sitting around the house smoking and talking to anyone who might pass by—whereas the elder brother went often to the town to shop, involving not only the expense of bus fares, but also the diversions of the town. When these aspects are considered, it is clear that the schedule offered cause for the younger brother's wife's outburst, and the consequent strains in the household.

Divisions were also likely to occur if brothers were doing different jobs, of course, for this did away with the advantages of co-operation. In one Delanikoro Northern household three brothers were farmers, and the fourth was a carpenter in town. The land was not enough to support the farmers who gained extra but unequal earnings as labourers, and the carpenter was paid a different amount in cash. The household had divided amicably, the brothers recognizing that it was better to do so than be forced to divide angrily later on.

In other divisions, cultural as well as economic factors were cited as the chief causes. One instance showed the gap in outlook between India-born and Fiji-born. A father and his son quarrelled for some time before dividing about the expenses considered essential by the younger man, but held to be extravagances by the elder. Such items as factory-made cigarettes, tinned pilchards, a sports shirt, and drinks of iced pineapple juice in town were normal for the young man, since most of his contemporaries shared the same tastes. But his India-born father characterized these as senseless, and castigated the Fiji-born as spendthrifts. Another case concerned a daughter-in-law who had been to school, and who was thought by her parents-in-law to behave without customary restraint in front of her husband and visitors to the household. Yet other cases centred around those temperamental incompatibilities which could be expected to loom large in households where members lived very close to one another.

The main protagonists in these divisions were the parents and their sons, and the sons' wives and *their* parents. Sometimes the friction was simply between a man and his sons, or between brothers. At other times the sons' wives quarrelled amongst themselves. The father might be able to prevent a division in such cases, but the old mother was more likely to have this power. As people said, the father could not go into the kitchen and talk seriously to his sons' wives, whereas the mother was able to do so and had in any case had considerable power over them from the time they came to the household after marriage. Hence, the two largest households in Delanikoro only divided after the mothers' deaths, and it was held that they would still have been joint had the old ladies still been alive. There was an opposite side to the mother's influence, of course. For she might cause a division if too dictatorial with a daughter-in-law who had influence over her husband.

In a joint household of brothers, the elder brother's wife might take the authoritarian place of the mother-in-law. Here, the elder brother could not mediate since he could not talk freely to his rebellious *chotki*, and the younger brother would take the latter's side. It was largely to avoid this situation that men commended the marriage of two brothers to a pair of sisters. There were ten such matches in the three settlements, but the force of the argument was vitiated by the fact that only two of these pairs were still living jointly; clearly, the ideal pattern of friendly co-operation between siblings could not here withstand domestic pressures.

The parents of the women who had married into the household could influence divisions. They might think that their daughter was being worked too hard in her new home; they might hope for a son-in-law in their own household who would provide extra labour; or they might merely wish to have such a man in their own settlement, to provide an ally in case of disputes. In each case, the wife's parents enticed the son-in-law away from his household with offers of work or land, or else encouraged their daughter to voice her discontent, in this way being responsible for divisions. Relations between the parents of the couple might, in any case, be beset with difficulties from the time of the marriage itself. The dowry given might not be thought adequate by the boy's parents, the behaviour of the groom's marriage party might anger the bride's parents and so forth. This was why most people preferred to have their wife's home at some distance from their own; and the behaviour of the respective parents tended to be either formal to the point of avoidance, or else to be extremely cordial when the marriage was going smoothly, and the couples were in close contact with each other.

The divisions of households show us that sons did not invariably obey their fathers, and that brothers were not always the best of friends. Nevertheless, almost one-third of people in the three settlements were in joint households, and this proportion would be greater if all those who never had the possibility of being in a joint household were excluded—for example, single sons whose fathers died during childhood. This seems to suggest that many people appreciated the four main advantages of joint organization. First, the economy which it represented was realized—'it takes only one match to light a fire for a big or small family'; secondly, the anxieties of management were placed on one pair of shoulders, and the rest of the members did not have to worry; thirdly, there was no aim for present work if, when a man grew old, his house remained empty and his money were only desired after his death; and lastly, a joint household could give its members more protection in factional fights.

It would be unwise to attribute adherence to every joint household to so positive a recognition of advantages. The data show that it was on the whole the younger men who remained jointly organized for a few years after marriage, and that divisions occurred when they had gained enough experience to manage their own affairs, and their wives had grown old enough to wish for undisputed authority in homesteads of their own. Until then, they tended to take joint family organization as a matter of course.

Members of a joint household usually worked land leased in the name of the senior member. Divisions did not involve an automatic partition of this property and other belongings, however, for joint households were not legal 'joint families', with the property 'owned' by coparceners, as are found in India. The idea of a joint family of men with legal rights to interests and, at a partition, to shares in the common family property was certainly held by the older men, and many of these tried to maintain a similar family structure by leaving property in equal shares to their sons, though this was not always possible in the case of leased land. But this was only a personal decision which might be nullified by events in the next generations— by a will disinheriting a son, for example—whereas in a joint family the coparceners, by virtue of their 'birthright', always have a legal right to a quantifiable share in ancestral or other joint family property.

Sometimes, too, the value set on joint organization was abused by men willing to expose the purely customary nature of the arrangement by recourse to British law. In one case, a substantial lease of cane land was held by a father, who farmed it with his four sons. The man's wife died, and he took another spouse. There were disputes in the family and, although his sons had worked the farm for many years, the father was able to evict them, since the lease was in his name and they had no legal rights such as they would have had, had they been coparceners.

No statistics are available to support the opinion of people in Vunioki that the joint organization of kin was decreasing. But it is significant that the problem of aged destitutes in Fiji was growing, and that many of these people had children capable of supporting them.[1] This suggests that sons no longer took their responsibilities towards their parents as seriously as traditional teaching enjoined, and points to an increase in simple households without the addition of older relatives as residents.

KINSHIP BETWEEN HOMESTEADS

The reader will recall that most people in each settlement formed a number of extended families comprising several homesteads.[2] These had evolved partly by the division of households, partly by the arrival of kin from other settlements, and partly by inter-marriage within the settlement. Did these kin feel that they were members of a group, and what were the ideal and actual obligations and rights which governed relations between them?

When people talked of their kin, they used one of several Hindi words. The most common were *parivar*, *rishtedar* and *natedar*. The first denoted a group of kin, the second and third referred either to specific people with whom there was a relationship, or could be used collectively. The definition of all these words was extremely unclear. *Parivar*, for example, was said by different people to include a man's paternal kin only, relatives on both father's and mother's sides, these together with the wife's close kin; people of the same caste, and people of the same homestead. The word had something of the meaning of the English term 'family'. A 'noble family' means a line of patrilineal descent, but the word in other contexts can include kin on the mother's or wife's side, or those living in a single household. Often only the context shows which meaning is used. In the same

---

[1] According to an interested official.
[2] See p. 34 seq.

way the other Hindi terms varied in the scope of the kin to which they referred.

The conclusion cannot be drawn from this that people saw no difference between their relations with paternal kin, maternal kin, and with affines. The implication is, however, that if there are no words to mark the difference, this difference may be slight. And a review of the various activities which brought kin together does, in fact, show that no single class of kin was actually pre-eminent in all spheres of life, though paternal kinship provided the nearest approach to this.

In economic activities, it was mainly neighbours who helped each other in the heaviest tasks of the year such as growing cane, and transplanting and weeding paddy. These people were not in any single kinship category. Some might be brothers, or sons of brothers, who had left the parent homestead and settled nearby. Others might be relatives by marriage, and yet others might not even be kinsmen. The whole conception of a family-sized cane block was designed precisely to provide work for one man and his dependants, and there was thus little emphasis on agricultural co-operation. Loans were made from both kinsmen and others, though the mother's brother and the wife's father had a greater obligation to lend if a request were made to them.

In day-to-day affairs it was the agnates (sons, brothers' sons) who felt most strongly that they should help each other. The daughter's husband and the sister's son would help if they happened to be living in the same settlement, but their aid came more because they wished to keep in the good books of their wife's father or mother's brother than from a sense of duty as kin. For agnates, this duty transcended the bounds of the settlement. An example concerned a youth who was involved in a fight at his home some twenty miles from Vunioki. As soon as news arrived there, three men went off to stand guard and prevent him being attacked again. Two of these were members of the 'parent' household, from which the youth's father had split some years before, and the third's paternal grandfather was the youth's paternal great-uncle. The immediate aid given by these agnates to a person in a quite distant settlement illustrates the ideal pattern of co-operation, in which a man should call first on his brothers and father, then on parallel cousins, and lastly on more distant relatives through his father or mother. Only if none of these respond should he approach his affines for help.

The notion that agnates should have especially strong obligations to help each other was part of the belief that paternal descent ties were stronger than maternal ones. The duty of sons to propitiate the spirits of the father and his ascendants in the annual *sraddha* rite was the most important symbol of this tie.[1] The marriage and settlement patterns were also based on the notion that the son's link to the father was closest; for marriages were held at the husband's homestead, and the couple continued to live there.

Inheritance, too, was organized around agnatic descent. Its importance had not hitherto been very great as a social factor in Fiji. For one thing, there were many cases in which the India-born father still lived, and where there had consequently never been any question of inheritance. For another, much of the land was leased and could not be divided among heirs (though informal divisions could, of course, take place on all but CSR Company blocks). Nevertheless, what inheritance there had been had followed patrilineal lines. Cane blocks were passed on to sons as tenants, or to widows to hold for their sons if these were still minors. Other property, money and goods, was divided among sons, or passed on to them all if they were living jointly. The claims of daughters to their father's property were said to have been met in their marriage expenses, particularly those of the dowry. Only if they were still unmarried might a dying man exact a pledge from his sons that they would arrange for their weddings in return for the sole inheritance. Intestate property followed the rules of British law—and only a minority of men made wills. According to this law, the wife could receive one-third of the estate, and the daughters could also claim shares. But not all people appeared to realize this, and an official said that many daughters renounced their claims in favour of their brothers.

Agnates were most strongly expected to attend each other's rites, although other kin had duties, and neighbours also came to build the marriage booth, or dig the grave and mourn with the stricken household. In *panchayats*, too, a wide circle of people took part; indeed, the neutrality of such councils was thought to be assured by the selection of people who were not kin of the disputants, and often not of the same caste or cultural group either.

Though agnates had the strongest obligations to aid each other, it was realized that such help was not automatically forthcoming, but depended on personal relations between them. An advantage of staying in a joint household was that one would always be helped by fellow members. A Southerner in Vunioki, when asked to discipline his son, said that since the latter had left the household he took no responsibility for his actions, and, it may be added, he felt no responsibility to support him. In this case, the son had left after

---

[1] In accordance with traditional Indian practice, a daughter's son could perform this propitiation if there were no sons or sons' sons; in this way the common blood passing through close female relatives was recognized, though it was considered to be minor to the agnatic line by all save a few Southerners.

quarrels; when agnates had parted amicably, they would still aid each other, an example being the four Northern brothers of Delani-koro.[1] Disputes might, however, cause men to ally themselves with maternal or affinal relatives against their paternal kin; an example would be that of Dharmraj's alliance with Chinsami against his brother Appa.

This account indicates that kin groups were often no larger than households, if by 'group' is meant a number of people bound by clearly defined rights and duties with a mechanism for penalizing people who ignored these. Kin in a settlement or a region might feel 'groupish'—especially if they were paternally related—but these feelings were subordinated to exigencies of distance, past histories of quarrels, personalities and so forth, and there was no council of kin to uphold the ideal of co-operation.

The idiom of many actions in the settlements was one of kinship. Not only did this exist amongst people who were really related to each other, and who said that they helped each other because they were in the same 'family', or were hostile because their opponents had not lived up to the required standards of behaviour for kin. It also extended to men of other castes and cultural groups by what can be called fictitious kinship, and by the existence of 'shipmate brothers'.

India-born men who had come over on the same ship under in-denture considered themselves brothers, and were supposed to be-have with the friendship and help that this betokened. A few cases of this shipmate tie still existed in 1951 in the settlements; in other in-stances Fiji-born inhabitants considered themselves classificatory brothers since their fathers, now dead, had been shipmates. These ties did not present over-riding obligations to help each other; but they strengthened any friendship already existing on other grounds.

As to fictitious kinship, a stranger coming to a settlement would at once try to find some kin tie, however distant, with the people there. This he could usually do, since Fiji is a small place, and people knew most of their caste mates in the district in which they lived. By finding this tie, the stranger acquired recognized norms of behaviour towards others in the settlement; he had to be formal with some, with others he could joke and so on. If he came from such a distance that no tie could be traced, he would have no links with anyone and would at first be treated with formality and even suspicion. Then, when the in-habitants had, as it were, 'approved' his tacit application for mem-bership of the settlement, he would start to call a few men of his own age 'brother'. From that relation would spring the remainder of his fictitious ties. Many of his 'brother's' relatives then became his own

[1] See p. 169.

relatives. These existed both inside the 'brother's' caste and in other cultural groups, some being shipmates and others fictitious kin whom the 'brother' had made of his friends in the settlement.

For example, a newcomer arrived in Vunioki without any kin ties. After a while, a neighbour made him his younger brother, to 're-place' a brother who had died. The newcomer thereupon treated the man's sister's husband with jokes, and his brother as a brother; the son of the latter was not treated as a son, as nephews should be, for he and the newcomer were of approximately the same age, and they continued to call each other by name. The fictitious ties did not there-fore necessarily extend to all relatives, but only so far as was con-venient. Again, this same newcomer—a Hindu—became a brother of a Muslim of the settlement; but the Muslim's brothers were not treated as fictitious kin, but as any other men of unclassified rela-tionship to whom behaviour of distance and a certain respect was due.

People were quite aware of the advantages of fictitious kin ties, saying that they minimized the chances of dispute. Without them behaviour would have been a matter of individual temperament and momentary change; with them the pattern was more predictable.

The account contrasts the loose nature of kin groups, and the much more precise ideas of how pairs of kin should behave towards each other. It is a situation to be expected in a society of only two, or at the most three generations depth, where kin groups based on descent could hardly have been expected to crystallize. At the same time, the contrast should not be drawn too starkly. For there *was* the idea that patrilineal descent bound people in kin groups with obligations and rights towards each other; and on the other hand, the rules of be-haviour between pairs of kin were not so binding as to be unbreak-able. Perhaps the conclusion that in Fiji Indian rural society there was no individual or group behaviour which over-rode the exigencies of the moment, emerges from these very qualifications. The society was fluid enough for its members to be free to follow their own ideas of what was expedient for them, even if this conflicted with ideal and accepted patterns of behaviour.

VIII

THE SETTLEMENTS AND THE OUTSIDE

THE previous chapters have dealt with each of the settlements as a microcosm within Fiji Indian rural society. The descriptions of important activities have brought in outside factors only in so far as they affected events within the settlement. Thus, the merchants in the town have been mentioned, not in the context of the Fiji-wide economy, but because their existence affected economic and social contacts within the settlement.

It is time to place the settlements in the framework of the outside world; to see how people regarded the Fiji Indian community at large; what these Fiji Indians thought about Fijians and Europeans and what the relations between those communities were; and lastly, what attitudes they had towards other countries and especially towards India, the country of their origin. It must be stressed that the account is based on information given by the people of the settlements alone, and is therefore not a general analysis of Fijian–Fiji Indian relations, etc. at the time of fieldwork.

THE SETTLEMENT AND THE FIJI INDIAN COMMUNITY

There were few stereotyped views about other settlements in the region. Occasionally, people remarked that the people of X were hot-heads, good farmers, etc., but the history of settlement may have been too short for the reputations of entire settlements to be made. For these, inasmuch as they reflect any reality, are concerned with an atmosphere in a settlement which can only grow over a period of time. There was nothing to compare with the reputations attributed to different villages in India.

Instead, people assessed the characteristics of individual inhabitants of nearby settlements. Some of these were kin, to whose homesteads visits were paid in the normal course of events. Others were people met in the market or the hotel of the town, often on some business such as match-making, or the purchase of livestock. Many men also frequently paid visits to other settlements as members of a marriage party. At such times, they came into contact not only

177

with those people with whom they had specific relations of friend-liness and dependence, but also with the general population of other settlements whom they did not know well. The feelings of superiority which often found expression in the behaviour of the marriage party arose partly because of the dominant position of the bridegroom whose supporters they were; but they came also from the visitors' feeling that the people of the other settlement tended to be hostile to outsiders. In spite of the fact that many settlement inhabitants seldom saw each other, when they were on 'foreign soil' they all felt a comradeship which came partly from an unsureness of outsiders.

Marriage parties were the commonest form of this kind of inter-settlement activity. The song contests before Holi were another.[1] A third occasion was presented by football matches. Vunioki took part in a league of teams from the region around the market town, and in 1951, having beaten several town teams, stood first. People said that the townsmen had been ashamed at losing to a team of farmers, and the competition was in abeyance during 1951. Delanikoro had also fielded a team, but this had been disbanded after the sons of Kanni and Virasami had come to blows in an affray which had spread to others of the team and the spectators.[2] Again, Southerners in Delani-koro helped to organize the fire-walking ceremonies near Suva; and there were at least nominal representatives from Vunioki Muslims on the board of the Urdu school in town, which was designed to serve the Muslims of the region.

In these ways, people from a settlement came into contact with the outside under some kind of organization rather than just casually. The boundaries of both kinds of contact mainly coincided with the hinterland of each town—the area within which the town was the economic and administrative centre—and this helped the inhabitants to think of this area as a separate region. A certain degree of regional patriotism was even engendered, with the market town as a social focus.

In other contexts, the entire Fiji Indian community could be seen as a single unit. One such occasion was the tournament of the Fiji Indian Football Association. This organization had been founded in 1938, and teams in 1951 came from all districts containing any num-ber of Fiji Indians. The tournament lasted two days, and collected an impressively large gathering. On no other occasion in 1951 was there a meeting of this size and representation. The competition was held in a different market town each year. When it was not too far off, many youths from Vunioki and Delanikoro went to watch. They did not make any wider contacts than they would have had at the Ramlila fair, for few of them knew people from the more distant regions. Only

[1] See p. 89. [2] See p. 128.

XV (*a*). India-born.

(*b*). Fiji-born.

XVI (*a*).   India-born.

(*b*).   Fiji-born.

the schoolmasters renewed acquaintance with colleagues who had been with them at the Training College, and had later been sent to schools throughout Fiji. But the gathering represented to them the whole of the Fiji Indian community, and in this way provided evidence of its unity. This was heightened by the fact that association football was mainly a Fiji Indian game.[1]

Other institutions, of course, had an all-Fiji coverage. Socio-religious bodies like the Sangam and the Arya Samaj were represented in each region, and trade unions spread over several districts, if not the whole of Fiji. But many of these bodies made people aware of the differences within the Fiji Indian community, rather than of its unity. Farmers continually criticized all politicians and cane union leaders for being unable to agree and present a solid front to the Europeans and Fijians, and politics were seen mainly in their significance for settlement loyalties rather than as concerned with the affairs of the whole community.[2]

People talked of other differences within the community. An example concerns the attitudes of the people of Viti Levu and Vanua Levu to each other. Those of the larger island said that their compatriots on Vanua Levu were at least a decade behind the times, since they had retained customs from India which the Viti Levu people had jettisoned under the impact of modern influences. This was contradicted by a subsequent visit to Vanua Levu, for it was found that in all important respects settlements on the two islands were similar. Vanua Levu people, on the other hand, considered the Viti Levu people to be over-interested in money and to lack sincerity. A similar feeling prevailed in Delanikoro about Suva inhabitants. These were said to be mean because they did not offer hospitality on the proper Indian scale, which was of the most generous kind. Suva people replied that their entertainment of country cousins cost them a great deal more than the latter believed; for all goods had to be bought at the store, whereas country folk could always kill a spare chicken if guests arrived.

The solidarity possessed by the Fiji Indian community did not come so much from positive *internal* features, such as Fiji-wide organizations, as from feelings of difference from other communities (i.e. from *external* relations). Fiji Indians felt part of a separate community when they participated in activities exclusive to themselves, such as voting for a Fiji Indian candidate in the Legislative Council elections, attending the Ramlila fair, etc. But few of

[1] Fijians and Europeans played rugby football; all communities played cricket, but only in the towns.

[2] The introduction of political parties, if it replaces the allegiance to individual politicians, might alter this.

these occasions were designed to cover the whole community. Co-operation was restricted to a single constituency in the case of the elections, or to the region around each town in the case of the Ramlila. There was nothing equivalent to the Fijian's Great Council of Chiefs, which represented the entire Fijian community.

ATTITUDES TOWARDS FIJIANS

In none of the three settlements was there any sustained contact of Fiji Indian and Fijian. A single Fijian cane farmer lived in Vunioki, doing his share in the Gang but making few demands on Fiji Indians for economic co-operation since he was aided by his relatives, and taking no part in the rituals or factions of the settlement. Contacts between Fiji Indians and Fijians were mainly limited to trading expeditions by the former to Fijian villages in the hills, to occasional loans of bullocks and labour to Fijian landlords who cultivated paddy, and to encounters in the store, the bus, the hotel, cinema or market in the town, when people of both communities found themselves with the same object of trade or entertainment.

The lack of contact can be explained in several ways. The initial settlement of Fiji Indians in the 'lines' and their later leasing of un-occupied land in separate homesteads ensured that they lived physically apart from Fijians. Though in some areas Fiji Indian homesteads and Fijian villages might be close to each other, the policy of early Governors kept Fiji Indians, and Europeans, from settling in Fijian villages.[1] Official policy divided Fijians and Fiji Indians administratively, for the Fijian Administration contained a hierarchy of authorities with judicial and local government powers which ran parallel to, but quite separate from, the government of non-Fijians.

Other reasons were occasioned by the wide cultural differences between Fijian and Fiji Indian. Language and religion were different; but neither need have been a serious barrier, for most Fiji Indians could speak some Fijian,[2] and religious tolerance existed in the Colony. The real gap can be described by the labels of Fijian 'communal' and Fiji Indian 'individualistic' social organization.

It will be recalled that the Fijian land-holding unit was not the single person, but rather the *matanggali*, a descent group of perhaps tens or scores of people. The responsibility for working the land and for sharing its produce fell on all members. Also, Fijian farmers lived

[1] Urban development, in which there was much closer mixing, had been a recent phenomenon.
[2] English as a common language had been a fairly recent development, and was confined to the educated minority of each community.

in villages where all co-operated in public works under the supervision of the headman. The programme for these labours (housebuilding, maintenance of paths, etc.) was discussed at the annual Provincial Councils of the Fijian Administration. Every person in the village had to work, and only under special circumstances could these communal services be commuted by a payment of cash.[1] A person's effort if it was for his benefit alone, was discouraged in traditional Fijian society. A man could not refuse requests for his belongings from relatives under the custom of *kere kere*,[2] and this diminished the attractions of commercial or salaried occupations.

In contrast to this, Fiji Indian social organization had from the first been more individualistic than in the parent society in India. In Fiji there were at first no kin whose demands for help had to be met, no local leaders of settlement or caste whose orders had to be obeyed. The CSR Company's post-indenture policy had made land into blocks so that families were territorially separate and most of the Fiji Indian economy was based on cash transactions by individuals with the town traders and the CSR Company, rather than on a more self-sufficient economy in each settlement, in which there might have been an exchange of different goods and services.

There were, in 1951, Fijians who thought that their own interests were opposed to those of their kin and village and who tried to break away from the communal system; and a Fiji Indian might well sacrifice a good deal of his time and assets for the sake of friends, or faction leaders, or kin. But this broad difference existed, and underlay the stereotype held of the Fijian by the Fiji Indians of the three settlements.

The most often cited characteristic of the Fijian was his attitude towards money and property. The Fijian economy had been until recently based on a largely subsistence production in each village, where little money was earned by the sale of crops and where, because of community endeavour, it was not needed for payment for services. Hence, the Fijian had had until recently little money sense. He would buy articles at more than market price if he suddenly desired them, and would sell at less if he needed cash. He knew that his basic maintenance was assured by the village, and so could afford to be reckless with whatever money or possessions he had. Some Fiji Indians took advantage of this, and a favourite time for one Vunioki trader to go to the hills was just before Christmas, when Fijians needed supplies for their celebrations. In 1951 he went to a village for two days, coming back with *yanggona* for which he had paid £3, and re-sold for £6, and a horse, on which he made a substantial profit.

The attitude towards money, and the Fijian tendency to share

[1] Roth 1951: 6.   [2] Derrick 1951: 126.

assets among a large group of kin, was apparently a major reason for keeping the two communities apart. Several Fiji Indians gave as a reason for the almost complete absence of inter-marriage the fact that the Fiji Indian kin of mixed matches would be fair game for the demands of their Fijian relatives, a situation which they considered to be impossible. The few matches recorded were of Fijian girls to Fiji Indian men.[1] This not only suggests an adaptation of inter-caste hypergamy to such unions—with the implication that the Fiji Indian was the superior side—but also an effort to surmount the *kere kere* obligations, inasmuch as these weighed on the mother's brother, who would here be a Fijian rather than a Fiji Indian.

Economic matters provided the focus for comments by Fiji Indians on Fijian ways; partly because it was here that the divergence between the two communities was greatest; partly because here the Fiji Indians felt themselves to be on the firmest ground, since their individualistic cash economy fitted best into the wider system of the Colony; and partly because a major pre-occupation of the Fiji Indian community had been that of raising its economic status in the Colony.

Besides this, Fiji Indians had a general view of the superiority of their own culture. They pointed to the pre-Cession custom of cannibalism among Fijians, and some Vunioki residents believed that several Fiji Indians had disappeared during the indenture period for this reason, though there was absolutely no substantiation of their stories. They contrasted Fijian culture with its lack of writing to the antiquity and range of Indian civilization. And they went on from this to suggest that the Fijian had been living in a rough, tribal society whose continuing elements militated against his entry into the 'modern' democratically-run world of which Fiji Indians were themselves a part.

This, however, was only one side of the picture. For there was at the same time the recognition that the Fijian was in some ways in a stronger position than the Fiji Indian, and that he had some customs, which were good, anachronistic though they might be.

As has been shown, Fiji Indians placed great store on unanimity within associations. They therefore regarded with approbation the common efforts of a Fijian village under its headman, and of the whole Fijian community under its chiefs. These contrasted with divisions of their own leaders which, though democratic, were sometimes held by the people of the settlements to weaken the influence of Fiji Indians in the Colony.

Besides this, there was the belief that the Fijian was favoured in

[1] Unfortunately, none of the couples were interviewed during fieldwork. They did not live near the three settlements.

some spheres. Though Fiji Indians were equally citizens of the Colony, Fijian welfare was specifically entrusted to the Government by the Deed of Cession through which Britain had taken over the country. The Government was therefore felt to be more concerned with, and more sympathetic to, the Fijian than the Fiji Indian. These were only the feelings of the people in the settlements, but it was nevertheless true that in 1951 a greater number of European officials spoke Fijian than were able to speak Hindi, and this was held to indicate a lack of interest in the community.

The major factor in this belief, however, was that Fiji Indians could not own land, apart from the relatively small amounts of available freehold. In a primarily agricultural country, the Fijians had the privilege of controlling the basic resource. Opinion had been little changed by the recent policy of reserving the lands to be needed by the Fijians, and giving a more secure tenure to non-Fijians on the remainder. As several people said, this was not the same as having freehold property; for however secure tenure now was, some tenants would be evicted if the reserves were enlarged in the future. Feelings over land tenure differed from settlement to settlement. Where land was mostly owned or leased by the CSR Company there was least insecurity. For a CSR Company lease was 'almost as good as a freehold' since tenants and their descendants were not evicted except for rank mismanagement, and leases were sufficiently easily transferred as to be a negotiable asset.[1] On the other hand, considerable emotion was generated in settlements with a large amount of Fijian leasehold land, where the question of reserves had not, in 1951, been settled. It was those people, who were most uncertain about their land, who made the only really hostile comments about Fijians. When the reserves have been finally demarcated, and people know how they stand, these feelings may subside. But the attitude of Fiji Indians towards Fijians must always be considerably influenced by the latter's ownership of the land.[2]

[1] From 1939 to 1943 the CSR Company evicted only one tenant, and refused to renew eight other leases. Thirty leases were transferred by the CSR Company because the tenant was unsatisfactory. This total of 39 changes at the CSR Company's initiative contrasts with the 963 transfers made at the tenant's request, as well as an unstated but presumably larger number of renewals (Shephard 1945: 50).

[2] Fijian ownership of all save freehold or Crown land was re-affirmed by the Burns Commission (Leg. Council Paper No. 1 of 1960, p. 18). At the same time the Commission recommended far-reaching changes for the Fijian community, including the gradual abolition of the parallel Fijian Administration in favour of a system of local government catering to all communities equally, and the fostering of economic individualism. The latter supported the view of Prof. Spate that a future Fijian rural society should consist of independent farmers (Leg. Council Paper No. 13 of 1959, p. 9). Such economic and administrative policies would have great significance for Fijian–Fiji Indian relations, of course.

The views of people in the settlements about the Fijian were thus of two kinds. On the one hand, they felt superior to the Fijian in some respects; on the other, they acknowledged good points in Fijian society and were conscious of the power held by the Fijian in the constitution of the Colony. This ambivalence indicated a lack of social pressure in Fijian–Fiji Indian relations up to the time of field-work. For it is when there is strong competition, or serious opposition between groups, that people tend only to see one side of the relation. This would be borne out by the observation that the hostile people were those who feared eviction from their leases. In sum, contacts of Fiji Indian farmers with Fijians were fairly infrequent and marginal to their activities; mixing was on at least outwardly friendly terms and several cases of good friendship existed, whatever the gulf of custom and outlook which everyone acknowledged between the two communities.

ATTITUDES TOWARDS EUROPEANS

Fiji Indian farmers had few opportunities to meet Europeans[1] resident in Fiji. Most of the latter lived in the towns, and were in such senior positions that they rarely saw people from the settlements though they might meet the Fiji Indians in their offices. Government administrative officers had few contacts with the people of the three settlements studied. There was no system of local government for them to supervise, the only official link being through an Indian Advisory Committee in each town which drew representatives from the countryside, but which was a body with little prestige or influence in the settlements.

The only close contacts were with the CSR Company's Field Officer, and with any European lawyers having clients in the settlement. The former was far from being the autocratic overseer of indenture times, and in the three settlements he played the parts of adviser and guide, rather than of ruler. He held considerable power, of course, under the terms of the Tenancy Agreement and Memorandum of Purchase of Cane. In addition, he had a key role in the transfer of tenancies, for it was largely on his recommendation that these were made. Yet he was not seen to step outside these duties to rule his tenants. For example, when a *sardar* was elected in Vunioki of whom the Field Officer did not approve, he did not push his choice into the post, as he could well have tried to do. People of the settlements remembered many of the Field Officers who had been sta-

---

[1] By 'European' is meant, of course, people coming from Australia and New Zealand, etc. as well.

tioned there. Tales were told about them—how some were bad-tempered, how others helped the farmers outside their official capacities—and, apart from the overseers of the indenture period who were often portrayed as brutal, the memories of farmers about these Field Officers were generally good. Again, European lawyers had their clients in the settlements, for some of whom they had fought several cases; and both lawyer and client often knew each other's capabilities and characteristics thoroughly.

The main feature of the relations of both the Field Officer and the lawyer with Fiji Indians was that they regarded the latter as individuals, and assumed this in their relations with them. Both knew that some Fiji Indians were honest and others were rogues, or that some were belligerent and others timid. To a large extent this was a departure from the attitudes of other Europeans, who had only a minimal contact with Fiji Indians. Such people tended to view the Fiji Indian as a stereotype, often of the lowest common denominator, whereas men having more to do with the community would always qualify their generalizations.

There is nothing unusual in the contrast just made; for it is usually the observer standing at a distance who feels able to make generalizations about the 'average man' of a community. It was the same with the Fiji Indian farmers themselves. Whilst talking in detail about Europeans whom they knew, they had only the most general ideas of the other members of that community.

Europeans in general were regarded as very rich[1] and efficient people, whose punctuality was proverbial and admired, though seldom emulated. They had the experience and techniques of the modern world at their finger-tips and were constitutionally incapable of manual labour. Several people refused, for example, to believe that Europeans were labourers in England—one man kept repeating, 'but not in the capital, it could not be so in the capital'. Fiji Europeans were regarded as aloof, particularly after a few years in the Colony, and as indifferent if not hostile to the affairs of Fiji Indians. This view was based to quite a large extent on the published opinions of some Europeans, and in particular on the advocacy of the deportation of the entire Fiji Indian community to India.[2] It also derived from informal incidents, such as one in which the author was involved. During 1951 there was a shortage of onions, an essential

---

[1] This idea might be modified if the nearest European countries were, for example, Spain and Italy, rather than Australia and New Zealand, for many ideas were based on impressions given by people returning from these highly developed countries.

[2] E.g. Mr. A. A. Ragg's proposals (outlined in *Pacific Islands Monthly*, March 1953, p. 125).

ingredient for curry. A man from the settlement went to the European-owned town store, in which he had an account of long-standing, to buy onions. He was told that they were out of stock, and reported this to the author when they met a short time later. The latter's wife had in the meantime gone to the store and had been given two pounds of onions. It is possible that supplies arrived during this short period, but the Fiji Indian regarded it as a case of discrimination in favour of fellow Europeans.

Such incidents were added to the knowledge of many farmers about the difficulties made for Fiji Indians in visiting, even temporarily, the neighbouring countries of Australia and New Zealand. This was disliked not only on the grounds of race discrimination, but also because it restricted a profitable form of labour. For in recent years a number of young men had managed to work in New Zealand for a short time. One man said that he had returned with savings of £200 after six months, and tales like this quickly made others wish to go, not all of whom found it possible to do so. The United Kingdom was known to be without landing restrictions, but its distance made a journey expensive and rare.

To some people in the settlements—in particular those on Viti Levu —it seemed as if the Fiji Indians and the Fijians were on common ground in being non-European in a world in which so much power lay with the European. This view was supported by an article to the effect that the ancestors of the Fijians had come from India.[1] Yet, the fact that the Fijians were indigenous, whereas both Fiji Indians and Europeans were recent immigrants, tended to prevent such an alignment from becoming clearer and to class all 'immigrant' communities together. An example of this emerged during a discussion of the role of Fiji Indians in World War II. The community as a whole refrained from military service on the grounds that there should be equal pay for all three communities—a fact which some men in the settlements later regretted as having created a great deal of ill-will towards Fiji Indians from the rest of the population. When a man was asked why he did not follow the example of the Fijians, who enlisted regardless of pay, he replied that Fijians were literally fighting for their land; since Fiji Indians could not own the land on which they lived, they should have been classed with other immigrant communities having loyalty towards Fiji, and should therefore have been given conditions equal to those of the Europeans.

An analysis of relations between Europeans, Fiji Indians and Fijians would be the subject of a separate book and would focus on the towns in which these relations were more complex. The rural aspects of these relations have been mentioned because they are

[1] *Pacific Review*, March 4, 1950.

relevant to the chapter's theme. For they show how Fiji Indians in the settlements saw themselves as part of a separate community. Distinct in their individualistic ways of life and their status in the Colony from the Fijians, they were also separate from the other newcomers, the Europeans, since their culture as well as their occupation, education, wealth and power in Fiji society differed so greatly from those of Europeans. From this feeling of separateness had come the wish to retain Hindi and other regional languages in place of English as a *lingua franca*, and also the consciousness of Indian civilization. This consciousness might not be backed by any great knowledge of traditional custom, but it was a criterion of difference formed by conditions in Fiji and connected to the attitudes people had towards India.

ATTITUDES TOWARDS INDIA: CONTACTS THROUGH THE INDIA-BORN

Two more or less contradictory feelings existed about India. These to some extent corresponded to the ties with India through people who had lived in both India and Fiji, and those which were the result of cultural ties with India—notably through the cinema and radio.

Since between 5 and 10 per cent of the settlements' populations were India-born in 1951, the younger men had good opportunities to hear about the regions from which their forebears had come. Yet there was almost no such talk. It may be that many of the Fiji-born had already heard these tales *ad nauseam*. But people who were willing audiences for other oft-repeated tales showed no interest when the talk centred on the birth-places of the India-born. Any comparisons made between customs seen in India and their Fiji variants met with no response, or the reply that the people were Fiji Indians and did not care what was done in India.

This reaction was, it seems, partly a genuine lack of interest in India, born of a knowledge of similar cultural features in Fiji, for people were very interested to hear about life in other countries. In part, however, the general attitude of the Fiji-born to the India-born affected the former's interest in India.

One element in this was a different approach to money. Several of the disputes within homesteads, and the splitting of the joint households there, started with criticism by the India-born father of the Fiji-born son on this score. The India-born were, on the whole, more frugal and thrifty. They had spent their lives in difficult conditions in India—for many had been recruited because of poverty—and then in working and slowly saving to better their status in Fiji. Their sons had known none of these struggles, and their way of life presupposed a pattern of expense on what the India-born considered luxuries. The Fiji-born picture of the India-born as a person hostile, or at least indifferent, to the new ways produced a lack of interest in the old ways, that is, in his experiences of India.

Another element had to do with the position of the men who had come to India since indenture. Most of these had gone into urban occupations, notably retail trading.[1] As middle-men and creditors, they were disliked by farmers for their powerful economic position. Moreover, they were felt to constitute a separate, almost 'alien' element in the Fiji Indian community. Not only did they come from regions of India from which few indentured immigrants had been recruited, and so formed a distinct cultural group, but they had retained close ties with India and in some cases appeared to regard Fiji merely as a place to make their fortune. The Fiji-born felt that, on the one hand, these people did not share their values and that, on the other hand, they prejudiced the degree to which the Fiji-born were regarded by other communities as having sole allegiance to Fiji. Some people in the settlements went so far as to advocate the re-patriation of all post-indenture migrants, and others supported the prohibition of any further immigration.

Thirdly, the visits of important Indians were not the subject of unbounded enthusiasm among Fiji-born, since the visitors often appeared critical of the community. Thus, a delegation of Indian parliamentarians paused briefly in Fiji in 1951 and held several meet-ings in which they exhorted the Fiji Indians to unite so as to better their economic and social position in the Colony. Though Vunioki men had themselves often voiced these views, their reaction was that outsiders should not have told Fiji Indians how to manage their affairs after such a short stay.

The closest contact with India through the India-born occurred when the people paid visits to the mother country. Under the terms of their indenture, the Fiji Government paid for the repatriation of all those who had been recruited, as well as their children.[2] There were in 1951 still people in Fiji who were eligible for this free return to India. Several of these said that they planned to return in 'the next boat'. Some had relatives to whom they were sending money, urged on by a succession of family needs detailed in each letter. Others had lost contact with their families, but said they still hoped to return to see what had become of their kin. In many cases these were only empty wishes, for the old people were alleged to have been talking of the 'next boat' for years. In other cases, pressure from the family in

[1] See p. 46.
[2] The option on repatriation for those recruited after 1906, which had been ex-tended on two-year terms, was finally cancelled in 1958.

Fiji restrained the India-born head from returning. In Vunioki, for example, an old Southerner badly wanted to return to his home in Nellore District of Andhra Pradesh. But his educated son tried to dissuade him with all the arguments he possessed. He told his father that things had changed and the customs he had known had died out, that he would no longer be well received but merely milked of all the money he had,[1] and that he might never be able to return to see his family in Fiji. When the father appeared adamant, the son 'lost' the letters which arrived from India, so that the old man missed the boat which came in 1951 and started to lose heart for the journey. In such ways did the Fiji-born show their attitudes towards India.

Nevertheless, some old people returned to India, and numbers of them came back to Fiji after a visit there. Some were passengers on the *Sirsa*, which docked at Suva in March 1951. The appearance of those who crowded the rails and later disembarked indicated that formerly indentured people did not number more than thirty or forty of the three hundred passengers. The remainder were kin of post-indenture immigrants, mostly Punjabi and Gujarati women and children.[2] There was quite a large crowd to meet them, and about a dozen Delanikoro men had come, since a Northern resident of the settlement was arriving on the boat after having spent two years in India. The day had been taken as a holiday, and all had reached Suva in time for drinks at the hotel. As the passengers started to disembark an old man shouted: 'If there are any old men wanting to go to India, I say do not go.' A passerby added: 'That is why all these indentured men (*girimitvale*) are returning.' The Delanikoro resident disembarked and was greeted quite off-handedly by his son; in fact, all the meetings took place with little outward emotion. Neither did the traveller's return to his homestead call for any more recognition than that accorded to any close kinsman coming from a distant part of Fiji.

Early next morning, the old man unpacked his luggage. His son, two other India-born men, and the wives of two India-born residents were present. There were no Fiji-born outsiders. The men were smoking Indian cigarettes and reading an Indian newspaper. Meanwhile, the father had unpacked a sweater as a present for his son, and school satchels for the two grandsons. The only other apparent personal purchase was a two-volume edition of the *Ramayana*.

There was nothing particularly Indian about these presents, for they could all have been bought in Suva. The remainder of the

---

[1] Returning immigrants had, in fact, often been treated in this way. In 1929, it was said, there were no fewer than 650 destitutes in Calcutta who wished to return to Fiji (Fiji Leg. Council Paper 33 of 1930, quoted in Gillion 1958).

[2] No case existed in the settlements of a Fiji-born person visiting India.

traveller's purchases, on the other hand, were more distinctive. These he intended to sell in Fiji. There were *papier-mâché* masks of Ravan and Hanuman for use in the Ramlila, some tinsel hangings, sandalwood beads, brass shoe buckles, and copies of a booklet which he had written about his travels in India and hoped to sell at fairs to other India-born people.

Later, there was talk about the journey. Most of the questions concerned the accommodation on the *Sirsa*, rather than conditions in India. The traveller was asked about the food, the time taken for the journey, the provisions made for sickness and so forth. His travels in India were dismissed with a short discussion of the food shortage there, the general prevalence of poverty and beggars, and one or two stories of how he had foiled pickpockets on the crowded trains. No public notice was taken of the man's return, although it was the first for some time in the settlement. This, again, is in contrast to the welcome given at the Youth Association's hall to young men returning after a few months in New Zealand; and the talk of life there was a constant topic at Delanikoro gatherings.

ATTITUDES TOWARDS INDIA:
CONTACTS THROUGH MASS MEDIA

The picture suggests that India was not a centre of Fiji Indian interest, in so far as it was represented by people who had actually been in India. But there was another side to the relations between Fiji and India, shown in the attention given to the mass media emanating from the latter country, where, in contrast, the influence of India was great.

Each of the settlements was near a town cinema which exhibited Indian films almost exclusively. These films—in Hindi—were divided by people into classes; religious (*dharmik*), historical and social. The former portrayed stories from the Hindu epics, the second the lives of great figures of Indian history. Social films were concerned with contemporary India, and followed a familiar 'boy meets girl—boy loses girl—boy finds girl' pattern, or the Indian variant in which a boy was to be forced by his parents to marry against his wish but managed to triumph in the end. In general, the older men preferred the former types of film, whereas the younger men went to all types. Women went only to see religious films.

The intensity of film-going varied with each settlement. Few people went from Namboulima, since the town was a long way off and a special trip would have been expensive. Delanikoro was much nearer, but the active younger men appeared to be more concerned with the Ramayana Society, and both they and others went only when they found themselves in town. Vunioki provided the largest body of inveterate film-goers, since the storekeeper ran a special evening bus twice weekly to town, and there were usually at least half a dozen Vunioki men on it.

The main influence of the 'social' films was that of the relative equality of the sexes. In them, women spoke freely to the men they met, with modesty but with none of the traditional avoidance; couples fell in love and, after many trials, managed to get married. It is true that the occasional women who behaved in an exaggeratedly Western way, wearing slacks and drinking whisky with the men, came to a bad end; but the amount of freedom allowed to women contrasted with a society in which marriage was arranged, mostly without the prospective spouses having spoken to each other. Coupled with this freedom were the songs which spoke of falling in love and of couples who flirted as they did so.

These songs were often roundly condemned in the Fiji Indian press as being corrupters of youth; but they were on everybody's lips and, together with the films from which they came, built up a picture of an 'advanced' society in India. This was helped by the press and radio. All three settlements possessed at least one homestead with a radio; and this was tuned exclusively to Indian and Pakistani stations, except for the extremely short Hindi broadcasts of the Fiji station.[1] People therefore heard not only the news—and thereby became well-informed, and partisan, over such Indo-Pakistani issues as Kashmir —but also heard reports on the economic and social developments in these countries. Though listening was restricted to the owner and sometimes his closer neighbours, such news spread in casual conversation. In the press, too, news items provided by the Indian Commissioner's office[2] in Suva tended, naturally enough, to stress India's achievements rather than her difficulties.

The image of India gained from these three sources, was of a country in which caste and the 'subjection' of women had been abolished, large plans for economic and social development put into practice, and world prestige regained after independence. It was a country of enormous new dams and steel mills, of increased agricultural production, and of liberating forces in the field of social relations. Besides this, India was the land of Rama and of Arjun, the cradle of a way of life to which most Indians adhered at least in sentiment. Religious films had the largest audiences of all, and a film like *Ram Rajya* (Rama's Rule) drew crowds of both sexes and all ages for weeks at a time. The picture of modern India excited the

---

[1] The time given to Indian programmes has been considerably lengthened since 1951.

[2] The first Commissioner for the Government of India in Fiji arrived in 1947.

interest of the educated people of the settlements; the picture of the past golden age renewed people's faith in their history and religion. In neither case was there any place for the knowledge of India provided by the old India-born or the new Gujarati immigrants with their apparently conservative ways.

Influences of social change came partly from India, though often Western in origin, and partly from European ways of life in Fiji. For example, the changing relations between the sexes amongst the younger Fiji-born (e.g. talking to a fiancé) could be connected not only to the influence of Indian films, but also to the knowledge of European customs in Fiji as well as to Western books and films. For it must not be forgotten that, though the average Fiji Indian farmer might have little to do with other Europeans, he always had a Field Officer living fairly close to him, about whose domestic life he was often well-informed. A study of urban conditions in particular could assess which form of social change was the most readily assimilated by the community—that coming from Europeans or that from the parent country, though originating in the West.

Not all the influences emanating from India were Western. There were also returns to traditional customs. The *sari*, for example, had been adopted as the dress of Fiji Indian women, though it had been in danger of being supplanted by the dress some twenty-five years previously. But the adoption of Indian ways was discriminate, and only occurred when it was in people's interests to do so. To wear a *sari* harmed nobody; but it would have been impossible for Fiji Indians to have re-adopted the caste system as it was practised in India. Western ways, it seems, were more indiscriminately adopted, without such a clear idea of their implications for the community.

The links with India made Fiji Indians feel a separate community. Just as the Europeans looked to England or Australia, so did the Fiji Indians think of India as providing the basis for their culture. Devotional songs praised the heroes of the past and the gods of the Hindu pantheon; and such a view of India included contemporary events too. This song, for instance, was sung at the Holi festival:

> Now, being free, we will say 'Jai Hind' [1]
> And will always remember Gandhi's name.
> Many thousands of patriots have sacrificed themselves in saving India;
> Today we shall gather to read their history.
> Gandhi, Tilak, our leaders, they died
> And will always remain in our memory.

[1] 'Jai Hind' may mean 'victory to India' or 'long live India' and can be used as a form of greeting.

All those who died to awaken India
Will always live in history.
Now, also the Indian Commissioner has arrived to keep watch;
He, too, will work for Fiji.[1]
The glory of India is contained in all hearts,
And now to all will Ram Lakhan say 'Jai Hind'.

The song is taken from a book entitled *Sudharas Phag*, published in Fiji in 1950, and composed by men whose names appear in traditional fashion in the last line of their song. A majority of songs are about Mahatma Gandhi and all are about events in India. There are, it is true, occasional references to Fiji, but on the whole the verse symbolizes a continuing cultural dependence on the parent country.

The degree of influence of India could, to some extent, be seen as a reflex of any insecurity felt by the Fiji Indian community. As members of the newest and politically least powerful of the three major communities in the Colony, Fiji Indians needed a feeling of reassurance and background, the knowledge that they originally came from a country which was becoming a great and influential nation, and so had no need to apologize for their ways of life or their aspirations. This the Government of India gave them. For, while telling overseas Indians that they should identify themselves with their countries of birth, it stressed the pride that they should have in their ancient culture, and had championed their interests where there had been discrimination against Indians as such, on the grounds that issues of this sort transcended national boundaries.

For all that, it was a Gujarati India-born in one of the settlements who advocated closer ties with India, to prevent Fiji Indians being deported under some future policy and to give them a place to settle if ever this policy eventuated. His Fiji-born hearers could not believe that they would ever have to leave Fiji. They felt themselves to be *Fiji* Indians, proud of their heritage, but equally proud of their place in the new society described in this book.

---

[1] In fact, the Indian Commissioner had a status similar to that of a consular representative, and had under his charge only those Indians not permanently residing in Fiji. But he was regarded by many Fiji Indians as a representative-at-large in Fiji.

IX

TWENTY YEARS AFTER

A person returning to a place after a long absence is struck primarily by the visible signs of change that meet his eye. It is only after he has stayed for some time that he can assess what other, less tangible changes have occurred, and the degree to which these are manifested in, or produced by, the visible changes.

Short as they were, my visits to Vunioki and Delanikoro produced impressions of change and continuity which were very much based on what I could see; and this, in turn, led me to see change in the settlements as related to economic and technological change, since this had produced the manifestations which were most apparent. In my account, then, I shall start with these economic factors, and will then go on, so far as I dare, to indicate other social changes which are at least partly linked to these factors.

In 1951 both Vunioki and Delanikoro[1] were overwhelmingly agricultural settlements, dependent to a very considerable degree on a single crop, sugar cane. It might be expected that changes in the place of that crop in the settlements' economies would have far-reaching consequences. Indeed, one could argue that the decision to close the sugar mill and thereby cease the production of cane in the Rewa valley was the most important single change to take place in Delanikoro during the twenty years, and that the extension of the cane-growing area in Vunioki—made possible by technological improvement and by the increased world demand for Fiji's sugar—was the most widely ramifying change in that settlement.[2] I shall therefore start my account of each settlement with the changing place of cane-growing in the settlement's economy and then proceed to consider the broader implications of this, and link it with a theme of the previous chapters of this book—the degree to which the settlements are social entities, and the kind of interaction taking place within them.

[1] I was not able to stay long enough in Namboulima to permit me to gain impressions firm enough to write about. I therefore limit my comments to Vunioki and Delanikoro.

[2] This is to except the independence of Fiji which occurred in October 1970 at the very end of this period and which was clearly the most important change for the future.

XVII (*a*). Vunioki 1971: cane fields on high ground

(*b*). Vunioki 1971: new style cane harvest (see Plate VI)

XVIII (*a*). Vunioki 1971: old and new house styles

(*b*). Vunioki 1971: fuel pump and customer

XIX (*a*). Vunioki 1971: one of the settlement's cars

(*b*). Delanikoro's market town 1971: traffic and shops

XX (*a*). Twenty years on (see Plate XVI (*b*))

(*b*). Delanikoro 1971: birthday party (note cake)

What I have just said about the central part played by cane cultivation certainly had relevance for the three main impressions I had of Vunioki settlement on the day I arrived there in late January 1971.

The first impression, gained as soon as I entered the settlement, was that there had been a great development of communications. The main road through the settlement had been widened and a proper bridge built over the river; and from the main road three or four all-weather roads branched off where previously there had been only dirt tracks or even footpaths. The roads were well used too, as private cars, taxis and especially lorries piled high with cane, passed on their way to and from the market town. Sitting in one of the stores at the settlement's centre (which now boasted a pump for tractor fuel) I was constantly aware of vehicles, some of which stopped to let passengers out or to enable their drivers to shop.

The second impression came when I stood on the site of the house where I had lived, and later walked over to see friends in several nearby homesteads; it was that the whole settlement appeared curiously overgrown, and that the views were far more constricted than I had remembered them. I put this down at the time to the growth into mature trees of what had been saplings in 1951.

My third impression came after I had gone to the Field Officer's office, from where I could get a good view over the countryside. I could now see the homesteads, and realized that these were in the same places and that few new ones had been built; from enquiries, it appeared that most of the families I had known still lived in them.

These impressions, I later realized, all had to do with the extension of cane cultivation. The new roads had been built in response to the extension of cane cultivation to the hillsides; the views were restricted by walls of waving cane, where previously there had been open land or fields of paddy or vegetables, and there had been little mobility or emigration from the settlement because cane cultivation was attractive enough for farmers to maintain their holdings. Let me expand on this position as it revealed itself.

THE ECONOMIC SITUATION

Over the past twenty years there had been a tremendous expansion of cane cultivation both in Vunioki and in the surrounding settlements. In 1951 only thirty-five of the fifty-seven farms were producing cane (see p. 42); but in 1971, I was told, every one of the Vunioki farms was a cane farm, and in most cases there was a virtual exclusion of every other crop, whereas in 1951 some farmers had cultivated pulses and paddy. Only three farmers were now said to be growing vegetables for sale, for instance. Moreover, cane had been extended into other settlements in the valley and into the hills for several miles, on land which in 1951 was used for mixed farming or was simply 'jungle'. The Vunioki cane sector, of which the settlement formed part, was now one of the largest in Fiji, with 573 farmers producing over 100,000 tons of cane each year.

The increase in cane acreage was due to several factors. First was the closing in 1959 of the Nausori sugar mill. This meant that the whole Rewa region in south-eastern Viti Levu stopped producing cane, and its proportion of Fiji's national basic allotment was shared out among the western districts of Viti Levu and the Vanua Levu region. But this opportunity could not have been fully utilized had not the second factor been present, namely the development by the SPSM[1] of new varieties of cane which would grow on land hitherto unsuited to the crop. Thus the hillsides of Vunioki and the surrounding countryside came to be planted with cane, and the size of the crop greatly increased. This expansion also coincided with the collapse of the International Sugar Agreement and a consequent need for Fiji to keep production up so that she would have a reasonable national quota when a new Agreement was negotiated. The increase in the world demand for sugar also worked towards a raising of production in the 1960s, so that Fiji's national basic allotment under the terms of the 1970 cane contract was 340,000 tons of sugar (and hence some 2,516,000 tons of the cane required to make this amount). This can be contrasted with the production in 1951 of about one-third of this amount.

This expansion would not have been realized, however, without a demand from farmers for increased cane acreage. This demand stemmed from two factors. First, it became easier to grow cane. The new strains of cane could produce many more rattoon crops of acceptable quality, and the cost and time spent in planting and nurturing new cane was thereby very much reduced. Moreover, the application of weedkiller and fertilizers almost completely took the place (for at least some farmers) of the long and costly weedings and cultivations that had formerly been necessary.[2] Some farms that I visited had produced up to fifteen rattoon crops and were still

[1] South Pacific Sugar Mills Ltd. (SPSM) was incorporated in Fiji in 1961 as a wholly-owned subsidiary of the CSR Company to take over its milling assets in Fiji. The SPSM went public in 1964 but only 2·2 per cent of the shares were owned by the public in 1971. It is now in the course of being taken over by the Government of Fiji. The SPSM's Agricultural Experiment Station has been responsible not only for the development of new strains of cane fitted to Fiji conditions, but also for supervising the control programme whereby the disease in cane has been greatly reduced.

[2] Further, much cultivation was now done by tractor. There were eleven tractors in Vunioki in 1971, which could be hired by the day.

yielding around 25–30 tons per acre, although other farmers told me that an optimum yield would be gained from more frequent plantings —but even these should be only every five to six years, i.e. half as frequently as in 1951[1]. Hence, cultivating cane became an attractive proposition. As one observer told me, 'When the new varieties of cane and mechanization came in, the cane farmers had a choice: they could go on getting the same income from less exertion, or they could raise their incomes by working as hard as before and taking advantage of higher yields.' Whichever they chose, there was improvement.

The second factor was an increase in the price paid for cane. I need not go into details of the price fluctuations and negotiations of the past decades, but need only say that very high prices in the early 1960s (during which there was an open world market in sugar) attracted farmers to cane production, and that the award by Lord Denning in 1970 of a price of $F7·75 per ton of cane or 65 per cent of the proceeds of sale (whichever be the higher) meant a rise in the price then being received, and hence stimulated a demand for even greater cane production.[2]

Vunioki had, then, been turned into a settlement with a single crop. It was this change, and the way it had altered the landscape, that impressed me on my arrival. But cane-growing was only one, though the most important, feature of Vunioki's economy. What about the other aspects, and had these changed?

In 1951 I had classed fifteen of the ninety-five adult men as having non-agricultural occupations (see p. 45). Not all of these had permanent work (i.e. some worked at the mill only during the crushing season)

[1] The latitude allowed to the farmer for such decisions about his cultivation is in contrast to the close control exerted by the CSR Company over its tenants in 1951 (see p. 39). In 1971 a farmer had only the obligation to cultivate enough cane to fulfil his farm's harvest quota and co-operate in removing diseased cane from his fields. However, the farm extension services of the SPSM were accepted voluntarily because the farmers saw that these increased their efficiency. The SPSM's extension officers were now highly mobile (the picture of the CSR Company's officer on his horse had been replaced by that of men in Land Rovers or pick-ups); and the fact that almost all were local people may also have helped to extend the influence of the services that the company was able to provide.

[2] Each farmer is given a basic allotment for his farm for the period of his contract with the SPSM (in this case from 1970–80). Each year, the harvest quota for that farm is calculated with reference to the national harvest quota. It may be above or below the farm's basic allotment. In turn, at the time of harvest, the amount harvested may be above or below the farm harvest quota—below due to drought, etc. and above due to miscalculation or, as is frequently the case nowadays, due to deliberate over-planting, in the hope that the extra tonnage of cane will be taken by the SPSM, as is allowed for under the sugar cane contract. Although it has sometimes seemed likely that maxima would have to be imposed, in fact, up until 1971, this has never been necessary: hence, the demand from farmers for increased production has so far been met. The wisdom of this kind of expansion is discussed by Fisk (1970: 23–4).

but their main focus was non-agricultural. In 1971 I found thirty-four men and seven women who could be thus classified.[1] In terms of the number of men of working age in the settlement, this gave an increase from 16 per cent in 1951 to 17 per cent in 1971[2] of men with non-agricultural occupations, not a significant change. There had been a rather greater change within this category, between men with work in Vunioki (e.g. the storekeepers and employees of the SPSM) and those who went out of the settlement to work, as regular commuters to the market town. In 1951 only four of the fifteen had been commuters, but this had risen in 1971 to eleven out of the thirty-four (i.e. from one-quarter to one-third) and there were seven other men who worked as drivers on lorries which took them out of Vunioki for most of the time.[3] Of the women, five had work as teachers or typists outside Vunioki and two taught at the settlement school.

It might be thought that a doubling of the male work force, without a corresponding increase in opportunities to find work elsewhere, would have resulted in considerable unemployment. It was hard to measure the extent of unemployment, which was frequently rather under-employment. But two things had helped to prevent this from being more explicit. First, the extension of cane to almost the whole settlement now supported a higher density of population, since a smaller area of cane was said to produce at least as much income as had the larger mixed and non-cane farms. Second, the crushing season was longer than it had been in 1951 and hence there was more work for younger men who were cutters in the cane harvesting gangs. The 1970 harvest only finished at the start of February

[1] I was not able to take a proper census of occupation, household composition, population size, etc., but while visiting people I was naturally told of family changes and so forth. Since I visited a considerable proportion of homesteads and saw most of the men whom I had known in 1951, their comments about their own and their neighbours' homesteads, work, etc., enabled me to compile the following informal figures, which probably approximate reality reasonably closely, though their tentative nature should be borne in mind.

[2] I classified 195 of the 446 males as being 'adult' in 1971, the criterion being whether they were said to be old enough to do full farm work. The doubling of this adult population since 1951, by contrast to a total population increase of 67 per cent (see p. 201) probably means that my informal census included younger males in 1971 than in 1951, or that I under-enumerated the total population, rather than that there was an ageing population in Vunioki to a degree which did not exist at the national level (see *Report on the Census* 1966, p. 20).

[3] One new element that urban occupation had brought was the existence of a few part-time farmers, men who cultivate mainly by employing labourers with some supervision at weekends and peak periods. This had been made easier, of course, by the less exigent demands of cane cultivation. There were few such men in 1971, but the number could rise if more urban employment were available to cane-growers.

1971 and there were now only some four months between harvests—hence, cane-cutting was becoming a fairly continuous occupation. Nevertheless, there was under-employment and some unemployment among the youths in Vunioki.[1] The further development of opportunities in the market town would find a ready supply of labour—and, as the educational standard rose, of potentially skilled labour—from settlements like Vunioki. But the optimal deployment of human resources is a national matter which can only be discussed at a higher level than that of this analysis.[2]

The presence of lady teachers in the Vunioki work force was the continuation of a trend noted in 1951, since teaching had for long been a profession for women. But the unmarried typists who now commuted to the town were a new phenomenon; and I was much impressed by the enterprise shown by a number of girls with whom I talked, who had had a secondary education and who were keen to do some sort of work before getting married and settling down. Not all the fathers I talked to approved of these ambitions, but changes in the economic and social position of country women seemed to be slowly evolving. The implications of this for family relations and for the upbringing of children need to be studied.

It is difficult to speak of the place of stores in the Vunioki economy without comparative figures on turnover and profit, which I was not able to gather. There were three stores in 1971; one run by the same Gujarati as had been there in 1951, and two by newcomers to the settlement in 1960 and 1966. The newest storekeeper was a young man, without much capital and with restricted stock. It would not be surprising if he were to withdraw from competition with the better established stores.

These rival storekeepers said that business was better than in former times; one told me that he did more business in a week now than he had done in a month in the 1950s. I was impressed by the range of items that they stocked, far more extensive than in 1951; and in each of the shops there was a deep freezer from which people bought frozen chicken and lamb for clearly run-of-the-mill rather than special meals. This increased business may have resulted from the larger number of people in the settlement, as well as from the greater ease of internal communication now that all-weather roads connected the central part of Vunioki (where the shops stood) with

---

[1] One group of farmers reckoned that an acre of cane required about one week's labour per year (three applications of fertilizer, one of weedkiller and one cleaning by hand). For the average-sized block, this would mean an annual cultivation of about three months. The rest of the time could be spent either in harvesting, or on other work—or without work.

[2] In fact, industries are being started in the towns of western Viti Levu.

the outlying areas, whereas in 1951 it was easier for some people to go to the market town than to come to the Vunioki shop, at least in the rainy season. Moreover, some men now had tractors or private cars to bring them to the stores, as part of a prosperity stemming from better cane prices and the extension of cane cultivation in the settlement.

Though statistics were not available, storekeeping appeared to be more secure, and the mortality of stores less than in 1951. The long-term social significance of the stores, which will increase with the growing importance of the fuel pump, and the opening of an off-licence liquor store (for which an application had been made shortly before my visit in 1971) is that they may provide the drawing power to become a social centre in the settlement.

A possible reason why stores were on a firmer footing than before was that they were said not to grant credit or give loans (other than small credit for a few days). The general picture of credit and debt that I was given was one in which most farmers had debts, through crop liens, mortgages of land where freehold, and bills of sale on houses. I was not able to make a detailed survey of the extent of indebtedness, but was told that a number of farmers who could clear their debts after a good harvest if they wished to, retained the custom of working on credit. One new technique was that those who had contracted over-large debts now tried to declare themselves bankrupt. Five men had been accepted as bankrupts by the courts in the two decades. The advantage was said to be that repayment was made without interest, and that the charge made by the Receiver for his costs was less than the interest they would have had to pay under normal terms of repayment. I was told that nowadays people were not ashamed of going bankrupt, since they saw that urban businessmen had done so; others said that bankruptcy still affected a man's prestige in the settlement, though less than before.

In general, the impression I received in Vunioki was of the existence of new amenities. In 1951 one man had owned a bus and another a lorry: in 1971 there were eleven cars, eleven tractors, twelve lorries and four motorcycles; three men had electricity, and seven had pumps for drinking water. The standard of housing had also risen. People said they preferred a house built of corrugated iron or wood to one built of thatch. In 1951 most houses were thatch (see p. 15); but in 1971, of fifty-seven homesteads only two had thatched houses alone, a further thirty had thatch together with iron or wood, and twenty-five had houses of iron or wood only.

Of course, not all homesteads showed changes: some people were clearly poor and were living in much the same style as in 1951. The changes in other people's visible standard of living may have been due to redistribution of income—less being spent on weddings, for example—rather than by an increase in it. Although the national average real income had probably increased since 1951 (Fisk 1970: 12), it was obvious that this had not affected everybody equally and farmers might not have shared to the same extent in this increase as had men in tertiary occupations. Finally, 1971 was the first year of increased cane payments, and everyone was feeling pleased about them and optimistic about future prosperity through cane, even if some were worried about the increasing pressure of their families on the land available to them, and the chances of their children finding work in the towns. These factors make it impossible to generalize with confidence on the standard of living—yet, my impression and the comments made to me suggest that it had increased in a significant number of cases.

KINSHIP AND CULTURAL GROUPINGS

My informal census shows that Vunioki in 1971 contained 858 people (446 males and 412 females), an increase of 67 per cent over the 1951 population. They lived in seventy-five homesteads, an increase of 19 per cent over the previous figure. Thus homesteads now contained considerably more people. There seemed to have been little mobility; some half a dozen people whose land was taken up by newcomers had left Vunioki during the twenty years. For the rest, the land (or lease of it) had passed at death to sons or other relatives, again not more than half a dozen of whom had come from outside. The geographical distribution of homesteads was not very different from what it had been in 1951, as my first impression suggested. What population movement had occurred had changed the proportions of cultural groups in the settlement. Figures for 1971 are shown in Table 1 (with the 1951 figures in brackets).

TABLE 1

Cultural group	Population*		Homesteads
	Number	Per cent	Number
Northern Hindu	552	64·3 (53·7)	46 (33)
Southern Hindu	106	12·4 (21·2)	9 (13)
Muslim	200	23·3 (25·1)	20 (17)

* 1 person was a Gujarati. I have not included the single Fijian homestead.

Most of the decrease in Southern homesteads was caused by the emigration to other land (which it owned) of part of a large extended family, which in 1951 had occupied two homesteads with sixteen people, and by the emigration and transfer of land to Northerners of two further homesteads with twenty-one people, after the deaths of the homestead heads. The Southern group suffered a further decline in influence through grave and lasting illnesses of two other important householders. The main population increase had been among Northerners who had provided almost all the immigrants. The Muslim group had held its own. The major areas of concentration of each group were those of 1951.

The sociological significance of this changing proportion of cultural groups needs research. In 1951, it will be recalled, disputes within the Southern group were an integral part of the settlement's factional alignments. This had presumably become much less important. It would be interesting to assess in how far cultural differences *are* important in the settlement's activities nowadays. Cultural groups were in 1971 still largely endogamous and hence separate; but I cannot say how important they were.

The fact that there had been a larger increase in population than in the number of homesteads is qualified by an analysis of the different types of homestead. It was mainly the growth of the housegroup (from an average of fourteen to one of nineteen persons) that had produced this change. The reader will remember that I defined the housegroup (see p. 32) as 'a group living in a single homestead but with several separate kitchens and budgets'. The groups having these separate facilities are households; these are either simple or joint households, i.e. with one or several adult males having a single budget. The focus on a common budget rather than on kin ties was because in 1951 there were still households of unrelated shipmates. But already in 1951, simple households were mainly composed of elementary (nuclear) families and joint households mainly contained agnates and, less frequently, male affines.

In 1971 I did not hear of any household with adult non-kin. But a new feature had emerged. In 1951 there had been few cases of households with adult but unmarried sons; for boys were married around the age of seventeen to eighteen. In 1971 the later age of marriage meant that a considerable number of households contained young unmarried men in their late teens or early twenties, who were either earning wages or making an equal contribution to the farm and hence to the budget. At the same time, there were still those households with a father and his married sons, or with married brothers. The difference between these two kinds of household is, of course, the presence of daughters-in-law and of grandchildren. I think that they should be distinguished. I therefore classify the households with unmarried adult sons as 'joint' (with inverted commas) since they are not fully joint, yet have relationships different from those in which sons are young. A comparison of the composition of homesteads in 1951 and 1971 is shown in Table 2.

TABLE 2

Type	No. of homesteads		Population	
	1951	1971	1951	1971
Simple household*	40	26	234	185
'Joint' household (with adult unmarried son(s))	—	15	—	123
Joint household	15	17	169	227
Housegroup	8	17	111	323
Total	63	75	514	858

* This category includes households of incomplete families (e.g. a widow and her children) as well as the accretions to nuclear families (e.g. an old mother, a married sister and her children).

Both joint households and housegroups show the developmental cycle of the family. Most joint households in a single homestead are composed of married sons who stay with their father, or married brothers who stay together after their father dies. Later, the sons set up their own kitchens; where they do this in the same homestead, a housegroup is formed. This can be quite complex, such as when there are three sons in simple households, and their father in a joint household with his other sons. Later still, the sons will shift to new homesteads, often fairly close to the original one, but on the plot of land which will have been divided.

The main point is that the composition of homesteads tended to be more complex in 1971. This must have had an effect on the content of kinship relations and the degree to which they affected people's choices of action. Men who used to live in autonomous homesteads now tended more often to be near each other in housegroups or to live jointly. Does this mean that kin ties were more important and their co-operative component more stressed? Or does it mean, on the contrary, that kin ties were less important than before, and that other more instrumental means of underpinning joint settlement in homesteads were found? A full-length study would need to consider such questions.

ASSOCIATIONS

I was interested to learn about associations—in particular whether the position of the cane harvesting Gang had changed (and, if so, in what ways); for the activity of the Gang had been the most important context of co-operation in Vunioki in 1951.

Two possibilities stemmed from the increase in cane production. First, it was possible that all farmers were cane-growers belonging to a single Gang. If this were the case, I speculated, the settlement would have a much stronger organization, since to be a member of Vunioki would also involve playing a part in the Gang; all Vunioki growers would then elect a *sardar* who would be in some ways analogous to a village headman. The other possibility was that most or all farmers were growing cane but that they belonged to several Gangs. In such a case, I thought, there would be less 'unity' in the settlement than before—for there would be no single Gang for farmers to rival each other in; and one would have to look to other associations for common settlement activity.

In fact, the second development had occurred. Instead of a single expanding Gang, various Gangs and sub-Gangs had arisen. This, coupled with a change in the composition of the Gangs, had brought about a trend towards the individualization of cane-harvesting.

In 1951 Vunioki had had a single cane-harvesting Gang of thirty-seven members. In 1971, by contrast, this Gang, harvesting with permanent and portable line, had shrunk to seventeen members. The other fifty-nine growers (there was double the 1951 number of growers) belonged to eight other Gangs, all of which also had members outside Vunioki settlement, though within the SPSM's Vunioki sector (in four of them, the Vunioki men were in majorities of between 65 per cent and 90 per cent). All of these Gangs harvested by lorries which travelled directly to the mill. Hence, there was no longer a centre of co-operative harvest activity.

Two features characterized the new situation. First was the fact that the Company no longer had anything to do with the management of the Gangs; and, second, there was a diffuseness in the control held by the growers themselves.

In 1951 the Growers Harvesting Agreement had laid down many of the details of the Gang's operation (see pp. 98–101). It had been specific about such things as the rates of pay for cutters and other workers in the Gang; and it had laid down that the Company's official would decide upon the order in which fields were to be harvested. The current 1970 sugar-cane contract between Company and grower, on the other hand, stated only that 'the growers shall work together in harvesting gangs in a manner accustomed heretofore' (clause 5). It said little about specific actions, beyond stating that the Gang should elect a committee, which would appoint a *sardar* to manage the Gang, open a bank account, and 'arrange with the millers, a programme of harvesting for the ensuing season'. The questions of rates of pay, rates of penalties for absenteeism or non-contribution to Gang expenses, and order of fields to be harvested—all these matters were left to individual Gangs to decide. This they did at annual general meetings before the harvest, when the committee was elected too. Agreements of different Gangs varied in wage rates and in other clauses—one Gang agreement I was shown, for instance, included a clause that 'no worker shall stage strike or participate in political activities during the harvesting period'.

In effect, then, the Company had largely withdrawn from the daily harvesting scene, only requiring the Gangs to fulfil their harvest quotas and to deliver cane by rail or road according to an agreed programme, so that the mill could keep running at full capacity. Officers of the Company played no part in the Gang's daily work, and in fact, the committee of each Gang signed a bond which bound them to indemnify the Company against any claims which Gang members might make against the Company over advances which the Gang might ask the Company to make to individual growers. The only harvesting duty of the Company staff was to allocate daily harvesting tonnages to the Gangs in its sector. There were twenty-seven Gangs in Vunioki's sector, and allocation was thus a complex business, in which Gangs competed for available quotas. The Company officers had power in this and also the power to reduce a Gang's quota if it did not return full lorries or trucks.

Where did authority lie within the Gang? The main difference between 1951 and 1971 was that, whereas previously this had been focussed on the *sardar*, it was now diffused between the president of the gang, the secretary, the rest of the committee, and the *sardar* as their appointee. Each was responsible for different parts of the Gang's activity. The *sardar* made out the accounts, handled all the paper work with the mill, and represented the Gang in its daily dealings with local Company officials as regards quotas, etc. That is, the *sardar* was the operational manager of the Gang. But in any dispute between members, it was the president and the committee rather than the *sardar* who were expected to act; and the president was said to have the ultimate sanction, in that he could close the Gang by telling the sector office not to give it a quota. The president was also the key person in deciding the order of fields to be cut, often a major issue. If there were conflict between president and *sardar*, which could not be settled through the informal good offices of Company officials, then the case would go to the local member of the Sugar Advisory Council,[1] I was told. But this was said never to have happened in Vunioki, because problems could not stay unresolved for so long; in fact, the *sardar* would defer to the president, since the former was only the appointed servant of the committee.

[1] This is an all-Fiji body whose members are appointed from men chosen by the *sardars* of each region.

The diffusion of authority within the Gang had been accompanied by the formation of several Gangs. The contract of 1970 provided for the splitting of Gangs, or for their amalgamation, 'provided always that the new gang and the old gang will, after the change, be efficient and workable units . . . ' (clause 5c). As I have noted, the number of Gangs to which Vunioki men belonged had risen from the single Gang in 1951 to no fewer than nine in 1971. Two of these new Gangs had split from the first lorry Gang to have been formed in Vunioki;[1] but sometimes new Gangs had to remain as sub-Gangs, with their own *sardar* for internal organization, but with a single president and *sardar* for external relations. This was because both the Sugar Board (whose consent was required for a split) and the Company were against a multitude of small gangs, and hoped to keep harvesting within fairly large units.

There was thus in 1971 a trend away from large organization, especially in the case of lorry Gangs, which had no technical compulsion for co-operative effort, unlike the rail Gang which needed a group large enough to provide linemen from within itself.[2] Lorry-cut cane could, in fact, be simply hauled from field to mill by individual growers without a co-operative organization at all. But if that were done, the supply of cane to the mill could not be so easily regulated in an adequate daily flow: the mills might be flooded one day and starved the next unless there were a co-ordination of cutting and transport. If individual growers cut separately, then such co-ordination might devolve on the Company's officials—thereby making a complete circle back to the early days of cane harvest when the system had been entirely in their hands.

Discussion over the need for Gang organization was stimulated by the events of the cutting season which was drawing to a close when I visited Vunioki. The mills were crushing a record amount of cane, and the season had lasted for an exceptionally long time, due partly to this and partly to delays at the start of the season. Towards the end of the season, when bad weather had also set in, absenteeism in Vunioki Gangs grew to epidemic proportions, the Company allocated tonnage to individuals cutting their own fields with family or privately-recruited labour[3]—and the Gang system more or less dissolved for

---

[1] An individual could change his Gang membership, in case of dispute, if both Gangs agreed to it; the possibility that they would not was a major sanction for good behaviour in a Gang, as was the power of a Gang to expel.

[2] But some Gangs had all but dispensed with linemen, and hauled the cane by tractor-drawn trailers, on which the rail trucks were placed.

[3] Sometimes men took these jobs rather than cutting in the Gang because they were paid more; they should have been penalized by the Gang members, but such disciplinary action was hard to take since it might have triggered off disputes between growers and cutters.

a few weeks. But in general, the farmers were being held to their contracts and it seemed unlikely that the Gang system would disappear, although several men told me that the problem of Gang splits was now the major concern of the Sugar Board.

The prestige of Gang officers did not seem to be as high as it had been in 1951, and the diffusion of authority had had an effect on leadership in general in the settlement. For there was no longer a single post for which many major figures in the settlement could compete. In fact, there were almost as many president's and *sardar's* posts as there were men who wished to fill them.

A change in the Gangs which struck me was the large proportion of alternates now in them. It will be remembered that some growers used in 1951 to hire alternates to do their share of the work, and I noted (pp. 102–3) that these men were usually youths who did not themselves have any cane land, and that they tended to form an interest group of cane cutters within the Gang. At that time, one-third of the Vunioki Gang was composed of alternates; the other two-thirds were growers themselves. By 1971 only 17 per cent of the Vunioki rail Gang were growers, the rest were equally divided between their kinsmen and unrelated alternates. Growers said that they were not members for several reasons—for instance, that the crushing season was now so long that, were they in the Gang, they would have no time to look after their property, and that the cane price was now high enough for them to be able to afford alternates. At the same time, growers complained that alternates did not work well as cutters, would not listen to orders about how to cut cane, were too eager to burn it before cutting it, and so on. The cutters, on the other hand, considered themselves underpaid for what they saw as the dirtiest and hardest work in the settlement, which growers were no longer capable of doing for themselves. The 1951 difference of interest was now sharper because of the longer season and the greater polarization of growers' and cutters' roles. I was told of the possible future organization of a cutters' union; if such a union were to start, its demands might be high enough to force growers to cut their own cane again; or else, the growers who had been union supporters in 1951 might find the roles reversed vis-à-vis their young cutters. But though there were grumbles on both sides, such a position had not yet crystallized.

One result of the lack of growers in the Gangs was that the field from which to select officers and committeemen had greatly shrunk. I was told that these men could only be selected from growers, since only these had leases, etc., which acted as security for their operating the Gang's bank account and other financial affairs. There was, indeed, discussion during my stay in Vunioki about how one president (who had become seriously ill) was to be replaced. Such difficulties about leadership could reinforce the tendency already noted towards smaller and smaller Gangs, which would not need outstanding men to lead them.

If leadership of the Gang was no longer the position of power and prestige that it had been in 1951, had any other position replaced it? The school had grown enormously (from 200 to well over 500 pupils in daily attendance) and the responsibilities for running it had correspondingly increased. Vunioki residents had subscribed for new buildings for classrooms and for staff, and their maintenance posed constant problems. The men with whom I talked about the position of the committee thought of service on it as an onerous task for which few were qualified. There was apparently no great rivalry for posts on the committee, and though there were said to be complaints from parents at each meeting, nobody new could be found to do the work. The committee's most active officers were one Gang *sardar* and two residents who were employees of the Company and well experienced in accounts and office work. I attended a meeting of the committee, which was businesslike and during which it became clear, over issues like the way to collect overdue fees, that it had little real power in the settlement.[1] The school committee, then, did not provide a prize for competition amongst settlement leaders though, as in 1951, it was a context for added prestige.

Another context of leadership mentioned in Chapter V was the *panchayat* or council of arbitration. Such councils appeared to have been convened over the intervening decades, both on an *ad hoc* basis and more formally. There was said to have been a dispute-settling (*sudhār*) committee founded in the early 1950s, which had six members and held several meetings over various disputes brought to it. Some of these it was able to solve by 'binding over' the culprit to behave himself, by making him apologize, and so forth. It levied no fines, nor could it enforce its decision when this was ignored, though it had a sanction in the threat that its members would bear witness of its proceedings in any ensuing court case. The committee did not seem to have been very active, however, especially in recent years; nor had it been called in to solve any very important cases. Some people said that they had never heard of it; others were uncertain whether it still existed or not; and though it can be compared to the Youth Association in Delanikoro (see p. 109) whose aims were similar to its own, its influence seems to have been considerably

---

[1] I was told that no child had ever been excluded because of overdue fees, and parents clearly knew this. But the majority did pay up, mainly at the exhortation of the headmaster rather than of the committee members.

less. But it was an attempt to create a more formal and effective form of *panchayat* than purely *ad hoc* bodies.

In 1951 Vunioki had been represented on a district-wide Indian Advisory Committee (see p. 184). A year before my re-visit, this Committee had been superseded by a structure of rural development committees. The lowest rung was the local committee made up of representatives from three or four settlements; these selected a member to represent them at the district level, and the district committees were then grouped at the divisional level. Vunioki's representative had been chosen unanimously at a meeting attended by about two dozen men. (The fact that he was *sardar* of the rail Gang and had been the chairman of the dispute-settling committee just mentioned, shows an expected overflow of prestige derived from the settlement's various associations.) According to him, the local committee had already drawn up a list of priority development projects for the settlement (e.g. the installation of electric light and piped water, the widening of the main bridge, the tar-sealing of the main road in the vicinity of the shops), but the scheme was too new to have produced results by the time of my visit. One interesting feature was that in the minds of the local people I talked to, these committees were not merely advisory and restricted to development, but were also to be arbitration committees. In fact, it was suggested when speaking of a local quarrel within an extended family, that the representative should go and settle the matter; he replied that he would do so if the chairman of the local committee (who lived in a nearby settlement) would go with him. Whether the future will see statutory duties of minor arbitration given to these committees, I cannot say; but the comments of people suggest that this might be welcomed, as giving a statutory basis to the kind of committee which settlement people had already tried to organize on their own. The representative, commenting on his role, thought that the next election might well be contested, since by then the committee would have assumed some importance in the eyes of local people.[1] If so, the importance of the representative might rival, and even surpass, that of the Gang *sardar*, and provide an important focus for leadership and settlement organization.

My discussion of leadership and the contexts in which it can be shown should be linked to a discussion of factions which had played an important part in settlement affairs in 1951. But it is impossible to give a balanced account of local factions after only a fortnight's stay. I was told of disputes over land, some of which had been

---

[1] In some cases, elections were held for the first representative; for instance, in Namboulima, Ramnath beat an opponent to become representative.

serious; of domestic quarrels; of allegiance to different political parties. But I cannot evaluate how important these were in forming and maintaining factions, nor can I outline in any detail the membership of factions or say how many people were able to keep neutral or even that there were factions of the kind I described in an earlier chapter. Nor can I assess the required attributes of leadership (see pp. 137–42) and show whether these had changed.

I have, in fact, focused largely on the aspects of life which were at once visible to me and on changes easily identified. Here, I think, the most important change in Vunioki was from cane farming as a way of life to cane farming as one of a number of different ways of gaining a livelihood. Perhaps now, for the first time, cane had become a truly cash crop—that is, it was really seen in terms of the cash it brought and less as the symbol of an agricultural way of life. As one young man remarked to me, 'Our fathers knew only how to cut cane; I and my friends cut it too, but many do, or want to do, other jobs as well. They only cut cane because they have to, in order to live well or save up for something.'

For the older generation, often ill educated and striving to build a firm base for their families' lives, there had been no other possibility than farming—if possible, cane farming. Some of the young men in the settlement were still rustics in this sense. But others had had at least eight years of schooling, and a knowledge of urban life. They tended to be cutters for other men; but their interests and aspirations often lay outside the settlement. For them, the *sardar's* or Gang president's post was not very important; and to the extent that this was the case, the web of relations within the settlement depended more on personal predilection than it had done in 1951. What will this changed attitude do to the quality of rural life? Again, perhaps even more important for the next generation than changes in cane farming economics, what changes will stem from the fact that many mothers-to-be have now completed secondary or at least full primary education and that some have held jobs with earnings comparable to those of men? Fashionable though it may be to say so, the difference between the generations, broadly defined, now appeared greater than it had in 1951. Perhaps with better internal communication the area around the shops will become a real settlement centre—evening gatherings of young men there indicated that this might be happening. But an unchanged settlement life, with no meeting place and drink a main male recreation, will surely not meet present aspirations for a more interesting life, ill-defined though these may be.

DELANIKORO IN 1971

To visit Delanikoro after twenty years was to notice both continuities and changes. The scenery and the atmosphere were the same and the change from cane to paddy was not obtrusive in summer, when much of the land near the settlement had in any case been under paddy and much was being ploughed for new cane. My early impression of change centred on the houses and their distribution. I looked in vain along the settlement's eastern side for the clusters of thatched houses which had marked major groups of homesteads: instead, a few iron and wooden houses stood rather forlornly in the valley between the bluffs. On the western side, however, there was the glint of new corrugated iron roofs, and the whiteness of cement and vivid green and blue of painted walls: here, the hillside seemed almost entirely covered with houses, and amongst them stood a long low building, clearly a new school.

The second change became apparent as I walked around the settlement. There was hardly anyone in the fields or the house compounds. In two of the three shops the counter was being kept by a small boy; only in the third was the proprietor present, busy with his sewing machine. Where were the holders of the fields in which only one or two families were out weeding the paddy? The answer was provided that evening. Throughout the day there had been a desultory arrival of buses, some of them passing through the settlement on the new road that led to Fijian villages in the hills. But now there was what can only be called a traffic of buses, private cars and taxis. The men left them and walked to their houses, back from work in the market town or in Suva. On asking, it appeared that the great majority of the settlement's 135 adult men (i.e. 71 per cent or ninety-five of them) commuted to work outside Delanikoro; only fourteen out of the seventy-five homesteads did not have a commuter.[1] Twenty years ago only 23 per cent (twenty out of eighty-eight adult men) had been commuters. Why had this change occurred?

At the time of my previous visit there had already been a trend away from cane to paddy growing, and by the end of the 1950s the Company had decided that it would close its mill serving the Rewa delta cane area (see p. 42). Although the trend had been away from cane, the actual closure in 1959 produced difficult economic conditions in Delanikoro and the surrounding region. At the same time, many people feared that the land they farmed would be reserved for Fijian use. They therefore searched for work outside the settlement.

---

[1] Not included are three homesteads for which I do not have information. The reader should apply to these figures the same qualifications as he was asked to give to those for Vunioki.

211

The main standby became short-term work in New Zealand. Already in 1951 a few men from Delanikoro had been there; but New Zealand was then enough of a novelty for their reminiscences to be popular subjects of talk and debate. In 1971 there was hardly anyone who had not been there, often several times, as well as to such places as the New Hebrides.[1] In three months one could save in New Zealand enough for a useful adjunct to the year's income, and a year in the New Hebrides would allow the saving of a capital sum.

Towards the mid-1960s it became harder to obtain permission to work in New Zealand; but at that stage the expanding city of Suva and its environs provided more work for men who were by that time used to leaving their farms for outside jobs. So it was that by 1971 only forty-two of Delanikoro's seventy-five homesteads held any land beyond the house site; and of these twenty-three had no full-time farmer, but simply a commuter who farmed on weekends, taking a few days off at times of peak activity. This left only nineteen homesteads with full-time farmers.

The commuters had a variety of occupations. There were labourers and men working in cafés and bookstores; there were accountants and foundrymen, artisans such as carpenters and plumbers and painters, and construction foremen with responsibility over as many as several hundred men. In addition, I noted three women having jobs, two as teachers and one as a typist. One homestead had become a small carpentry and blacksmithing shop, making components on piecework for a Suva firm; it had even engaged a labourer from another homestead—the only evidence I saw of a 'rural industry' developing, although many of the necessary skills were represented in the settlement.

Some men regretted having gone into urban work; others, and these appeared to be the majority, were glad at being delivered from what they remembered as back-breaking toil in the fields, for rewards which had often been no larger and were certainly a great deal less certain than their weekly wage packets.[2] To some extent, the difference stemmed from whether the person had been a cane farmer (with a reasonable income) or not, as well as from his present occupation; but it was uncertain how many would have gone back to full-time

---

[1] At the time of my stay, four and five men were in New Hebrides (this may be a generic term and include New Caledonia, etc.) and New Zealand respectively, having left their families in Delanikoro. They are not counted in the number of adult men in the settlement; but their part in forming a joint household is taken into account.

[2] So far there had been no slump in, for instance, the construction industry that would make urban employment also seem uncertain.

agriculture, had the land been available and the crops to support them.[1]

Most households, then, had one or more men with non-agricultural incomes. When supplemented by the household's own paddy, and by the occasional sum saved by a member's work overseas, there was frequently an amount of money to be saved, invested or spent on consumer goods above the bare necessities. Without a full survey, I cannot report on the patterns of investment and expense. But there did appear to have been a change in the standard of living. For example, in 1951, forty-five of the ninety-one houses were made of thatch; by 1971 there was not a single thatch building, only partly explainable by the absence of cane tops for thatch. Fifty-six of the houses I counted were of corrugated iron, twenty-one of wood, and three of cement blocks in the most modern style. Most houses now had windows instead of wooden shutters, and their condition was generally better than I remembered it. Partly, this was because of available money; partly it must have been because so many owners were themselves working as carpenters or other craftsmen in Suva, and could help themselves and their neighbours. Many houses were well-furnished too, with sofa sets, cabinets with ornaments, and at least one with tiled floors. Every house possessed at least one radio (in 1951 there had been two sets in the whole settlement), and even the poorest I visited had a sink. People were, in fact, living more comfortably than they had done. Their wives were aware of this; more than one told me that, with piped water (brought to the settlement since 1951), soap suds, kerosene cookers, ready-made curry powder and so forth, their lives had considerably less drudgery. Other amenities included six cars (whose owners might cover running expenses by taking commuters to Suva); several men had motor grass mowers, and several more were considering buying them, an indication of the need for labour saving devices for weekend farming, paid for out of the proceeds of urban jobs. People dressed better, and there seemed to be more purchase of consumer goods generally, since there were three stores in place of the single store of 1951 (although people doubted that more than two could survive, and

---

[1] This may not be an academic question in the near future. Irrigation schemes allowing the double-cropping of paddy and hence a good income from a moderate sized block of land were being experimented with by the Government and the FAO in a region nearby. A few Delanikoro farmers were involved in this; they had all promised to become full-time farmers (since double-cropped land needs constant attention) but not all of them had done so, or else they had assigned the farming to a younger and not very efficient son. (A few had turned into successful farmers, however.) The planners were concerned to find out whether, if the irrigation were extended to Delanikoro, and the land made available, enough men would change back to farming to make the scheme a success.

it was clear that the two stores in the western end of the settlement were in sharp competition).

One could argue that these changes had resulted from a re-deployment of the same sized incomes rather than a growth in them —and it was true, I was told, that some spending had been made possible by a reduction of expenses for weddings. Only a full survey could uncover the whole position. One facet of such a survey would be to see what changes there had been in the place of credit and debt in Delanikoro. An important consequence of urban employment was that people were now on weekly, or in some cases monthly, wages and salaries. No longer did they have their incomes from two large cane payments or a paddy harvest each year. As a result, they no longer needed to run up debts at the stores but paid for their purchases either each week in arrears or by monthly cheque if they had bank accounts and monthly salaries. This, I was told, had stopped storekeepers from adding items to bills for long forgotten purchases and had kept people to their current incomes more strictly. I was not able to find out a great deal about the sources for long term loans; perhaps because people less often had the security of long-term leases or of cane crops, large loans were apparently not often contracted. I was repeatedly told that there was almost no serious debt in the settlement any more.

For whatever reasons, most people conceded or asserted that they were better off in 1971 than they had been in 1951, and many saw the closing of the mill as a blessing in disguise that had led to more diversified incomes. Delanikoro was now part of south-eastern Viti Levu's 'periurban' zone. An introduction of irrigated paddy land would give it an economy balanced on both rural and urban income. It is, of course, impossible to say that urban occupations were taken up only because of the abolition of cane cultivation; for the move to these occupations could have occurred in any case, because of increased education, better transport, and the growth of demand in Suva. But it is at least tempting to see, just as in Vunioki, the change in the settlement's most important crop as a key factor in subsequent changes in the economic and social spheres.

KINSHIP AND CULTURAL GROUPS

Delanikoro's population had increased over the two decades from 457 to 562 (an increase of 23 per cent) living in seventy-five[1] as against fifty-four homesteads (an increase of 28 per cent). That is, there had been a decrease in the size of homesteads from an average of 8·5 to one of 7·5 people, and an increase in both total population

[1] I do not include the homestead of a single part-European.

and number of homesteads. It is interesting to compare these figures with those for Vunioki; the Delanikoro population increase is only one-third of Vunioki's, whereas the increase in the number of homesteads is 50 per cent higher.

One reason for the smaller population increase is that emigration from Delanikoro had been greater. At least eleven householders had moved away during the period, as well as substantial sections of a large joint household and a housegroup. Some men moved when they were afraid that their land was going to be reserved for indigenous Fijians; others moved after the sugar mill closed; yet others moved because of family disputes or because they wanted to live nearer to their work in Suva. This loss of people was only partly offset by immigration. I estimated that fifteen new homestead heads had arrived; of these, nine were affines (sons- and brothers-in-law) of men already living in Delanikoro, and all but two already had relatives in the settlement. Most of these men, however, were starting their families, whereas those who emigrated tended to be older men with many dependants—hence there was not the population increase which this number of immigrant households suggests.

Another explanation for the slower rate of increase in Delanikoro may be family planning. It may be no coincidence that the settlement with the slower rate of growth is the one nearer to Suva, from where the stimulus to family planning has emanated. In addition, it is the settlement which has had more contact with a foreign country in which family planning is widely practised, whose value migrant workers may have brought back with them.

Although homesteads contained much the same numbers of people as in 1951, they had changed in the important respect that, as in Vunioki, the later age of marriage had meant that a new category of 'joint' households had arisen, in which there was at least one adult unmarried male contributor to the family budget. The change in Delanikoro can be seen from Table 3.

TABLE 3

Type	No. of homesteads		Population	
	1951	1971	1951	1971
Simple household	37	52	221	169
'Joint' household (with adult unmarried son(s))	—	20	—	156
Joint household	14	19	184	186
Housegroup	3	4	52	51
Total	54	75	457	562

The table shows that simple households had decreased; that 'joint' households had become a major category;[1] and that joint households had increased in number but decreased in size. Regarding 'joint' households, there is an important difference between Delanikoro and a farming settlement like Vunioki. In the former, such households may contain a farmer, and one or more commuters, or they may have several commuters. In either case, the common income comes from distinct sources. This contrasts with many Vunioki farming households where the income derives from a single source—the cane cheque—which is worked for by several men.[2] Where separate wages are paid into the common budget by an unmarried youth, there is the problem of how much he should be able to keep for his own expenses and entertainment. The difference is between an allocation by the family head to a son, and the retention by the son of part of what he is bringing home.

I discussed this situation with people in Delanikoro, and the consensus seemed to be that, although there were quarrels from time to time about the amount that young men should contribute, most households managed to keep an agreed distribution of wages—the amount varying from household to household, from those in which the son kept almost all he earned to those in which he gave up almost everything. Men were aware that the unmarried men might wish to leave home rather than pay a share; but since it was difficult to live alone, since parents often took only a fraction of the pay, and since they might well pay for a man's marriage if he were living with them, this had not become a pressing problem. People were, however, agreed that though the joint system had worked so far, the basis was much more on 'rational agreement' than on the traditional authority of parents, and that it could lead to an increased individualism of young men.

The movement of families in and out of Delanikoro had produced a noticeable change in the physical distribution of homesteads, as I had noted on my arrival, and as the map shows when compared to the one of page 19. In social terms, there had been a marked shift of the relative numbers in the different cultural groups, as Table 4 shows:

---

[1] Even supposing that a few households in 1951 contained single sons who might be classed as adult but were not then classified as such because of the general marriage of youths at the age of seventeen or eighteen years, the increase of 'joint' households would still be notable.

[2] The increase of youths working as cane cutters would increase the number of households with separate incomes for at least part of the year, since cutters are paid separately. This may be an important trend in Vunioki household organization.

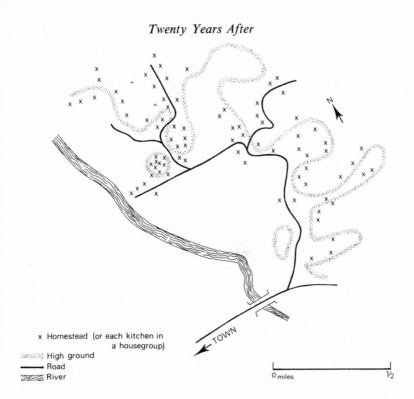

x Homestead (or each kitchen in
a housegroup)
High ground
Road
River

0 miles   ½

DELANIKORO SETTLEMENT: 1971

TABLE 4

Cultural group	Homesteads		Population	
	1951	1971	1951	1971
Northern Hindu	28	34	240	240
Southern Hindu	17	35	164	273
Muslim	6	5	41	37
Sikh	3	1	12	12
Total	54	75	457	562

The change was mainly due to the pattern of emigration (mainly non-Southern) and of immigration (mainly Southern). The incomers had settled near their kinsmen in the western part of the settlement, and the departure of Northerners had to some extent denuded the

217

eastern part. The degree to which this movement had affected settlement life can be explored in two ways. First, in so far as Southerners and Northerners had different cultural features, the content of, and emphasis on, activities had presumably changed. An examination of this aspect (which would bring in, of course, the degree to which Southerners and Northerners *were* in fact culturally distinct in 1971) needed more time than I spent in Delanikoro. The second aspect is concerned with the relation of these cultural distinctions to the organization of group activities in the settlement, and I turn to this subject.

ASSOCIATIONS

There had been several contexts of associational and parapolitical activity in 1951. On the one hand, there had been the Youth Association and the Ramayan Mandli as formal contexts: and on the other, there had been the informal *panchayats* and the factional groupings into which at least part of the settlement's population had been grouped. Activities in these had involved co-operation, competition, and sometimes a rupture of relations in a boycott. To what extent could this pattern be seen in 1971?

Three main factors lie behind the answers to this question. First, most of the major leaders of 1951 had either died or left the settlement; second, Delanikoro had had a school since 1961, and hence there was now a compulsory association—the school committee—in the settlement: and third, in the new occupational situation most men spent most of their time outside the settlement in a variety of work-places. Together, these factors (and possibly others of which I was unaware) had made for a different pattern and intensity of local activities.

Of the leaders mentioned in my earlier account, Kanni had died, and Gopal, Sundar and Lakhan had left the settlement in the late 1950s and early 1960s. Two of their major lieutenants, not mentioned by name in the account, had also passed from the scene in the early 1960s—one had died and one had emigrated to Suva. Of the people named in the boycotts, both Baburam and Sahdeo had died. This very considerable change in the personnel of local leadership must be coupled with the change in weightage of the cultural groups. Much activity was in 1971 centred in the Southern group for demographic if for no other reasons. Affairs were in the hands of new men: some were new immigrants, and others had taken over from former leaders. It is impossible to judge from a short visit how much they were influenced by past history.

Let me take the formal associations to show what had happened.

After my departure, I was told, the Youth Association continued to function with vigour. On several occasions, it was said, youths were called to account for their actions, and were even corporally punished. The supporters of the Association looked back to those days as ones in which rowdy behaviour was kept in check, by comparison with today.[1] Opponents, of course, saw the period as one of unfair and even despotic domination of the settlement by Sundar, Lakhan and their supporters.

In 1958 the Youth Association leaders decided to start a school. Children were having to go to the neighbouring settlement for their education, at some cost and trouble. Money was collected, land obtained, an application made and authorization given. By that time, Sundar and Lakhan had both left the settlement, and the committee was composed of men who had been associated with the Youth Association, but had not been among its major leaders. They formed the first operating committee when the school was opened in 1961. A Southerner was president, but most of the rest were Northerners. Since that time, the composition of the committee had changed several times; at the time of my visit, three of the four main offices were held by Southerners, thus reflecting the change in the settlement's cultural composition.

The building of the school was not unaccompanied by argument. One section of Southerners wanted the money to be used for the more traditional purpose of building a proper temple (since Delanikoro was then dependent on a temple as distant as the school). The question of whose land the access road was to run upon also produced dissension. But opposition was eventually overcome, and the 1971 position was that the school committee was the major forum for settlement activity and, when it occurred, of settlement competition among leaders. The school had developed until it had, in 1971, an enrolment of about 150 children, housed in a new building which was being added to, and with a good playground around it. Teachers mainly commuted from town.

As in Vunioki, running the committee was somewhat arduous; the collection of fees,[2] the management of accounts and the organization of workers to keep the building in good repair was not always easy. The nature of the committee's work ruled out those people who were

---

[1] It appeared that drink and consequent disorder was a problem in the settlement in 1971; several youths appeared to me to be drinking too much and too regularly. This may well be as much connected with their having separate incomes as with the ending of restrictions on drinking. When they were working for common household incomes the opportunity for expenditure on drink was less.

[2] Since 1969 the public had not paid any part of teachers' salaries; hence fees were now devoted to maintenance and equipment—this could be done by *ad hoc* collections if the committee preferred it.

219

not qualified to be officers or who did not wish to spend time on committee work, though it by no means always stopped their criticism of the committee's work.

At the same time as the school committee was starting, the Youth Association was ending. This may have been because its founders and chief luminaries had left the scene, and with them had gone the notion of a settlement-wide organ of social control. It may also have been because the school committee came to provide a context adequate enough to engage the energies of active and responsibility-if not power-seeking men. Because the school committee was a compulsory committee, and because it did not seek to 'interfere' in the private lives of settlement members as had the Youth Association, but only to enforce a certain discipline necessary to accomplish a task that everyone admitted was necessary, the committee was not the centre of such strong factional disputes as had been the Youth Association. The most that disturbed its functioning were disputes about administration and financial control. Though such disputes were linked to quarrels between kin-groups (especially the two main Southern extended families) there seemed to be less dissension at the settlement level than there had been in 1951.[1]

This change was reinforced by the disappearance of formal and active boycotts—perhaps again with the end of the Youth Association. The boycott against the single Sikh household had ended and members of it now went to settlement functions. The Muslim households did not appear to play any part in settlement affairs (their children went to Muslim schools in town); the men said that they were in theory invited to settlement functions though they chose not to attend them; others said that they were not invited. But, if there were still a boycott of them, it was not at all an active one, and the position was accepted by both sides.

Again, there did not appear to be any more than minor *panchayats;* when the chairman of the school committee offered to call a *panchayat* over a case of alleged assault, the plaintiff refused and went instead to the police to lodge a complaint. In short, there were no sustained activities at the settlement level other than the school committee. The new development committee was known about but had not started to make any impact. The Ramayan Mandli still had its prayer hall, and had been registered as a religious body in 1965; its president and vice-president were Southerners, marking the shift from an earlier, mainly Northern, leadership. But its membership was limited. Individual Southerners maintained shrines, and the cultural group participated in their annual festivals—the Mariamma

[1] This is not to say that school committees have not become the centres of strong factional rivalries in some settlements.

festival and procession was now organized by Subramaniam (see p. 90) at his shrine, and another shrine, at which Lakshman (see p. 91) officiated, celebrated Sivaratri. But Lakshman, who had been a chief participant in the Mariamma procession, now took no part in it, and it seemed that there had been a division of allegiances within the cultural group. Finally, political parties did not appear to have formal branches in the settlement, though different opinions on this topic suggested that there might be some formal organization at times of activity such as elections.

The picture that emerges is one in which there might be localized disputes (e.g. there was clearly a rift between two sections of Southerners at the time I visited the settlement) but in which such disputes tended to be confined to the kin group or cultural group at most. The lack of more widespread factions may well be because men did not in fact have much time for such contacts. One man working in Suva, for example, left Delanikoro at about 5.45 a.m. and did not return until 6.15 p.m. Such a routine allowed him hardly any time to see fellow residents except at the weekend, when he was busy on his land.[1] It may also be because the focus of interest had tended to change. Men were aware of wider issues in Fiji and the world, and settlement disputes seemed small beer to them unless they were directly affected.

This changed attitude is part of the impression I gained of an increased 'individualism' in the settlement. This goes with the general pattern of a divergence of economic interests, through the heterogeneity of occupations.

CONCLUSION

I hope to have shown that the two settlements I re-visited had changed since 1951 in at least those aspects that I was able to see for myself and discuss with residents. The directions of economic change had been different in each—towards an emphasis on an agricultural crop on the one hand, and towards urban employment on the other. This can be linked to such changes as the fragmentation of authority in the cane harvesting system, and the dispersal of Delanikoro's work force into different occupations with different

---

[1] It is important to note that few Delanikoro men appeared to have common work-places in Suva. Men might get jobs through neighbours or kinsmen who were in a position to recommend them—although I was told that people did not like doing this, lest the recommended person did not measure up to the work and thereby lessened the standing of the recommender—but they were equally likely to get work through direct applications. People might travel on the same bus or in the same car, but they dispersed when they got to the city.

interests in, for instance, pay and conditions. Some of the impetus for these changes was clearly economic: but in part it was a concomitant of increased education and a change in values, which had gone with a trend away from the 'paternal' aspect of society—whether in the political sphere (culminating in Fiji's independence), or in the economic sphere (shown by the increasingly advisory role played by the SPSM in Vunioki) or in the domestic sphere (shown in the greater independence of young men in earning and controlling their incomes in Delanikoro). One could view this as an overall trend towards what I have loosely called an increased individualism where, instead of people having relatively undifferentiated economic and social interests and the centre of co-operation and competition being in factions and associations within the settlement, people now tended to have different interests expressed in contexts outside the settlement.

Certainly, settlements appeared to be no more 'social unities' in 1971 than they had been in 1951. But one must not take the point too far. Not only were many people members of extended kin-groups with many of their links of reciprocal obligations within the settlement: there were also possible trends in the opposite direction. If, for instance, irrigated paddy farming were to come to Delanikoro at the same time as the expansion of urban occupations lessened, and the movement of young people on to the land were to increase,[1] one could imagine a sector of common agricultural interest developing. In Vunioki, too, I have noted the possibility of a more conscious grouping of cane cutters. Again, if the rural development committees were to become effective (with or without additional duties of conciliation) their leaders could use this local support to move into national politics.[2] The competition to be a committee leader might well then become an even more focal point of a settlement political system than was the struggle to be *sardar*.

Another way of looking at the future is in terms of a trend towards a 'modern' way of life. This is not only reflected in the consumer goods which were now being bought or desired; it is shown in the transition of Vunioki residents from being what could be called peasants (although even in 1951 they had been closely linked to a cash crop and were thus not as subsistence-based as some might

[1] The problem of the provision of land for Indian farmers is, of course, a national one. I have not considered it here because the growth of urban occupations in Delanikoro, and the recent availability of freehold land in Vunioki, had muted the subject; but some people did speak in Delanikoro about the rise in rents of Fijian land, and the difficulties in putting some of the reserved land to good use.

[2] The fact that Hindi is now a Parliamentary language may be a factor facilitating rural involvement at higher political levels.

define peasants to be) to what were more nearly commercial farmers
—men earning a living from the soil as a business rather than as a
family's way of life. I do not wish to exaggerate—some smallholders
in Vunioki had changed little; but a change seemed to be discernible.
In Delanikoro, of course, the growth of urban work had taken the
settlement much further along this road.

Other aspects of this trend are the education of boys and girls,
the later age of marriage and the broad acceptance of family planning
(whether practised or not, it was no longer the delicate subject I had
found it to be in 1951), and a general contact with the world at large,
personally and through the wide migration of people either on a
temporary or permanent basis.[1] Within Fiji, too, there was more
travel, more distant marriage ties,[2] and more extended contacts
with the Fijian and European communities than there had been.
In the Vunioki sector there was now a number of Fijian cane
farmers; I was told of co-operation between settlement members
and Fijian villagers in the loan of equipment, etc; and the settlement's representative on the rural development committee was
aware that, for the first time, Fijians and Indians were working
together in local government, at the district and divisional levels
of the structure.[3] In Delanikoro, men worked in offices and work-
shops with Fijians, Europeans and others. English was now more
widely spoken and understood in both settlements, and was part of a
general life style (which included dress) in which members of all
communities were converging in at least part of their lives. People
drew a cautious optimism about the future from this, and even
more from the successful attainment of Fiji's independence through
agreement and mutual understanding between communities. Difficulties there undoubtedly will be in the years that lie ahead in both
Vunioki and Delanikoro, the greatest of these perhaps being the
problem of employment for the rapidly increasing educated younger
generation, and the meeting of their social as well as economic
aspirations. But the decades between my visits have been ones of
adaptation to change, and one can reasonably hope that this will
continue.

---

[1] On my first day in Vunioki I met a man now residing in London, who had
returned for a holiday; and several men from both settlements had gone to
North America.

[2] Jayawardena (1971: 111–13) shows how marriage networks have become
more socially and geographically extended; he also discusses the place of caste
in settlements, a topic on which I do not have enough data to write about here.

[3] See Mayer (1963: 101–4) for the history of previous attempts to achieve this.

REFERENCES

BENEDICT, B. 1958. 'Cash and Credit in Mauritius', *South African Journal of Economics*, Vol. 26, No. 3, pp. 213–21.

COULTER, J. W. 1942. *Fiji: Little India of the Pacific*. Chicago, University of Chicago Press.

DARLING, M. L. 1947. *The Punjab Peasant in Prosperity and Debt*. Bombay, Oxford University Press.

DERRICK, R. A. 1951. *The Fiji Islands*. Suva, Government Press.

FISK, E. K. 1970. *The Political Economy of Independent Fiji*. Wellington, Reed.

GILLION, K. L. 1956. 'The Sources of Indian Emigration to Fiji', *Population Studies*, Vol. X, No. 2, pp. 139–57.

1958. *A History of Indian Emigration and Settlement in Fiji*. Unpublished Ph.D. Thesis, Australian National University, Canberra.

H.M.S.O. 1953. *Fiji: 1951*. London, H.M.S.O.

1958. *Fiji: 1956*. London, H.M.S.O.

JAYAWARDENA, C. 1971. 'The disintegration of caste in Fiji Indian rural society'. In L. R. Hiatt & C. Jayawardena (eds), *Anthropology in Oceania*. Sydney, Angus & Robertson.

MAYER, A. C. 1952. 'The Holi Festival among the Indians of Fiji', *Eastern Anthropologist*, Vol. VI, No. 1, pp. 3–17.

1953. 'The Organisation of Indian Settlement in Fiji', *Man*, Vol. LIII, No. 284, pp. 1–3.

1960. *Caste and Kinship in Central India*. London, Routledge and Kegan Paul.

1963. *Indians in Fiji*. London, Oxford University Press.

O'LOUGHLIN, C. 1956. *The Pattern of the Fiji Economy*. Council Paper No. 44. Suva, Government Press.

ROTH, G. K. 1951. *Native Administration in Fiji During the Past 75 Years. A Successful Experiment in Indirect Rule*. Occ. Pap. R. Anthrop. Inst. No. 10. London.

1953. *Fijian Way of Life*. London, Oxford University Press.

SHEPHARD, C. Y. 1945. *The Sugar Industry of Fiji*. London, H.M.S.O.

T'IEN, J.-K. 1953. *The Chinese of Sarawak*. London, L.S.E. Mono. on Soc. Anthrop. No. 12.

GLOSSARY

1. HINDI AND FIJIAN WORDS

barka husband's elder brother
bhatwan day in the programme of a Hindu wedding
bhauji elder brother's wife
bure, or *belo* a type of house
chautal type of song sung at the Holi festival
chotki younger brother's wife
devar husband's younger brother
dharmik socio-religious (used about films on traditional or legendary topics)
dhoti loincloth used as male dress over much of India
ghee clarified butter
halal lawful—hence, meat which it is religiously lawful for Muslims to eat
jagah place
jahazi bhai shipmate (used by former indentured labourers)
ianeo sacred thread, invested on Hindus of upper ('twice-born') castes
katha reading from Hindu sacred texts
kere kere Fijian custom of privileged demand for the belongings of others
kitab reading from Muslim sacred texts
kus species of grass used in Hindu religious ceremonies, believed to possess purificatory powers
marrit civil marriage
matanggali Fijian social unit, basic to the system of land tenure
maulvi learned Muslim, priest
natedar one or more kin
neem margosa tree
panchayat council for arbitration (or administration)
parivar family
parsad offering to deity, later eaten by worshippers
rishtedar one or more kin
sardar leader; used for elected head of cane-harvesting Gang
shadi religious marriage, wedding day
sraddha rite of propitiation of ancestors
tali thread dyed in turmeric, used in Southern wedding
taziya model of mausoleum used in Moharram festival
telwan day in the programme of a Hindu wedding
tilak mark made by Hindus with earth or unguents on forehead
toli ward within a settlement
yanggona Fijian drink made of infusion of *yanggona* plant (*Piper methysticum*) in water

2. SELECTED ANTHROPOLOGICAL TERMS

affine   relations, relationships by marriage
agnate   kin traced through males only
collateral   descent by different lines from a common ancestor
cousin, cross   mother's brother's or father's sister's child
cousin, parallel   mother's sister's or father's brother's child
endogamy   rule enjoining marriage within a specified social group
exogamy   rule prohibiting marriage within a specified social group
hypergamy   marriage with a woman from a social group of lower status
hypogamy   marriage with a woman from a social group of higher status
patrilineal   descent reckoned exclusively through males

INDEX

administrative divisions, 25
affines, and language differences, 145
  and joint households, 33
  relations between, 164ff.
agnates:
  and inheritance, 174
  and joint households, 33, 202–3
  and mutual help, 173–4
  relations between, 164ff.
  and ritual duties, 83
agriculture:
  importance of, 12, 210
  rotation of crops, 40
  techniques of cultivation, 38–45
Ahmad, Mirza Ghulam, 9
Ahmadiya Muslims, 9, 10, 28
altar, at weddings, 68, 72, 75
alternates, in Gang labour, 43, 102–3, 207
amulets, 85
Anglicans, 9
arbitration, 110–11, 114ff., 208
Arya Samaj, 9, 28, 130–2, 148–9, 161, 179
  weddings in, 75, 78
assaults, 114–15
associations, 98ff., 203ff., 218ff.
  outside, and settlements, 120–1
  'voluntary', 109ff.
  See also Gangs; Youth Association; School
    Committee; Ramayana Society
Australia, visits to, 186
authority, pattern of, 5

Bakr-Id, 95
banana cultivation, 12, 14
barbers, 45, 46, 47, 159
  See also caste
barka, 166
belo, 16
Benedict, Dr. Burton, 53, 73
Bengal, 3
bhauji, 167
Bihar, 3
bills of sale, 54
birth, ritual of second, 61–2
birth certificates, 73
bonuses, for alternates, 102
boycotts, 113, 118, 126, 220
brothers, fictitious, 175–6
bure, 15, 19
Burns Commission, Report, 183
Burns Philp Co., 46
bus services, 45–6, 49

Calcutta, 1, 2, 3, 145, 157, 189
calf, as child's ritual counterpart, 61
cane, sugar, 2
  areas of cultivation, 14, 194–7
  burnt, 100

cultivation methods, 38–40, 196, 199
cultivation statistics, 38
export value, 12
introduction of cultivation, 1–2
order of cutting, 100, 204
plantations, cycle of work, 4
plantations, Indians on, 4
  See also Gangs, cane-harvesting
cane farmers' unions, 11, 120–1, 133, 179
  and cultural groups, 149
cannibalism, 182
caste(s), 36, 37, 156–64, 223
  change of, 161–3
  of emigrants, 2–3
  and hostility, 161
  and leadership, 138–9
  loss of, by emigrants, 2, 157
  and marriage, 63, 160–2
  and occupation, 158
  rules, and agriculture, 158
  specific:
    Barber, 45, 159
    Brahman, 3, 156, 157, 159, 161, 162, 163
    Dairyman (Ahir), 160
    Potter (Kumhar), 161
    Rajput, 160, 161, 162, 163
    Sweeper, 156
    Tailor, 159
    Tanner (Chamar), 156, 161, 163
  weakening of, 157
  See also untouchables
Central Organization, 10, 121
change, social and economic, 194ff.
Chatthi, 60
chautal, 87, 88, 89
Chiefs, Great Council of (Fijian), 180
child-parent relationship, 165–6, 170
chilli, use at funerals, 80
Chinese traders, 46
Chinsami, Vunioki leader, 123–5, 137, 138, 139,
  140, 141, 142, 175
chotki, 166–7
Christians, 9
Christmas, 87
cinemas, 190
circumcision, 61, 151
clan membership:
  and marriage, 63
  unimportance of, 84
coconut oil, 12, 51
co-education, distrust of, 66
cohabitation, unmarried, 165
Colonial Sugar Refining Co. (CSR), 1, 6, 14,
  15, 20–1, 24–6, 38ff., 98ff., 181, 183, 196
Commissioner for India, 191, 193
committees, 106. *See also* School Committee
communal relations, 149ff.
conversion, religious, 151

227

Index

228

Index

Field Officer, 100, 104, 107, 184–5, 192
Fiji:
  cession to Britain, 1
  climate, 13–14
  first arrival of Indians, 1
  geography, 13ff.
  imported labour, 1
  political status, 10, 194
Fiji Indian Football Association, 178
Fijians:
  economic activities, 12
  Fiji Indian attitude to, 180–4
  social relations of Fiji Indians with, 11–12, 223
  and World War II, 186
films, 190–1
fire-walking, 93–4, 178
Fisk, E. K., 197
flagellation, 90–2, 146
flags, ritual, 84, 85
football matches, 128, 178–9
funerals:
  attendance at, 81–2
  rites at, 81–3

Gandhi, 192–3
Ganesh, 85, 95
Ganeshlila, 95, 130, 132
Gangs, cane-harvesting, 26, 40, 43, 58, 98–104, 143, 149, 204–7
  average age, 103
  rates of pay, 99
  sardars, 103–4, 123–4, 134, 205
  size, 101, 206
  See also alternates; *sardar*
ghee, 71, 80, 83
gifts at wedding, 71, 76
Gillion, K. L., 2, 3, 4, 12, 46, 119, 145, 157, 162, 189
Gordon, Sir Arthur, 1
government, participation in, 10
  administrative officers of, 25, 132, 184
graves, 80
groups:
  formation of, 5
  minority, 138
  and religious obligations, 96–7
  See also cultural group; house group; kin group
Gujarat, 3
Gujaratis, 28, 46–8, 192, 193

hair, shaving of baby's, 61
halal, 152
Hanuman, 85, 94, 190
Hardayal Singh, Vunioki leader, 108, 119, 123–5, 137, 139, 140, 141, 142, 161
Harvesting Agreement, 98–101, 102, 204
headaches, curing, 85, 151
healing, 85–6
Hindi language, 67, 144–6, 222
  Southern Indians and, 144
Hindus, relations with Muslims, 149ff.
Holi festival, 87–9, 178
  communal dispute over, 152–3

homesteads, 31–3
  and crop types, 44
  definition, 31
  distribution, and cultural groups, 29–31, 148
  growth and splitting of, 34, 203
  types, statistics, 32–3, 202–3, 215
  See also housing
house group, defined, 32
  statistics, types, 32–3, 203, 215
household, joint:
  advantages of, 171
  composition of, 164–5, 216
  defined, 31–2
  division of, 168ff.
household, 'joint', 202–3, 215–16
household, simple, defined, 31
housing, 4–5
  in Delanikoro, 18–19, 32, 213
  in Namboulima, 16
  in Vunioki, 15–16, 200
'husbands, depot', 3
hypergamy, 160–1, 182
hypogamy, 161

illegitimacy, 165
immigrants, Indian:
  age, 3
  classification, 3
  first arrival, 1
  'free', 2
  marital status, 3
  Northern and Southern, proportions, 3
  numbers, 2
  places of origin, 3
  post-indenture, 46, 188
  women, 3
income:
  per head, 8
  rural, 52, 201, 214
indenture system, 1ff.
  abolition of, 6
  abuses of, 6
  advantages and disadvantages, 6
India:
  attitudes to, 187–93
  contacts with, 188–9
  image of, 191
  importance of labour from, 1ff.
  visits to, 188–9
India-born, 21, 22, 33, 82, 90, 121, 137
  and Fiji-born, differences, 169–70, 187ff.
Indian Advisory Committees, 184, 209
Indian Association, 10
Indian Reform League, 10
Indians, Northern and Southern:
  distinctions, 28, 30, 144
  factors separating, 144ff.
  intermarriage, bars to, 144
Indians, visits from, 188
inheritance, 174
interest, 54, 58
intermarriage:
  Fiji Indian–Fijian, 182
  Hindu–Muslim, 150
  Northern–Southern, 144–5
'inviter', 45, 61
Islam Teaching Society, 9

229

Index

Index

231

Index

repatriation:
  of indentured labourers, 2, 188
  of post-indenture immigrants, 188
rice, cultivation of, 14, 16
  See also paddy
rishtedar, 172
rites:
  birth and infancy, 60–1
  cost of, 56, 61, 81, 84, 94
  festival, 86–96
  funerary, 80–3
  household, 83–6
  marriage, 62–79
  'rebirth', 61–2
rivalry, inter- and intra-settlement, 107–8
Roman Catholics, 9, 28
Roth, G. K., 181
Rural development Committee, 209, 220, 222–3

Sanatan Dharm, 9
Sangam. *See* Then India Sanmarga Ikya
  Sangam
Saraswati, Dayanand, 9
sardar, 5, 99, 159, 204–8
  election of, 103–4, 123–4, 134, 184
  qualifications, 5, 104, 139
sari:
  use in Fiji, 192
  at wedding, 72
School Committee, 98, 104–9, 124–5, 208,
  219–20
schools, 9, 104–5
  See also School Committee
settlement(s):
  boundaries of, 24–6
  criteria of membership, 26
  economy of, 58–9
  histories of, 20–4
  kin groups and, 34–7
  and outsiders, 177ff.
  patterns of, 13ff.
  See also under names of settlements
Seventh Day Adventists, 9
shadi, 72, 73
Shephard, C. Y., 23, 24, 38, 39, 40, 48, 53, 56,
  99, 183
'ship brothers', 6, 175–6
sibling relationships, 166
Sikhs, 28, 46, 50
Sivaratri, 89, 221
social welfare associations, 9–10
solidarity of community, basis of, 179
songs:
  at Holi festival, 87, 192–3
  from Indian films, 191
South Pacific Sugar Mills, 196–8, 204–6
Southern Indians:
  divisions among, 122ff.
  marriage rites, 75–6
  marriage rules, 63
  proportion among immigrants, 3
Spate, Prof. O. H. K., report of, 183
specialization, lack of, and caste rules, 4,
  158
spirits:
  Fijian, 84, 86
  propitiation of, 83–4

spouse(s):
  desiderata in, 65
  selection of, 62–6
  relations between, 164–5
sraddha, 82, 83, 173–4
stereotypes:
  caste, 161
  cultural, 147–8
  of Fijian, 181–2
  communal, 149
stores, storekeepers, 8, 45, 46–52, 59, 199–200,
  213
stores, as social centres, 49, 50, 210
  stock of, 47, 52, 199
  See also credit
strikes, 149
sub-caste, 156
sub-districts, 25
sub-sectors, CSR, 25–6
suffrage, qualifications, 10
sugar. *See* cane
Sugar Advisory Council, 205
Sundar, Delanikoro leader, 69, 89, 112, 126–9,
  137, 139, 141, 218–19
Sunni Muslims, 9, 28. *See also* Muslims
Suva, 8, 13–14, 45, 179, 189, 211–13, 221

tailors, 46, 52
tali, 75, 146
Tamil language. *See* languages
taziyas, 96, 151
teachers, 108–9, 179, 199
Telugu language. *See* languages
Temple Committee, 109, 130, 131, 134, 141
Then India Sanmarga Ikya Sangam, 9, 10, 11,
  179
thread, sacred, 61, 162
T'ien, J.-K., 52
tilak, 67, 70, 85
tobacco, 41
toli, 28
towns, 8, 47ff., 57, 59, 95, 128. 140, 178, 212
  See also Suva
tractors, 44, 196, 200, 206
traders, 49, 50
  See also storekeepers
transport drivers, 45, 198
Trinidad, 40
turmeric, ritual use of, 68–9, 70 83–4
'twice-born', 61, 138, 162

unanimity in decisions, 112, 116, 117, 182
  See also elections
unions. *See* cane farmers' unions
United Kingdom, visits to, 186, 223
untouchables, 3, 157, 158
Urdu. *See* languages
  school, 106, 178
Uttar Pradesh, 3

Vanua Levu, 13, 95, 133, 149, 179, 196
vegetables, 41–2, 195
Victoria, Queen, 1
Vishnulila, 94
Viti Levu, 13, 133, 149, 179, 186, 196, 214

232

Index